This is an astonishing volume of essays: articulate, frank, insightful, and suffused with fraternal respect; an exercise in ecumenical engagement at its best. Joseph Ratzinger is one of the great Catholic theologians of the last 100 years. To encounter him anew through the eyes of gifted Protestant scholars is a deeply satisfying revelation.

Charles J. Chaput

O.F.M. Cap., Archbishop of Philadelphia

Joseph Ratzinger—His Holiness Pope Emeritus Benedict XVI—is the greatest theologian elected to the papacy since the age of the Reformation. This volume, written by a scholarly team of convinced Protestants, show why this is the case. An exercise in ecumenical theology at its best.

Timothy George

founding dean of Beeson Divinity School of Samford University, general editor of the *Reformation Commentary on Scripture*

This is a remarkable collection of essays, deep and sympathetic. Benedict's achievement is broad and uniquely significant because of the important roles he's played in recent history. The contributors to this volume have, together, produced a constructive and luminous engagement of the whole breadth of Benedict's theology. This is a landmark study and a model of authentic dialogue.

Scott Hahn

Father Michael Scanlan Chair of Biblical Theology and the New Evangelization at Franciscan University of Steubenville, founder and president of the St. Paul Center for Biblical Theology

The writings of Pope Emeritus Benedict XVI have nourished my thinking and devotion for years, and this collection of thoughtful Protestant engagements with those writings proves that I'm far from alone. Even though our communion with the See of Rome is impaired, we Protestants can still receive the gift of Benedict's profoundly Scriptural, Christocentric work and allow it to enrich our study, preaching, worship, and evangelism too. This book shows us how.

Wesley Hill
associate professor of New Testament, Trinity School for Ministry

These essays represent ecumenism at its best. In a spirit of obvious sympathy and appreciation, the Protestant authors of this book offer an in-depth investigation of key aspects of Joseph Ratzinger's theology. Differences remain, to be sure. But The Theology of Benedict XVI demonstrates that in Ratzinger, Protestants have found a theologian with whom they deeply resonate. Tim Perry has placed Protestants and Catholics alike in his debt.

Hans Boersma
St. Benedict Servants of Christ Professor in Ascetical Theology,
Nashotah House, Wisconsin

Protestants owe an enormous debt to Pope Benedict XVI. With an unmatched breadth of clarity, wisdom, and insistence, he recalled the larger Church to her Scriptural center, her essential theological vocation, and her apologetic responsibilities in an age where Scripture, theology, and witness are often debased afterthoughts to ideology and personal religiosity. This collection of outstanding essays—written by a range of Protestant luminaries—presents Benedict's rich, sometimes intricate, but always Christologically grounded contributions with an unparalleled balance of understanding and critical sympathy. Compendious in scope and accessible in style, it is both a marvelous introduction to his theology as well as an act of thanksgiving for its profound value.

Ephraim Radner
professor of historical theology, Wycliffe College, University of Toronto

The THEOLOGY *of*
BENEDICT XVI

A PROTESTANT APPRECIATION

The THEOLOGY *of*
BENEDICT XVI

A PROTESTANT APPRECIATION

Edited by Tim Perry

LEXHAM PRESS

The Theology of Benedict XVI: A Protestant Appreciation

Lexham Press, 1313 Commercial St., Bellingham, WA 98225

Print ISBN 9781683593461
Digital ISBN 9781683593478

Lexham Editorial: Todd Hains, Jeff Reimer, Abigail Stocker, Jim Weaver
Cover Design: Joshua Hunt, Christine Christopherson, Brittany Schrock
Typesetting: Sarah Vaughan

DANIEL WESTBERG
Ex umbris et imaginbus in veritatem

REVEREND PROFESSOR DR. DANIEL WESTBERG OF NASHOTAH HOUSE WAS
CONTRACTED TO CONTRIBUTE TO THIS VOLUME. WE WERE ALL SADDENED
AND SHOCKED BY HIS DEATH. DAN WAS A GOOD FRIEND TO SOME
OF US AND A WELCOME COLLEAGUE TO MANY MORE IN BOTH
ANGLICAN AND EVANGELICAL CIRCLES. HE WILL BE
REMEMBERED AS A FAITHFUL PRIEST AND
THEOLOGIAN OF THE CHURCH. IT IS
TO HIS MEMORY THAT THIS
VOLUME IS WARMLY
DEDICATED.

Contents

Contributors

GREGG R. ALLISON (PhD, Trinity Evangelical Divinity School) is professor of Christian theology at The Southern Baptist Theological Seminary. He is author of numerous books, including *Roman Catholic Theology and Practice: An Evangelical Assessment, Historical Theology: An Introduction to Christian Doctrine,* and *50 Core Truths of the Christian Faith: A Guide to Understanding and Teaching Theology.*

ANNETTE BROWNLEE (DMin, Wycliffe College, University of Toronto) is chaplain and professor of pastor theology at Wycliffe College. She is author of *Preaching Jesus Christ Today: Six Questions for Moving from Scripture to Sermon.*

CHRISTOPHER R. J. HOLMES (ThD, Wycliffe College, University of Toronto) is associate professor of systematic theology at the University of Otago in New Zealand. He is author of The Lord Is Good: Seeking the God of the Psalter, *The Holy Spirit* (New Studies in Dogmatics), and *Ethics in the Presence of Christ.*

PETER J. LEITHART (PhD, University of Cambridge) is president of the Theopolis Institute in Birmingham, Alabama. He is author of numerous books, including *The Ten Commandments: A Guide to the Law of Liberty, The End of Protestantism: Pursuing Unity in a Fragmented Church,* and *Athanasius.*

MATTHEW LEVERING (PhD, Boston College) is James N. and Mary D. Perry Jr. Chair of Theology at Mundelein Seminary. He is author of numerous books, including *Participatory Biblical Exegesis: A Theology of Biblical Interpretation, Predestination: Biblical and Theological Paths,* and *Dying and the Virtues.*

BEN MYERS (PhD, James Cook University) is director of the Millis Institute at Christian Heritage College and a research fellow of the Centre for Public and Contextual Theology at Charles Sturt University in Australia. He is author of *Christ the Stranger: The Theology of Rowan Williams* and *The Apostles' Creed: A Guide to the Ancient Catechism.*

DAVID NEY (ThD, Wycliffe College, University of Toronto) is an Anglican priest and assistant professor of Church history at Trinity School for Ministry.

PRESTON D. S. PARSONS (PhD, University of Cambridge) is rector of the Church of St. John the Evangelist in Kitchener, Ontario and teaches political theology and ethics at Waterloo Lutheran Seminary.

TIM PERRY (PhD, Durham University) is adjunct professor of theology at Saint Paul University (Ottawa, ONT) and Trinity School for Ministry (Ambridge, PA). He is author of *Mary for Evangelicals: Toward an Understanding of the Mother of Our Lord* and editor of *The Legacy of John Paul II: An Evangelical Assessment.*

TRACEY ROWLAND (PhD, University of Cambridge; STD, Pontifical Lateran University) is St. John Paul II Chair of Theology at University of Notre Dame Australia. She is author of numerous books, including *Ratzinger's Faith: The Theology of Benedict XVI, Benedict XVI: A Guide for the Perplexed,* and *Catholic Theology.*

THE RT. REV. JOEY ROYAL is suffragan bishop in the Diocese of the Arctic in the Anglican Church of Canada. He oversees theological education for the Diocese as the director of the diocesan theological college, Arthur Turner Training School.

FRED SANDERS (PhD, Graduate Theological Union) is professor of theology at Torrey Honors Institute (Biola University). He is author of *The Triune God* (New Studies in Dogmatics) and *The Deep Things of God: How the Trinity Changes Everything.*

KATHERINE SONDEREGGER (PhD, Brown University) is William Meade Chair in Systematic Theology at Virginia Theological Seminary. She is author of *Systematic Theology*, Vol. 1, *The Doctrine of God*, 2015; Vol. 2, *The Doctrine of the Holy Trinity*, forthcoming 2020.

R. LUCAS STAMPS (PhD, The Southern Baptist Theological Seminary) is associate professor of Christian studies at Anderson University. He is author of *Thy Will Be Done: A Contemporary Defense of Two-Wills Christology* (forthcoming) and co-editor of *Baptists and the Christian Tradition: Toward an Evangelical Baptist Catholicity* (forthcoming).

CARL R. TRUEMAN (PhD, University of Aberdeen) is professor of biblical and religious studies at Grove City College. He is author of numerous books, including *Grace Alone: Salvation As a Gift from God, The Creedal Imperative*, and *Luther on the Christian Life: Cross and Freedom.*

KEVIN J. VANHOOZER (PhD, Cambridge University) is research professor of systematic theology at Trinity Evangelical Divinity School. He is author of numerous books, including *Hearers and Doers: A Pastor's Guide to Making Disciples, Biblical Authority after Babel: Retrieving the Solas in the Spirit of Mere Protestant Christianity,* and *The Drama of Doctrine: A Canonical-Linguistic Approach to Christian Doctrine.*

JONATHAN WARREN P. (PAGÁN) (PhD, Vanderbilt University) is associate rector at Church of the Ascension in Pittsburgh, Pennsylvania.

Foreword

After agreeing to write this foreword, I remembered meeting a Calvinist doctor at a luncheon during the pontificate of Benedict XVI. This doctor played the organ at Catholic Mass because his wife was Catholic. After joking about why Catholics can't sing, he described Pope Benedict as "a good Lutheran lad," and over the course of the luncheon he enumerated points of convergence between the theology of Joseph Ratzinger and the spiritual preoccupations of Martin Luther. He praised Ratzinger for his knowledge of Scripture and for his understanding of the Reformers' theological sensibilities. His conclusion: "You Catholics don't have a monopoly on him; he belongs to us, too."

In the spirit of a Calvinist who plays the organ so that Catholics can sing, I will offer some comments on this work compiled by scholars from the Reformation traditions.

I agree with Tim Perry: far from being God's rottweiler, a more appropriate metaphor for Joseph Ratzinger would be God's border collie. Ratzinger's most outstanding qualities are his fidelity to his Shepherd and his concern for the welfare of his sheep. These qualities do rather set him apart from many of his contemporaries, who had other priorities. I also agree that "for over 40 years, the small, quiet, brilliant German found himself at the center of every major theological controversy in the Catholic Church." This explains why he has been the victim of so much vicious commentary.

What makes him of broader interest, however, is that the controversies for the most part were not limited to the Catholic Church but relate to what Ratzinger once described as the most serious crisis in twentieth-century theology: the mediation of history in the realm of ontology. As he explained in his book *Principles of Catholic Theology*, in the twentieth century Catholic theology faced the question of the relationship between salvation history as presented in the Scriptures and the metaphysical heritage in Catholic theology, with a subsidiary question of the extent to which scriptural mediation could exist together with ecclesial mediation as well as an anthropological question about the value to be given to human achievements in the economy of salvation. The Catholic engagement with these issues in the first half of the twentieth century was acutely mindful of the Protestant scholarship in these fields, especially the work of Oscar Cullmann and Karl Barth.

Although Protestants have long avoided entanglements with ontological issues, the cultural revolution of the 1960s fostered the same crises within Protestant communities as in Catholic parishes. Ratzinger found himself amidst these crises because he believed, among other things, that the faith is something received, not something constructed, and that Christ's teaching as recorded in the Scriptures is normative for all time. Protestants who were similarly attempting to hold the ground for the principle of the normativity of Scripture found that they had an ally in Ratzinger.

Today, Christian scholars contending with the intellectual fallout of the 1960s need to engage with postmodern philosophy. To a large degree this philosophy defines itself by its opposition to the Greek heritage in Western culture. As is evident from the essays in this volume, Protestants are now very aware of the need to defend the reasonableness of Christianity and, indeed, the very notion of reason along with its shadow concept, truth. When struggling with a post-truth culture dominated by fake news and ideological prejudice, reason is no longer the "devil's whore" (to use Martin Luther's colorful metaphor) but a much-needed healing antidote.

However, even in his defense of Greek heritage and his interest in truth and rationality, Ratzinger is mindful of Protestant caveats. Because reason has a wax nose, he insists that it needs to be linked to a loving heart and to the purifying insights of revelation. As he argued in his commentary on Vatican II's *Guadium et spes* (1965), there is no such thing as pure reason, only impure reason and purified reason. While Ratzinger believes that Scripture has significant things to say about being as such, he makes the point that in contrast to the Greek concept of being, the biblical idea of creatureliness means having one's origin not in a passive idea but in a creative freedom. Ratzinger's anthropology is not Aristotle with a Christian gloss. Rather it begins with his understanding of the Trinity, especially the notion of personhood which flows from Trinitarian theology.

The high scholarly value of this collection is such that young Catholic scholars will no doubt have recourse to it to better understand their own tradition and Ratzinger's place within it. Almost every theme in contemporary theology has been covered: theological method; revelation; tradition and biblical interpretation; the relationship among faith, reason, and love; the theological virtues; Christology; theological anthropology; Eucharistic theology; ecumenism; prayer and preaching; Mariology; Trinitarian theology; catechesis; the theology of the priesthood; and liturgical theology.

Ratzinger himself models the humble posture of this collection's essayists. For example, Peter Leithart suggests that Ratzinger might have a "cleansing of the temple" moment, were he ever to attend a megachurch service with its sacro-pop music. Very possibly! But Protestant scholars like Calvin M. Johansson have helped Ratzinger to sharpen and strengthen his own arguments against the banality of sacro-pop music and its general unworthiness for liturgy. Ratzinger is willing to acknowledge truth wherever it may be found.

I hope that a copy of this work reaches the Pope Emeritus and that it becomes a standard text for students of ecumenism.

Tracey Rowland
University of Notre Dame Australia

Twelfth-century pulpit relief in the Cathedral of Santa Maria Assunta in Troia, Italy

Introduction

A Lion or a Dog?

TIM PERRY

In *The Nature and Mission of Theology* Joseph Ratzinger draws his readers' attention to a strange and unsettling relief on the cathedral pulpit in the Italian city of Troia.[1] It depicts three beasts locked in a deadly struggle: a lamb, a lion, and a dog. The lamb—still living—is being devoured by the lion. Atop the lion, however, a small dog—though clearly outmatched in size and power—is struggling if not to kill the much larger lion, to at least distract it long enough to rescue the lamb.[2]

On Ratzinger's reading, the referent for the clearly symbolic lamb is obvious: it is the church or the church's faith. What the artist saw as true of his day remains so: the faith of the church (*not* to be confused with her hierarchy) is always exposed, threatened with destruction, vulnerable to the point of death. The lion and dog, however, are more ambiguous. Unable to locate any interpretation of the relief in art history, Ratzinger suggests that the lion may represent the devil or heresy and the dog fidelity or perhaps, as a sheepdog after all, the Lord himself.

Where, Ratzinger wonders, does the theologian and theology fit in this disturbing image? His following assessment is, for me at least, just as unsettling:

> Only the significance of the lamb [as the faith of the church] is clearly defined. The other two animals, the lion and the dog—do they not stand for the two possible forms of theology, for the opposite courses

1. Joseph Ratzinger, *The Nature and Mission of Theology: Understanding Its Role in the Light of the Present Controversy*, trans. Adrian Walker (San Francisco: Ignatius, 1995).
2. Ratzinger, *Nature and Mission*, 69–72.

which it can take? The lion—is it not the embodiment of the historical temptation of theology to make itself the lord of faith? ... As for the brave hound—it stands for the opposite choice, for a theology which understands itself to be the servant of faith and for that reason agrees to make itself a laughingstock by putting the intemperance and naked tyranny of naked reason in their place. [3]

The relief, carved into a pulpit, is thus a constant challenge to preachers and theologians to a continual examination of conscience. Will they, in their theological and catechetical work, be "ravening predators or protectors of the flock?"[4]

At this stage in history, this question may perhaps uniquely be posed with regard to the Emeritus Pope. Will history and providence remember Joseph Ratzinger as a ravening lion or a protective dog? There is no doubt that he was and remains a polarizing figure. At one level, perhaps it's odd that this is so. He's hardly a captain of industry, a celebrity, a pundit, or a wielder of political power. He's a theologian. And a theologian—any theologian—may be many things, but polarizing is often not one of them. However disagreeable they may be, there is simply too small an audience that cares anymore. Add to that the fact that in Ratzinger's case we are dealing with a small, soft-spoken academic who, throughout his long public career in the hierarchy of the Catholic Church, pined at times for the quiet life of an academic priest, for his Bavarian home, for solitude, and for reading and writing in relative anonymity.

But the life of quiet reflection was not to be. His association with Cardinal Frings and the German delegation at the Second Vatican Council marked him as someone who would, for good or ill, be at the forefront of the debates that would follow the council's conclusion. And that is what happened. Ratzinger rose quickly to become cardinal archbishop of Munich in 1977, prefect for the Congregation of the Doctrine

3. Ratzinger, *Nature and Mission*, 71.
4. Ratzinger, *Nature and Mission*, 72.

of the Faith in 1981, dean of the college of cardinals in 2002, and finally pope in 2005. For over forty years, the small, quiet, brilliant German found himself at the center of every major theological controversy in the Catholic Church—a place that found him many supporters and many opponents.

His opponents seem to have had the better press agents. After all, the popular image of Joseph Ratzinger is that of the *Panzerkardinal*. As head of the Congregation for the Doctrine of Faith (CDF) from 1982 to 2005 Ratzinger was labelled Pope St. John Paul II's "Rottweiler," tasked with maintaining doctrinal fidelity around the world. He is recalled as the staunch revanchist who wished if not to overthrow the texts of the Second Vatican Council—texts he himself was instrumental in drafting—then at least to restrain its reforming spirit. Many, to use the image of Troia, would insist that the man was, in fact, a lion. As a separated brother and ardent admirer of his papal predecessor, I demur. Such depictions, however popular they were or are, are so one-sided as to be a caricature of the man and his legacy.

Consider three important examples.

First, under his direction, the Holy Office produced the *Catechism of the Catholic Church*, signaling that the Catholic Church was still, in some way, a dogmatically ordered faith with a particular intellectual shape and content that both forms and requires the assent of the faithful.[5] The intellectual core of the Catholic faith was not up for constant revision. Doctrine, as Ratzinger well knew, does indeed develop, and the *Catechism* can be and indeed has been revised since its introduction. The question that the Catechism framed was, What would development look like? And its answer was equally clear: Wholesale revisions of Catholic teaching were not possible, for that was not how the teaching office of the church worked; doctrinal development reflected a deepened understanding of the past and a continuity with what was received, not a rupture or departure from it. For good or ill, this may well be his singular achievement while in this role.

---

5. See *Catechism of the Catholic Church*, http://www.vatican.va/archive/ENG0015/_INDEX.HTM.

4

THE THEOLOGY OF BENEDICT XVI

More controversially, it was also under his direction that the CDF produced the document known as *Dominus Iesus* (2000). It announced that the true church subsisted in the Catholic Church. Orthodox bodies in which apostolic succession and a valid Eucharist were preserved were accorded the status of "true Churches" even if, in their denial of Petrine primacy, their communion was not full. But Protestants—although rightly called Christians by virtue of baptism—belong not to churches but to "ecclesial communities" whose participation in the true church is impaired.[6] The document caused widespread consternation among some Catholics and non-Catholics alike. And yet, as the footnotes of the offending paragraph (§17) make clear, the document itself merely repeats positions set forth in the Second Vatican Council declarations *Unitatis redintegratio* and *Lumen Gentium* as well as those of Pope St. John Paul II's very positively received encyclical *Ut Unum Sint* (1995).[7] I remember expressing my confusion to people who, on the one hand, believed passionately that Catholics were not "real Christians" and, on the other, were outraged when they found out that convinced Catholics thought similarly (indeed, more generously!) about them. Reactions aside, a careful reader will see in *Dominus Iesus* the *Catechism's* central conviction at work: Whatever development in ecumenical relations have taken place in recent years, whatever may take place in the future, they must do so in a way that received, deepened, and passed on magisterial teaching; they would not simply reject or ignore it.

The (mis)conception of Ratzinger as reactionary was given further weight at his reinstitution of the Latin Mass in 2011.[8] Widely regarded as another attempt to undo Vatican II,[9] the move was understood by then Pope Benedict XVI himself as an expression of the deep continuity between the two rites. The new rite was, for Benedict neither a

---

6. Congregation for the Doctrine of the Faith, *Dominus Iesus*, August 6, 2000, http://www.vatican.va/roman_curia/congregations/cfaith/documents/rc_con_cfaith_doc_20000806_dominus-iesus_en.html. The controversial paragraph is §17.

7. *Dominus Iesus*, §17, notes 59–67.

8. See "Pope Asserts Order to Reinstate Old Latin Mass," *National Post*, May 15, 2011, https://nationalpost.com/holy-post/pope-asserts-order-to-reinstate-old-latin-mass.

9. See, e.g., Ron Schmitt, "Attempt to Resurrect pre–Vatican II Mass Leaves Church at Crossroads," *National Catholic Reporter*, December 8, 2012, https://www.ncronline.org/news/spirituality/attempt-resurrect-pre-vatican-ii-mass-leaves-church-crossroads.

repristination of nor a revolution against the old, but a preservation of and a deepened insight into the truth articulated for a new and different situation; accordingly, it could not simply supersede the old. In his own words, "A society that considers now to be forbidden what it once perceived as the central core—that cannot be. The inner identity [the Latin rite] has with [the new Mass] must remain visible. So for me it was not about tactical matters and God knows what, but about the inward reconciliation of the Church with itself."[10] The restoration of the Latin rite was, once again, a reflection of the abiding theological theme of Ratzinger's entire oeuvre: doctrine develops in such a way the continuity with the past must be demonstrable. Hardly the reflection of an unflinching nostalgia, this theme was, when first expressed by John Henry Cardinal Newman, radically—even suspiciously—innovative.

These depictions of the Pope Emeritus have taken some truth and spun it in a way to suit a narrative that is at best unkind and at worst straightforwardly hostile to the man and his legacy. Each can be—and often has been—read in a way to support the Ratzinger-as-lion thesis. Each can be—and I think ought to be—read in a way to support the Ratzinger-as-faithful sheepdog thesis. Though his opponents may have called him God's Rottweiler, whenever I read his work, I encounter God's border collie. Small, tough, faithful to the Shepherd and to the ultimate welfare of the sheep. It is out of that conviction that I agreed to edit this collection of essays.

My conviction is, I hope, not naïve. I do not believe that in these and other of his actions the Pope Emeritus was immaculate. On the contrary, held up before not simply the light of history but the far more accurate light of the perfect judgment of the Holy One, the former pope's actions are and will be found lacking in many ways—as he himself would confess. Rather, this collection is my invitation to consider even the more controversial of the Pope Emeritus's contributions to the church more charitably than has sometimes been the case and leave the final judgment to, in Benedict's favorite phrase, the loving God. This treatment is

10. Benedict VXI with Peter Seewald, *Last Testament: In His Own Words* (London: Bloomsbury, 2016), 201.

no different from what we would wish for ourselves. That being the case, let us weigh as counterevidence the following gifts God gave both the Catholic Church and the global Christian faith through Joseph Ratzinger.

The primary instance is his prophetic insight into the ascent of godlessness and the eclipse of the Western churches following World War II. As early as 1958, when churches in Europe and America were full and the future of Western Christianity looked bright, then Fr. Ratzinger warned that it was, in fact, a hollowed out Christendom that would soon collapse.[11] But it is this quotation, from a talk first given in 1969—the heyday following the council—that now looks especially prescient:

> From the crisis of today a new Church of tomorrow will emerge—a Church that has lost much. She will become small and will have to start afresh more or less from the beginning. She will no longer be able to inhabit many of the edifices she built in prosperity. As the number of her adherents diminishes, so she will lose many of her social privileges. In contrast to an earlier age, she will be seen much more as a voluntary society, entered only be free decision. ... But in all [this] ... the Church will find her essence afresh and with full conviction in that which was always at her center: faith in the triune God, in Jesus Christ, the son of God made man, in the presence of the Spirit until the end of the world.[12]

In the light of the demographic cratering of European Christianity, both Catholic and Protestant, and the headlong rush of (North) America down the selfsame slope, it is impossible to argue with this now half-century-old assessment. It has come true in Europe; it is coming true here. And yet Ratzinger, whether as priest, bishop, cardinal, or pope, never submits to despair. It is his conviction that although Christianity may even disappear from some parts of what was once known as

11. Joseph Ratzinger, "The New Pagans and the Church: A 1958 Lecture by Joseph Ratzinger (Pope Benedict XVI)," trans. Kenneth Baker, SJ, *Homiletic and Pastoral Review*, January 30, 2017, https://www.hprweb.com/2017/01/the-new-pagans-and-the-church/.
12. Joseph Ratzinger, "What Will the Future Church Look Like?," in *Faith and the Future* (San Francisco: Ignatius, 2009), 116–17.

Christendom, the church will endure. Smaller, poorer, marginalized, and perhaps persecuted she will remain and become perhaps more fully the Bride, the temple, the vanguard of the kingdom.

In the following essays four themes continually reassert themselves. These themes could be read as Ratzinger's prescription for the future church on how not merely to survive but to thrive in its smallness.

First, *the future church will find her strength in holy Scripture*. It may strike some Protestant readers as odd to find in a pope of Rome a reminder of *sola Scriptura*, but it does appear to be the case. This is not to say that the Pope Emeritus is a closeted Lutheran (his well-known and long preoccupation with the Reformer notwithstanding), but it does point to their shared Augustinian heritage. Even as Augustine was a *biblical* commentator, preacher, and theologian, Ratzinger has from his earliest days understood his own calling not to be a scholastic but to be a theologian of the Bible and the fathers.[13] Specifically, Ratzinger teaches us through his constant biblical engagement that the Bible is one book that speaks to the present. In Protestantism in general, and perhaps most alarmingly in evangelicalism given its supposedly Scripture-centered piety, the notion that the Scriptures are to be read as the one work of one Author is increasingly rare. It has been declared, rather than demonstrated, that such a view is naïve and cannot stand against the explanatory power of historical-critical exegesis. Ratzinger's use of the Scriptures shows just the opposite: that properly understood and deployed, historical-critical methods are vital to opening up the text in its humanity so that the Christian reader may more accurately discern how these texts are taken up into the saving work of God such that they are at the same time God's saving Word. It is only as we recover an awareness of Scripture's divine authorship and, accordingly, its deep unity that it is released from its sequestration to the histories of its human authors to speak to today.

Second, *the future church will affirm that Christian faith is reasonable*. Again a central plank throughout Ratzinger's vast corpus, this conviction

---

13. He describes himself using just this language as he reflects on his work with the neo-Thomist Karl Rahner at the Second Vatican Council. See *Last Will*, 134–36.

was at the center of the much-maligned and, ironically enough, much misunderstood Regensburg address.[14] Far from being anti-Muslim, the lecture was a rejection of notions of God, found in Christianity as much as in Islam, that rendered rational discussion about theological claims impossible. Specifically, Benedict's allegedly inflammatory statement (which was actually a quotation of a long-dead Byzantine emperor) rejected the notion that the goodness or evil of moral actions was located in God's inscrutable will rather than in reason. This problematic theological development was known as voluntarism, or at least an extreme version of it, and Benedict insisted that it condemned theology to irrationality, rendered authentic theological debate impossible, and paved the way for violence. The only counter to such an end is reasoned discussion aimed at truth. Ratzinger's wide-ranging corpus is testimony that while (some of) the truths of Christianity are revealed and cannot be rationally discovered, all Christian claims can be rationally proposed, investigated, debated, and defended. In an increasingly religious world (the secularism of the West is hardly ascendant anywhere else), the only hope of peace rests in a common commitment to reason. Christian faith is a reasonable faith, capable of living reasonably and charitably with those who disagree, and for the sake of the world must be so.

Third, *the future church will depend much more on the visible holiness of her members.* Most if not all of the cultural trappings of its previous authority will have been razed. We must of course speak here of the sex abuse scandal that began in Canada in the 1990s, became the so-called Long Lent of 2002 in the United States, and is now erupting in the States (again), Argentina, Chile, Ireland, and elsewhere. The revelations of Cardinal McCarrick's abuse and the widespread knowledge thereof were especially disgusting. They invite questions about how far up the hierarchical chain such knowledge ascended—up to and including both Pope Francis and the Pope Emeritus. Both Francis and the Pope Emeritus have chosen to remain silent in the face of allegations, and people of

---

14. Benedict XVI, "Faith, Reason and the University, Memories and Reflections," September 12, 2006, http://w2.vatican.va/content/benedict-xvi/en/speeches/2006/september/documents/hf_ben-xvi_spe_20060912_university-regensburg.html.

goodwill now debate the wisdom of such a strategy. Nevertheless, it is my conviction (and my deep hope) that when all the information is out, Benedict will be shown to have been a man of his word when he committed his papacy to continuing the work he began when prefect for the CDF: cleaning up the "filth" that had infiltrated even the highest levels of the church.[15]

Finally, *the future church will be humble.* At one level, it will have to be—shorn of all the trappings of worldly power and success, downward mobility will be the only mobility left. More than that though, having weathered the storms of humiliation, the chastened church will be able again to grow in the grace of humility. And it will have no better example of the "simple worker in the vineyard of the Lord," the Pope Emeritus. Before his career path was set, Joseph Ratzinger had hoped to be an academic priest, but was prepared to be a parish pastor if that was the opportunity that came. It did not; and he moved at first in academic circles and eventually in curial ones. He seems to have longed for a life of relative anonymity in the academy rather than climbing the ladder into Catholicism's hierarchy, though the latter is what, in fact, transpired. And although he spent twenty-three years as the prefect for the CDF (and Pope St. John Paul II's "right hand") and eight years as pope, it is clear that he embraced these offices out of obedience to his superiors (and above all to the Lord); Ratzinger himself seemed to long throughout for solitude, silence, prayer, and his books.

In short, the chastened, small church of the future will learn again to be scriptural, rational, holy, and humble, and in all these ways, Ratzinger's life and thought will provide a heroic guide. He is an example of fidelity and accompaniment in times of great challenge. He powerfully lived out these themes in his ministry and explored them in his

15. The language comes from his Way of the Cross meditations of 2005, and specifically, station 9, http://www.vatican.va/news_services/liturgy/2005/via_crucis/en/station_09.html. We may also consider his strongly worded pastoral letter, "To the Catholics of Ireland," March 19, 2010, http://w2.vatican.va/content/benedict-xvi/en/letters/2010/documents/hf_ben-xvi_let_20100319_church-ireland.html. He has also spoken about the abuse scandals in *Benedict XVI, Light of the World: The Pope, The Church and the Signs of the Times; An Interview with Peter Seewald*, trans. Michael J. Miller and Adrian J. Walker (San Francisco: Ignatius, 2010), 184–86, and in *Last Testament*, 199–200.

written work. Both have much to teach those of us who, like all the contributors to this volume, live on the other side of the Tiber.

1

"Truth, not Custom"

Joseph Ratzinger on Faith and Reason

BEN MYERS

Our Lord Christ called himself truth, not custom.

—Tertullian[1]

T he hallmark of contemporary Protestant theology is its preoccupation with Christianity as a religion. The priority of communal belonging; spiritual formation through ritual practices; doctrine as the grammar of communal life; an emphasis on mystery and unknowability; the importance of narrative; the remythologizing of Christian belief; a profound yearning for the certainties of ancient traditions; the priority of desire over reason, praxis over truth, the Dionysian over the Apollonian: these are the great energizing forces of Protestant thought today.

Karl Barth rejected the nineteenth-century tendency (culminating most impressively in Ernst Troeltsch) to represent Christian faith as a sociological by-product of the Christian religion. A century later, the dominance of Troeltsch is evident even among theologians who invoke Barth's legacy. The word "religion" has not quite recovered from Barth's excoriating treatment. Hence Protestant theologians today prefer to speak of the priority of "the Christian community" and its "practices." An important clue to the new theological mood is the widespread sense among Protestant thinkers that the Reformation was a mistake. How could Luther have been so wrong-headed as to prioritize the pursuit of truth over communal belonging? Luther once said, "If I were the only one in the entire world to adhere to the Word, I

---

1. Tertullian, *On the Veiling of Virgins* 1.1; cited in Joseph Ratzinger, *Introduction to Christianity*, trans. J. R. Foster, rev. ed. (San Francisco: Ignatius, 2004), 141. Ratzinger calls this "one of the really great assertions of patristic theology."

alone would be the church and would properly judge about the rest of the world that it is not the church."[2] A scandalous sentiment. Nothing could so bluntly reveal the spirit of contemporary Protestant theology as our instinctive reaction to those words. Faced with a choice between Word and church, we would choose the latter, with some reassuring qualifications about the communally conditioned nature of all biblical interpretation and all claims to truth. For us, Luther's stance is not so much wrong as unintelligible.

That is our situation as Protestant theologians today. As theologians, we seek truth, but we seek first the community and its righteousness and trust that all these other things will be added as well.

In this context the theological work of Joseph Ratzinger seems a bit deflating at first glance. For over half a century Ratzinger has challenged the subordination of truth to communal belonging. From his academic career in the 1950s and 1960s to his papal ministry as Benedict XVI, one of Ratzinger's most consistent themes has been the priority of reason and truth over communal identity. In his analysis, the most urgent theological task is the recovery of reason. It is, he thinks, the most urgent social and political task too.

Ratzinger sees the split between faith and reason as inimical to both religion and secular society. Religion becomes pathological when its claims are reduced to private exhortations to insiders with no link to a universally accessible rationality or a shared conception of the human good. And reason, for its part, becomes pathological when it is confined to the sphere of fact, measurement, and technical manipulation with no accountability to moral considerations of justice, goodness, and the ends of human life. Ratzinger calls for faith to be animated by rationality and for reason to be open to its transcendent foundations as revealed to faith. Faith and reason alike, he argues, arise from the manifestation of the divine Logos, who is ultimately revealed as Love: a rationality that is living, personal, and directed toward us for our good.

---

2. Martin Luther, *Luther's Works*, vol. 2, *Lectures on Genesis, Chapters 6–14*, ed. Jaroslav Pelikan and Daniel E. Poellot, trans. George V. Schick (St Louis: Concordia, 1960), 102.

THE RATIONALITY OF FAITH

You would expect the bishop of Rome to be a champion of the Christian
religion. But Ratzinger argues that Christianity is true in spite of being
a religion, in the same way that Greek philosophy was true in spite of
being Greek. Greek philosophy was a product of its own culture, but it
became "philosophy" to the extent that it transcended its own cultural
limitations in the search for a universal rational order. In the career of
Socrates, philosophy achieved a stark critical distance from its own
cultural context. The search for truth necessarily entailed a critique of
the particular cultural conditions in which that search was carried out.
If philosophy had been an articulation of the grammatical rules of the
social order, why was Socrates condemned to die? And why did Plato
expend so much effort trying to imagine a completely new society in
which religion, myth, law, and education are reconfigured according to
rational norms? Ratzinger sees the self-critical aspect of Greek philosophy as its essential characteristic.[3]

The criticism of Greek culture by Greek philosophers has a striking
parallel in the prophets' criticism of Israelite faith, and in the ministry
of Jesus, which reaches through and beyond its own cultural context to
proclaim a universal divine order, the kingdom of God. Biblical faith, like
Greek thought, is directed toward a truth that transcends and relativizes
its immediate context. Ratzinger argues that this move toward self-crit-
icism—an unintended by-product of the search for universal truth—was
the real point of contact between the gospel and Greek culture.

Since the start of his career Ratzinger has carried out a quiet but
persistent polemic against the Protestant project of de-Hellenizing the
Christian faith. From Luther's repudiation of Aristotle to Kant's banish-
ment of metaphysics to Barth's denial of the analogy of being, Protestant
theology has policed the boundary between faith and reason, the God
of the Bible and the God of the philosophers. Adolf von Harnack argued
that the noble simplicity of biblical faith was contaminated by its contact
with Greek culture. Contemporary contextual theologians insist that it

---

3. Joseph Ratzinger, *Truth and Tolerance: Christian Belief and World Religions*, trans. Henry
Taylor (San Francisco: Ignatius, 2004), 198–201.

was purely a matter of historical accident that the church took root in the soil of Greco-Roman culture. The message of the Bible (in its original, pre-Hellenized form) can be enculturated into any number of contexts. Greek thought, we are assured, is no better (or worse?) than any cultural medium. Ratzinger replies that the synthesis of biblical faith and Greek thought "was not only legitimate but necessary" for the full articulation of the meaning of the gospel.[4] The gospel is a universal message. It is not gnostic but catholic: not a message addressed to a private spiritual zone but an interpretation of reality as a whole. Any truth, discovered by any means, is necessarily compatible with the truth of the gospel. This does not mean that Christianity holds in its grasp a synthesis of all knowledge. It only means that Christianity refuses to remain on one side of the border between faith and reason, since both stand under the one all-embracing manifestation of the divine Logos.[5]

Because Christianity is founded on knowledge, its message and mission are universal. This universalism emerged first in the witness of Israel's prophets and sages who reached beyond the boundaries of a particular worshiping community and made universal claims founded on knowledge of the one God.[6] The Christian message, like the message of the prophets, is not mythic and religious. It is not a communal and symbolic representation of an unknowable reality. It is a proclamation of the truth revealed by the divine Logos. As rational truth it commends itself to all. The earliest generations of believers understood themselves not as members of a new religious community with its own particular rites and ceremonies but as representatives of a new humanity. They proclaimed the risen Lord not as the founder of a sect but as the new Adam, the founder of humanity. The lordship of Jesus comprehended all things "in heaven and on earth and under the earth" (Phil 2:5–11). Christianity, Ratzinger observes, is a missionary faith only to the extent

---

4. Joseph Ratzinger, *Der Gott des Glaubens und der Gott der Philosophen* [The God of faith and the God of the philosophers] (Munich: Verlag Schnell und Steiner, 1960), 29.
5. Ratzinger, *Der Gott des Glaubens*, 29.
6. Joseph Ratzinger, *The Nature and Mission of Theology: Understanding Its Role in the Light of the Present Controversy*, trans. Adrian Walker (San Francisco: Ignatius, 1995), 24.

that it is more than a religion and so "transcends all traditions and constitutes an appeal to reason and an orientation toward the truth."[7]

In his 1954 doctoral dissertation Ratzinger drew attention to the
patristic understanding of faith as a fulfillment of the project of Greek
philosophy. Augustine categorized Christian teaching not as one of the
"mythic" or "civic" theologies but as one of the "natural" (that is, rational)
theologies. He ranked Christianity not among the religions, founded on
poetry and myth and oriented toward social cohesion, but among the
philosophies founded on reason and the quest for truth. Christianity
put itself forward not as a better religion but as the true philosophy.[8]

Ratzinger has returned to this theme throughout his career. His
1959 inaugural lecture at the University of Bonn criticized Pascal's claim
that the God of the philosophers is not the God of Abraham, Isaac,
and Jacob.[9] Based on his study of patristic sources, Ratzinger argued
that in fact "early Christianity boldly and resolutely made its choice ...
by deciding *for* the God of the philosophers and *against* the gods of
the various religions."[10] This was already St. Paul's decision in the first
chapter of Romans. Christianity is not based on myths; its justification
does not lie in its social usefulness. It is not an instrument for achiev-
ing communal belonging through ancient rituals and powerful stories.
The Christian faith is, like the philosophies, founded on knowledge.[11]
The early Christians were condemned not because they had a new religion—new religions were in vogue—but because they were perceived
as "atheists." They were a threat to the social order because they did
not honor the gods. They refused to locate their faith among the other
religious communities with their own stories, traditions, and practices.
They denigrated all myths, denounced all gods, and proclaimed the universal truth of the lordship of Christ. "The suspicion of atheism with
which early Christianity had to contend," writes Ratzinger, makes clear

7. Ratzinger, *Nature and Mission*, 26.
8. Joseph Ratzinger, *Volk und Haus Gottes in Augustins Lehre von der Kirche* [The people
of God and the house of God in Augustine's doctrine of the church] (Munich: Zink,
1954), chap. 9.
9. Ratzinger, *Der Gott des Glaubens*.
10. Ratzinger, *Introduction to Christianity*, 137.
11. Ratzinger, *Truth and Tolerance*, 170.

"its intellectual orientation, its decision against *religio* and custom devoid of truth, its option in favor of the truth of Being."[12]

In his extensive writing on the liturgy Ratzinger never retreats to religious and sociological conceptions of identity-formation through communal stories and practices. Christian worship, he argues, is ordered by revelation and oriented toward truth. It is rational service of the Logos.[13] To cultivate religious practices for the sake of personal transformation or communal belonging or some perceived cultural benefit is, Ratzinger says (invoking Barth), "the very opposite of faith."[14] Without its rational content and its ordering toward the truth of reality, Christian worship reverts to some variety of "mythic" or "civic" paganism.

Ancient Christianity dissolved the power of the pagan cults not by putting forward a superior method of communal formation but by announcing a truth that freed the mind from its captivity to falsehoods. If Christianity was in later centuries able to commend itself as the "true religion," it was only by laying hold of the hollowed-out shell of religion and investing it with a totally new content and a new orientation toward rational truth.

THE FOUNDATIONS OF REASON

When faith and reason are divided, Christianity loses its identity as a religion of truth. Reason, too, is affected by the division. Secular reason confines itself to an ever more efficient technical mastery while moral and metaphysical questions, including questions concerning the nature of the human person and the purpose of technology, remain unasked and unanswered. What Kant called "practical reason" is no longer admitted as a valid mode of reasoning. The domain of reason is restricted to whatever can be measured and manipulated.[15] Under these conditions reason becomes aimless even as its technical achievements advance on

12. Ratzinger, *Introduction to Christianity*, 143.
13. See for example the opening chapters of Joseph Ratzinger, *The Spirit of the Liturgy*, trans. John Saward (San Francisco: Ignatius, 2000).
14. Joseph Ratzinger, *The Feast of Faith: Approaches to a Theology of the Liturgy*, trans. Graham Harrison (San Francisco: Ignatius, 1986), 23.
15. For Ratzinger's account of these modern developments, see his *Introduction to Christianity*, 57–66.

every side. And the aimlessness of reason becomes destructive when its own tools turn irrationally against their maker. The most urgent challenge of our time, Ratzinger believes, is to address this "crisis of reason."[16]

Ratzinger has given particular attention to the way materialist ideologies, precisely in their exclusive commitment to reason, end up turning against human nature and ultimately against reason itself. Ratzinger's decades-long criticism of Marxist ideology centers on this point. The fundamental error of Marxism, he argues, is the denial of the priority of Logos. Irrational matter is at the basis of everything. The assumption of the priority of the irrational leads in turn to an application of scientific reason to the ostensibly raw materials of human nature.[17] The history of Marxist social experiments gives ample proof of the theory's delusions. Human nature proves to be peculiarly resistant to all attempts to remodel it technocratically. It breaks before it bends. There is a mysterious givenness to human nature. Its possibilities as well as its limitations need to be properly discerned. There is something in the human person that is not fully reducible to materiality and that frustrates the application of scientific techniques. Ratzinger's relentless opposition to liberation theology has to be understood in this context. Liberation theology, in his analysis, is not a cure but only a symptom of the ailment of modernity. It uncritically mirrors—and even sacralizes—the loss of rationality in secular social theory. It supplants the priority of the Logos with a theory of irrational materialism; it trades the rational persuasiveness of faith for the promise of violent revolution. Such a system, Ratzinger argues, is not really a theology of liberation at all but a liberation from theology: an escape from the freedom of the Logos into ideological captivity.[18]

The enthusiasm for Marxism among Western intellectuals led to widespread disillusionment after the collapse of Soviet communism and

16. Joseph Ratzinger, *A Turning Point for Europe? The Church in the Modern World*, trans. Brian McNeil (San Francisco: Ignatius, 1994), 122.

17. See for example Ratzinger, *Turning Point for Europe*, 88–98.

18. Joseph Ratzinger, *Politik und Erlösung: zum Verhältnis von Glaube, Rationalität und Irrationalem in der sogenannten Theologie der Befreiung* [Politics and redemption: the relation between faith, rationality, and the irrational in the so-called theology of liberation] (Düsseldorf: Westdeutscher, 1986).

the revelation of the degradations and horrors that had resulted wherever Marxist theory had been able to put its social-scientific methods to the test. The doctrine of inevitable progress through the application of social theory gave way to a climate of relativism. In contrast to the universalist pretensions of Marxism, the impossibility of obtaining universal truth now came to be seen as the necessary basis of a free society. A world-weary relativism in politics soon spread to other spheres of life, especially religion and morality. Ratzinger sees this mood of relativism as a threat to Western liberal democracies. He has written extensively in praise of the European project as a secularization of Christian universalism. More than a decade before the resurgence of European nationalisms and the rising tide of anti-EU sensibilities, Ratzinger warned of the threat that relativism posed to Europe's spiritual foundations: "The complex problems left behind by Marxism continue to exist today. The loss of man's primordial certainties about God, about himself, and about the universe—the loss of an awareness of intangible moral values—is still our problem, especially today, and it can lead to the self-destruction of the European consciousness."[19]

The dominance of relativism can be traced in the changing meaning of the word "conscience." The Protestant Reformers elevated the importance of conscience in the moral life. As the etymology of the word suggests, conscience is a faculty of knowing (*con-scientia*). It is the soul's interior link with divine justice. Calvin called it a midpoint between God and the human. It is a connection to a moral criterion that both resides within the individual and "pursues him" from outside himself. The soul is tethered to an objective moral order from which it cannot escape.[20] To contemporary ears this sounds like servitude. But to the Protestant Reformers the whole point about conscience is that it defends the individual against tyranny. Because we are accountable to a transcendent order of justice, we are freed from servitude to

---

19. Joseph Ratzinger, *Europe: Today and Tomorrow; Addressing the Fundamental Issues,* trans. Michael J. Miller (San Francisco: Ignatius, 2007), 29. The book is translated from the Italian original published in 2004.

20. John Calvin, *Institutes of the Christian Religion,* ed. John T. McNeill, trans. Ford Lewis Battles (Philadelphia: Westminster, 1960), 3.19.15.

earthly authorities, whether political or ecclesiastical. No human being has the right to bind the conscience of another. We can obey human authority without being spiritually subject to it, that is, with a conscience that is accountable only to God. Conscience, for the Reformers, designates knowledge, objectivity, freedom. And what is the meaning of "conscience" today? When the word is used at all, it is to designate the purest subjectivity. It concerns a choice or preference that is not accountable to rational norms. It is no longer a faculty of perception that connects me to the objective moral universe of which I am a part. An appeal to conscience means: this is what I want, this is what I choose. And I respect the conscience of others simply because it is that element in them with which I cannot reason. Conscience is no longer *scientia*, knowledge, but only will.

One might imagine that the reduction of conscience to subjectivity would enhance individual freedom. With no rational accountability to an objective moral order, the individual can choose anything, be anything, become anything. But freedom loses its foundations when life is reduced to pure will. Citizens are reduced to consumers. The notion of a "common good" becomes incomprehensible, a contradiction in terms. The pursuit of the good is replaced by a pursuit of power as a means of securing one's preferences against the encroaching preferences of others. Political leadership becomes the art of amplifying and manipulating the irrational desires of the masses. And political power without accountability to rational norms can ultimately descend into totalitarianism. At that point the horrors of naked desire and naked power are manifest, and the individual—deprived now of conscience as an anchor in objective reality—is enslaved and debased. It is no coincidence that every totalitarian regime wages war against the concept of truth.

No one who has witnessed the developments in Western political culture over the past few years would conclude that such fears are unfounded. What is needed today, Ratzinger argues, is a recovery of the rationality of conscience and the universality of social goods as bulwarks against social disintegration and political tyranny.[21]

It is here that secular modernity stands in need of faith. Not because the church is itself a social project or a political power. Ever since his doctoral work on Augustine's *City of God*, Ratzinger has emphatically maintained the necessary distinction between temporal and spiritual power. The church is not an alternative social order, nor does it have its own unique methods for dealing with concrete social issues. Practical reason has its own tasks. What faith offers is knowledge of the transcendent foundations of reason. Faith secures reason's capacity to reach beyond the domain of fact and to investigate deeper questions of meaning, truth, justice, and the good. The mystery of faith is Logos itself. Faith serves reason by opening the way to the underlying rationality of existence. So Ratzinger argues that "the Christian faith is not a limitation ... of reason: on the contrary, it is only this faith that sets reason free to perform its own proper work."[22] The Protestant jurist Hugo Grotius had argued that legal norms would be valid "even if God did not exist." Adopting Pascal's formulation instead, Ratzinger urges nonreligious people to live "as if God did indeed exist."[23] His apologetic for Christianity is not that the truth of faith can be proved but that secular reason is, in the long run, impossible without it.

Ironically, then, Ratzinger's message to secular modernity is not that it needs more faith but that it needs more reason. It needs a larger and more expansive rationality. And to that extent modernity also needs faith. It needs a guide to show the way back to the wellsprings of rationality. "In the crisis of reason that confronts us today, this real essence of faith must once again become visible, this essence that saves reason, precisely because it grasps reason in its whole breadth and depth and protects it from the restrictions of a merely experiential verification."[24]

---

21. See for example Joseph Ratzinger, *On Conscience* (San Francisco: Ignatius, 2007); and Ratzinger, *Christianity and the Crisis of Cultures*, trans. Brian McNeil (San Francisco: Ignatius, 2006).
22. Ratzinger, *Turning Point for Europe*, 42.
23. Ratzinger, *Christianity and the Crisis of Cultures*, 50–52.
24. Ratzinger, *Turning Point for Europe*, 112.

Ratzinger's apologetic for Christianity turns out to be an apologetic for secular modernity as well. He is a severe critic of modernity, but he has little in common with those thinkers who call for a new monastic withdrawal or a new medieval Christianization of society. Ratzinger wants a new Hellenization of Christianity. And he wants it for the sake of a stronger, more human, more secular Europe: more secular because reason has opened itself to the full *saeculum* of human life in all its breadth and depth.

Beneath the surface here is a strictly Augustinian conception of the two cities. The universality of the church's teaching never translates into political power or a superior theory of the ordering of society. The gospel supplies no template for government, law, or economics. Yet the gospel is essential to those spheres to the extent that it nourishes the moral depths of the human person and awakens secular reason to its own transcendent foundations.

REASON AND LOVE

Probably no other Christian thinker in recent times has given so much weight to reason, rationality, *logos*. Is Ratzinger too optimistic about the competency of reason? The Catholic theologian Hermann Häring speaks of Ratzinger's "unconditional praise of the Enlightenment and his extraordinarily high estimation of reason and rationality," as well as his relatively straightforward identification of the Johannine Logos with the Logos of Greek metaphysics.[25] Protestant readers may also wonder whether Ratzinger concedes enough to the noetic effects of sin. Can the world's problems be solved by reason when reason is so susceptible to the distorting influence of ego and self-interest? The scientific method itself first arose not as an expression of unbounded confidence in reason but as a corrective to the human mind's seemingly ineluctable tendency toward distortion, prejudice, and error.[26]

---

25. Hermann Häring, *Theologie und Ideologie bei Joseph Ratzinger* (Dusseldorf: Patmos, 2001), 45, 49.
26. Most clearly seen in Francis Bacon's account of the "idols of the mind": see *The New Organon*, ed. Lisa Jardine (Cambridge: Cambridge University Press, 2000), 1.39–68.

Whether or not Ratzinger responds directly to such criticisms, he takes pains to counterbalance the weight of reason in his thought. He does this not by downgrading reason but by setting it in creative tension with love. The polarity between reason and love, *logos* and *agape*, is in fact the centerpiece of Ratzinger's theological project. It has defined his work from the 1960s to the papal encyclicals *Deus Caritas Est* (2005) and *Caritas in Veritate* (2009).

In *Deus Caritas Est,* the pope returned to the theme that had preoccupied him since the start of his academic career: the synthesis of biblical faith and Greek philosophy. The Lutheran theologian Anders Nygren had posed a radical disjunction between (Greek) *eros* and (Christian) *agape*. Ordinary desiring, acquisitive love, he argued, is totally incompatible with Christianity and has to be set aside by self-sacrificial love.[27] The logic of Nygren's position has a natural kinship with the classic Protestant disjunction between faith and reason, the world of the Bible and the world of ordinary human experience. Benedict XVI's reply to Nygren corresponds closely to the Catholic doctrine of the analogy of being. He writes, "Biblical faith does not set up a parallel universe, or one opposed to that primordial human phenomenon which is love, but rather accepts the whole man; it intervenes in his search for love in order to purify it and to reveal new dimensions of it."[28] If there were an antithesis between *agape* and *eros*, then "the essence of Christianity would be detached from the vital relations fundamental to human existence and would become a world apart, admirable perhaps but decisively cut off from the complex fabric of human life."[29] Grace does not abolish nature but perfects it. God's love is totally *eros* and totally *agape*. It is a desiring love that finds its fullest expression in self-sacrifice. There is no opposition between Plato's *Symposium* and the Gospel of John: the latter absorbs, purifies, and perfects the former.

---

27. Anders Nygren, *Agape and Eros,* trans. Philip Watson (Philadelphia: Westminster, 1953).

28. Benedict XVI, *Deus Caritas* Est, Encyclical Letter, December 25, 2005, §8, https://w2.vatican.va/content/benedict-xvi/en/encyclicals/documents/hf_ben-xvi_enc_20051225_deus-caritas-est.html.

29. Benedict XVI, *Deus Caritas Est,* §7.

Benedict argues for the unity not only of *agape* and *eros* but also of *agape* and *logos*. Under the influence of Christianity, the philosophical concept of God underwent a profound change. Aristotle's ultimate being—immovable and incapable of desire or relation—was reinterpreted as an infinitely personal, creative, self-communicating love. The unmoved mover is also the One who hears and answers the cry of the human heart. God is pure love as well as pure reason. The foundation of knowledge and the foundation of morality are one and the same. If Christianity was Hellenized, even more so was Greek philosophy Christianized by this dynamic union of *agape* and *logos*.

In his later encyclical *Caritas in Veritate*, Benedict teases out the social and political implications of the unity of love and reason. Western societies today presuppose a separation between the domain of knowledge and the domain of morality. The first concerns reason; the second is confined to feeling and opinion. The first drives toward certainty; in the second everything is relative. The first delivers the social benefits of economic growth and technological progress; the second plays no real part in social progress but only provides charitable assistance for individuals who fall through the cracks. But this division of knowledge from morality, the pope argues, sets us on a path toward the disintegration of humanity. Scientific reason alone lacks direction. It has no access to the first beginnings and final ends of the human person. Only when knowledge is animated by love, when the scope of reason is broadened to encompass moral reflection, can the scientific method become a means to human flourishing and integration. "Intelligence and love are not in separate compartments: love is rich in intelligence and intelligence is full of love."[30]

Once more the influence of Augustine's *City of God* is clear. The church's social teaching is not a rival theory of society or an alternative method for obtaining human flourishing. The church respects the proper calling of secular reason and only seeks to support reason by elucidating

30. Benedict XVI, *Caritas in Veritate*, Encyclical Letter, June 29, 2009, §30, http://w2.vatican.va/content/benedict-xvi/en/encyclicals/documents/hf_ben-xvi_enc_20090629_caritas-in-veritate.html.

its deeper moral foundations. Love is not an alternative to reason. Love solves no concrete social problems. But love is a moral energy that gives direction to reason, so that reason can be empowered to work at finding technical solutions to problems within its own sphere of competency. As Benedict writes in *Deus Caritas Est*, "Faith enables reason to do its work more effectively and to see its proper object more clearly."[31]

CONCLUSION

Modern Western societies, according to Ratzinger, are dying from an insufficient use of reason. We are dying from community: or to be more exact, from communal identity drained of any universally valid rationality. A community without rationality is only a tribe. Its practices are self-authenticating. Its claims are unique and incommunicable. Its truths are myths, that is, the self-validating stories of one particular community. Its moral world is sealed off from any higher moral order. Its peculiar virtue of passionate allegiance is idolatrous to the extent that the group requires allegiance in its own name and for its own sake, not for the sake of a higher truth. In exchange for such allegiance the individual is rewarded with feelings of security, identity, belonging. But those feelings have no objective merit. From a psychological point of view the violent white nationalist and the local library volunteer both experience the same feelings of purposeful belonging. Only the question of truth determines the relative value of any particular communal belonging.

How are we to participate in a shared world if we can no longer appeal to a common rational order? How can we cross tribal boundaries in pursuit of the common good if each group supposes itself to be bounded by its own immanent rules and practices? What are we to do when communities seek mutually incompatible goals and proclaim mutually incompatible standards of justice? Have we no capacity for mutual critique, negotiation, and adjustment? In the absence of any group-transcending rationality, is it any wonder that social groups increasingly see power as the only conceivable way of pursuing their aims? And is it any wonder that, in our time, the great projects of

---

31. Benedict XVI, *Deus Caritas Est*, §28.

political universalism—Europe and what it represents—are breaking down?

Ratzinger's theology is addressed to this global situation. He approaches the question of faith and reason not primarily as a topic for theologians but as a question about the future of humanity. He is best compared not to the encyclopedic dogmaticians like Barth and Pannenberg but to a Protestant thinker like Reinhold Niebuhr, a theologian of culture who uses doctrinal resources to investigate the perplexities and contradictions of his society. Ratzinger is most critical of modernity at exactly the point at which he is most allied with it: in a commitment to the rational foundations of a properly human, properly secular order.

Ratzinger responds to the Protestant division of faith and reason by arguing that faith is necessarily rational. And he responds to secular modernity by arguing that reason is necessarily open to transcendence. Faith and reason both arise from the same divine Logos. The church needs a wider conception of faith, and the world needs a wider conception of reason.

If Ratzinger comes across at times as a champion of rationalism, the impression is tempered by his consistent emphasis on the mutually conditioning relation between reason and love. Reason gives love its content and direction. And love for its part anchors reason in reality. Love ensures that reason seeks not just abstract technical goals but the good of the human person. "The Logos became flesh" (John 1:14); "God is love" (1 John 4:16). All truth, all knowledge, all human wisdom are taken up and transformed—not abrogated but purified and elevated—by that revelation.

PART I

DOGMATIC THEOLOGY

2

Writing Theology in a Secular Age

Joseph Ratzinger on Theological Method

KATHERINE SONDEREGGER

I t is not a discovery of today that we live in a secular age: theologians have
been mourning the passing of the old Christendom since the Victorian
Matthew Arnold, in the gray tones of "Dover Beach," painted his elegiac
portrait of an ebbing tide of faith, "retreating, ... down the vast edges drear
/ And naked shingles of the world."[1] As professor of theology, prefect of the
Congregation for the Doctrine of the Faith, and as pope, Joseph Ratzinger
has thrown his considerable theological passions against the coming flood
of secularism in a modern world. It is sometimes said that as prefect and
pope, Ratzinger opposed *modernity*, or perhaps in more technical idiom,
*modernis*m in theology; but I think his writings show a deeper animus against
secularism, a world indifferent to the reality of God. Of course, the shaping of the modern world in the West—the division of the medieval church
during the sixteenth century; the rise of Enlightenment thought; the growth
and dominance of the nation-state—all these give vibrancy and depth to
secularism as a way of life. But as pope, Benedict did not turn a deaf ear to
modernity as a whole; indeed, we might say that certain prized possessions
of a modern conception of life—the dream of freedom, for example, or the
glory of the human and the humane—hold prime positions in Benedict's
theology. Secularism, on the other hand, can find no refuge in Ratzinger's
thought. From his earliest writings to his last encyclicals, Ratzinger insisted
that the only and true great hope for humanity is the reality of God and

---

1. Matthew Arnold, *New Poems* (London: Macmillan, 1867), 112–14 (here 113).

28

belief in him. Some scholars have considered Ratzinger a "cosmopolitan anti-liberal."[2] However intriguing a label—it has the pleasing air of an oxymoron—in truth, I believe Ratzinger might best be understood as a modern Christian, a theologian dedicated to exploring the present-day mystery of the human being in light of the Eternal Mystery who is God.

Those of us who take up the task of theology out of the churches of the Reformation might find, at first glance, Pope Benedict to be a formidable, perhaps implacable non-Protestant. Most certainly, as prefect, as cardinal archbishop, and as pope, he was a stout defender of the Catholic Church, its magisterium, and its faith. He is rightly seen as a traditionalist in this narrow sense: in his passion for Marian piety (the "inner culture" of European Catholicism), in the liturgy and ceremonial of the post-Tridentine church, and in the ideals of the ascetic and sanctified life, Benedict could brook no rival. He advanced a more dogmatic and conservative reading of the major constitutions of Vatican II, and was a decided critic of much liberation theology, especially as formulated in the immediate postconciliar period. He was more inclined to speak of Protestants as members of "ecclesial communities," as outlined in the ecumenical document *Dominus Iesus*, and he defended papal primacy and universal jurisdiction with great rigor. These well-defined traits of Ratzinger's *mentalité* as theologian might strike evangelical dogmaticians as unfertile soil for collaboration. But this assessment would overlook the great commonality all Christian theologians share—the proclamation of the gospel in a world indifferent, perhaps hardened, to its sweetness—and the remarkable strengths Ratzinger brings to this common task. And, in more careful exploration of Ratzinger's major works, we find a deep commitment to ecumenical ecclesiology, and an extensive, fine-grained knowledge of major Protestant theologians. Indeed, we would more likely find nuanced readings of Martin Luther and Immanuel Kant, and of modernist Lutherans such as Adolf von Harnack and Rudolf Bultmann, in Ratzinger's texts than in those of many leading Protestant theologians.

---

2. Tracey Rowland, *Ratzinger's Faith: The Theology of Pope Benedict XVI* (Oxford: Oxford University Press, 2008), 46.

In Ratzinger's work we will find rich resources for topics that have deviled Protestant theologians in the modern era: the place of authority, ecclesial and creedal, in the shaping of doctrine; the proper claim of philosophy, most especially metaphysics, in theology and exegesis; the long road of enculturating ancient dogmas in a startlingly new world; and the role and calling of the professoriate in Christian theology. Most pleasing, perhaps, to Protestant dogmaticians, Ratzinger was above all a *scriptural* theologian. He brought to Catholic theology a *ressourcement* for Augustine and Bonaventure, and he shared with those Doctors of the Church a passion for the sacred page. As pope, his encyclicals read as sensitive biblical commentaries, where Thomism is brought into a larger conceptual realm of deep reflection on a scriptural text. As one of the founders of *Communio*, the international journal of Catholic theology, Ratzinger exhibited his loyalty to the liturgical and biblical renewal movements of the Interwar years; he belongs to the thought-world of Henri de Lubac, Joseph Pieper, Romano Guardini, and Hans Urs von Balthasar. These are theologians of the whole church, gifts to any dogmatician who anchors the riches of doctrine in the fertile soil of holy Scripture. Ratzinger brings these vast holdings into modern theology, and we are all the beneficiaries. And in a gift above all, he shows us the world we live in, unvarnished, and as it truly is.

Let me begin with an address Pope Benedict gave at the Convent of Saint Scholastica, in Subiaco, Italy, at the beginning of his pontificate. In this address, Benedict outlines many of his most familiar themes about secularism in the modern world. (These we must unfold bit by bit.) But he ends the lecture on a wistful note:

> But at this point, in my capacity as believer, I would like to make a proposal to the secularists. ... Kant had denied that God could be known in the realm of pure reason, but at the same time he had represented God, freedom and immortality as postulates of practical reason, without which, coherently, for him no moral behavior was possible. Does not today's situation of the world make us think perhaps that he might have been right? I would

like to express it in a different way: the attempt, carried to the extreme, to manage human affairs disdaining God completely leads us increasingly to the edge of the abyss, to man's ever greater isolation from reality. We must reverse the axiom of the Enlightenment and say: Even one who does not succeed in finding the way of accepting God, should, nevertheless, seek to live and to direct his life "veluti si Deus daretur," as if God existed. This is the advice Pascal gave to his friends who did not believe. In this way, no one is limited in his freedom, but all our affairs find the support and criterion of which they are in urgent need.[3]

Here, the pope discloses an underlying *alliance*, a sympathy and empathy, with the modern condition. However prone this theologian has been to expose and relentlessly rebuke the foundations of the modern, Benedict firmly anchors Christian theology in that world and in the present day. His is no "Benedict option"! Rather he invites the secularist to examine the world that confronts us, the world we have made, with a clear eye and a pitying heart. This is a world, Benedict warns, where "the splendour of being an image of God no longer shines over man, which is what confers on him his dignity and inviolability, and he is left only to the power of his own human capacities."[4] Those capacities Benedict catalogs with a keen, but also solicitous spirit. The world we have fashioned is vulnerable to terrorism, a human "capacity for destruction which at times horrifies us."[5] Of course this malign "sign of the times" can be used simply to throw blame on others—nations, groups, individuals—and shore up the West as innocent but indomitable bystanders. But Benedict is not given to such cheap analyses. Immediately he notes how the very proper human longing for security and purpose in our world has led Western states to "adopt internal security systems similar to those that

3. Benedict XVI, "Appendix I: The Subiaco Address," in Rowland, *Ratzinger's Faith*, 156–65 (here 164–65).
4. Benedict XVI, "Subiaco Address," 156.
5. Benedict XVI, "Subiaco Address," 156.

previously existed only in dictatorships."[6] Benedict knows, too, the suffering of the present age. He notes rising inequality, searing poverty and famine, the ecological crisis that menaces the earth, and the "technical systems of control" that threaten to overwhelm the dignity, purpose, and nature of human beings, the embodied spirits who have engineered the technologies that now seem poised to rule us.

These themes pervade the 2009 papal encyclical *Caritas in Veritate*, a commemorative essay on Paul VI's celebrated treatise *Populorum Progressio* (1967). Here Benedict takes up the unfinished work of *Populorum Progressio*, the analytic task of measuring the reach of "globalization," and the technical financial instruments that make possible such an integrated, "articulated" world. Benedict is generous in his praise of Paul VI, but does not hesitate to rebuke an easy confidence in the rosy glow of "development," and a modern notion of "progress." "More than forty years after *Populorum Progressio*," Benedict notes, "its basic theme, namely progress, *remains an open question*, made all the more acute and urgent by the current economic and financial crisis. If some areas of the globe with a history of poverty have experienced remarkable changes in terms of their economic growth and their share in world production, other zones are still living in a situation of deprivation comparable to that which existed at the time of Paul VI, and in some cases one can even speak of a deterioration."[7] Benedict marshals an impressive roll call of modern economic actors: transnational corporations, cultural borrowings and mixtures, the porous boundaries of modern nation-states, juridical authorities replaced by authorities of the market, modern financial instruments (often computer driven), environmental degradation, and the great migration of labor from a new homeless and landless people. In bold face, Benedict underscores his major premise: "The world's wealth is growing in absolute terms, but inequalities are on

---

6. Benedict XVI, "Subiaco Address," 156. Benedict does not specify these menacing systems, but we might expect he would mention the greater security cordons at airports and train stations, the widespread use of surveillance cameras in public spaces, the quiet amassing of details on citizens through electronic means.

7. Benedict XVI, *Charity in Truth: Caritas in Veritate* (San Francisco: Ignatius Press, 2009), 63–64.

the increase."[8] Wealthy nations exhibit a kind of faceless consumerism, unchecked, shallow and wasteful, and they promote this form of secular development—"superdevelopment"—that moors a tiny elite, mirroring the bourgeois world of things, in a sea of utter despoliation and poverty. Benedict is as relentless a critic of modern economic cruelty as any liberation theologian: human beings, made in the image of God, are hungry, exploited, imprisoned, and even more deeply imprisoned by unemployment, abuse, and indifference; they are denied health care, freedom of movement, and freedom of religion, reduced to a life without beauty, love, and culture. This is not the whole of modern development, certainly. Benedict also recognizes the enduring significance of capitalism—he scorns the millenarianism of Marxist-Leninism—and the technological innovations in medicine, social mobility, and communication that enrich many lives. But ours is a godless world; and that brute fact undermines any claim to true human development:

> God is *the guarantor of man's true development,* inasmuch as, having created him in his image he also establishes the transcendent dignity of men and women and feeds their innate yearning to "be more." Man is not a lost atom in a random universe: he is God's creature, whom God chose to endow with an immortal soul and whom he has always loved. If man were merely the fruit of either chance or necessity, or he had to lower his aspirations to the limited horizon of the world in which he lives, if all reality were merely history and culture and man did not possess a nature destined to transcend itself in a supernatural life, then one could speak of growth, or evolution, but not development.[9]

Though hardly a long-standing admirer of his contemporary Karl Rahner, Benedict could readily echo Rahner's claim that a humanity without even the name God would amount to little more than "clever animals." *Caritas in Veritate* offers a somber assessment of our era: in

---

8. Benedict XVI, *Caritas in Veritate*, 41.
9. Benedict XVI, *Caritas in Veritate*, 56–57.

the midst of great wealth, we starve from a gnawing lack of love, most especially God's love.

Now much of this diagnosis sits easy with an ideological antimodernism, even a reactionary one. Some social critics long to return to some earlier, golden era—the postwar era, say, when US power was in ascendance; the global reach of empire for Great Britain, France, or Germany; the ultramontanism of Vatican I; or further back still, behind the Enlightenment or the Reformation to a time when the well of faith was brimful and pure—such nostalgia can seek little more than a removal of the modern, and a luxuriating in old times. Certainly, the line between criticism and reaction is obscure. In his melancholy investigation of the Weimar years, Peter Gay traces the ambiguity of European movements, secular and religious, right and left, seeking an organic wholeness, a purity to be found—where? in the past? in the inner emigration of a disenchanted generation? in a daring and revolutionary present?[10] The delicate maneuver of moving backward in order to move forward haunts the radicalism of the Interwar years—and not only they. Protestants will recognize the ambiguity of such movements in the widespread theological call to tear open modern capital's "iron cage," as Max Weber put it; or in some feminist theologians' censure of the "Enlightenment subject"; or in the frequent calls from the pastor's pulpit to become "countercultural"; or, again, in Karl Barth's repeated swings back behind the early moderns to find firm ground for fresh dogmatic work. Indeed, Barth's full-throated animus against certain forms of modernism has branded him, in some circles, a social conservative, even theological reactionary—a caricature, I believe, of Barth's actual theology and bearing. Such ambiguities, it seems, run clear only after close study. We might say that the entire program of Vatican II, summed up in the catchwords *ressourcement* and *aggiornamento*, carry in themselves the ambiguity of a modern church in a modern world, at times at ease and at times exiled and horrified. As prefect and pope, Ratzinger walked in this narrow hallway, and his writings exhibit at once a profound commitment to addressing and entering into the world of

---

10. Peter Gay, *Weimar Culture: The Outsider as Insider* (New York: W. W. Norton, 2001).

contemporary men and women, and an equal defiance of the misshapen and defiling elements of a world that has made its peace with poverty, violence, and despair. Present-day Protestants can learn much sitting at Benedict's feet here, because evangelicals and mainline Christians have found themselves caught between a longing for an earlier day, when "The Sea of Faith ... Lay like the folds of a bright girdle furled" and a longing for a future day, when the old wounds are healed, and the truth will be revealed in majesty and glorious light. We, too, need to learn how to be the church in the modern world.

Benedict has learned this lesson well. He expresses the modern moment in theology in a striking and vivid fashion, by examining and honoring the human subject: Benedict places the human being at the very center of theology. Catholics recalling twentieth-century theological movements will recognize the notes of personalism and a form of Christian phenomenology in this "turn toward the subject." And Protestants will immediately recognize such a starting point too: anthropology has been front and center in modern dogmatics since the pathbreaking work of Friedrich Schleiermacher's *Christian Faith*—and perhaps still further back, to Luther's profound examination of the troubled conscience and the *Anfechtung* of the sinner before the holy God. For Schleiermacher, as for the magisterial Reformers, theology is principally *gospel*: it is the good news of the sinner's rescue by a gracious God in Christ. To be sure, Christian theology must address other dimensions of the church's confession—creation, providence, cosmology—but in the end, each of these must exhibit a relation to the human being, redeemed. We know Christ—and all things in relation to him—"in his benefits," we might say. Modern theology of this stripe is fundamentally *religious*: it concerns itself principally and in the end with sin and grace. For this reason, Protestant dogmatics has been strictly christological; this mirrors the christological concentration of Vatican II, of Karl Rahner and Balthasar, and of Ratzinger.

Now, this is *not* the same as saying modern theology is "subjectivist," "constructivist," or "historicist"; not at all! Certainly, the architects of modern Western theology have seen Kant hovering over their shoulders, and they are preoccupied—far too zealously, I say—with showing in method how a focus on the redeemed sinner can square with the strictures of critical philosophy. But Protestant theology, evangelical and Reformed, has consistently sought to describe the world as it is, to trace back all creaturely goods to the sovereign creative will of God, and to direct the path of nations into the bright light of God's dealings with us. However divergent in doctrine, Schleiermacher and Herman Bavinck and Barth and Paul Tillich shared these marks of theological realism. Anthropology serves in these theologies as keystone; it holds up and integrates but does not replace the entire archway. Something of this pattern we find in the theology of Joseph Ratzinger.

In his book *The Nature and Mission of Theology,* Ratzinger places at the very center of theology the "new subject," a human life transformed by the encounter with the risen Christ. A biblical theologian, Ratzinger begins his examination of the human subject by a close reading of the Pauline Letters. Turning to the apostle Paul's account of his life in the Letter to the Galatians, Ratzinger compresses into one luminous experience the human person as radiant center of a community, a tradition, and a world transformed. "Beginning on the outside, this *apologia pro vita sua* leads him, so to speak, farther and farther inward."[11] Here the Augustinian notes are unmistakable. "Paul first presents the external events surrounding his vocation and the subsequent direction of his life. Finally, however, this one phrase, [who does not think here of *tolle, lege?*] like a sudden bolt of lightning, reveals in its light the inner event which took place in these outer events and lies at their very foundation."[12] Now Ratzinger draws together in tight compass the themes that will anchor his modern account of person and church: "This inner event is at one and the same time wholly personal and wholly objective. It is an individual experience in the highest degree, yet it declares what the essence of Christianity is for everyone."[13] Note the determined emphasis on realism here: the anthropology Ratzinger favors is unthinkable

11. Joseph Ratzinger, *The Nature and Mission of Theology: Understanding Its Role in the Light of the Present Controversy,* trans. Adrian Walker (San Francisco: Ignatius, 1995), 50.
12. Ratzinger, *Nature and Mission,* 51–52.
13. Ratzinger, *Nature and Mission,* 51.

without the "objective," the "external," and the universal. This is the elixir of modern philosophy, to move from the inner world of the human subject out into the world of external objects, collectivities, and things. "From the inner to the outer": this may well be the motto of modern philosophy. But note again, the move *away* from a Cartesian or perhaps Kantian foundation in the human. The apostle's experience is *at once* inner and outer, *at once* personal and objective; the two essentials meet in the one experience, and neither serves as prior condition to the other. (We may say that in truth this realist copresence may have been the aim of Descartes and Kant—and even Wilhelm Herrmann—all along.) Ratzinger underscores the radical nature of Paul's experience. It is not "conversion," though to be sure human lives are changed, reoriented, transformed by such an encounter. It is not quite "becoming Christian." In truth, no language this side of the Jordan can capture this revolution: "It is a death-event." Here Ratzinger begins to sound very much like his contemporaries Balthasar and Barth: "It is an exchange of the old subject for another. The 'I' ceases to be an autonomous subject standing in itself. It is snatched away from itself and fitted into a new subject. The 'I' is not simply submerged, but it must really release its grip on itself in order then to receive itself anew in and together with a greater 'I.'"[14]

This lightning bolt, this revolution? "It is no longer I who live, but Christ who lives in me" (Gal 2:20). Here we are brought to the very gold standard of modern, Western theories of the self—the territory of the human subject-in-the-world. Ratzinger understands the apostle Paul to undertake an introspection of his inner life, to plunge down into the roots of awareness, and encounter the identity of human selfhood, the "I." In this drive to the inner depths, the apostle is not simply recounting his own journey, though of course he does that. In truth, he exemplifies the human search for self-awareness. Every Christian, "in essence," makes this pilgrimage in and out of one's own inner chambers. What shatters this "turn to the subject" is the Revolution who is Christ. "It is the surrender of the old isolated subjectivity of the 'I' in order to find oneself within the unity of a new subject, which bursts the limits of the

---

14. Ratzinger, *Nature and Mission*, 51.

'I,' thus making possible contact with the ground of all reality."[15] The human subject is radically remade. The old self is shattered on the Rock who is Christ, and what was once seen as freedom—the "autonomous subject standing in itself"—has now, by dying to self, risen up into a new larger subject, the "Christ in me." Like Barth, again, Ratzinger spies trouble in the Enlightenment praise of an autonomous, self-directed, and self-determining life. This is a notion of freedom that both would consider a form of blindness, an Oedipal prison of our own making. Such isolated sovereignty in truth is not "in contact with the ground of all reality." This is a very strong claim indeed; but we see the whole compass of Ratzinger's theology in this sharp rejection of individual self-determination. Secularism cannot be a form of realism—his claim is that strong. What is necessary for the human subject, for the life and flourishing of the human person, is that this shell of atomized rights and liberties must be shattered, *killed*, so that a larger, "new subject" can be born, the person who has God as its ground, Christ as its *inner* subjectivity. We must become members of the body of Christ.

Protestant theologians who have been drawn to communitarian themes in ethics and ecclesiology will have much to like in Ratzinger's anthropology. Stanley Hauerwas has made these themes programmatic for many ethicists, but theologians as varied as Sallie McFague, Miroslav Volf, and Jürgen Moltmann have united in their opposition to an isolated, self-enclosed human subject. Freedom, a hallmark of self-determination, should no longer be defined as self-directed and self-caused action, they will argue, but rather as the relatedness, the joining of self with another, that lies at the heart of community. Of course, such themes will carry a certain poignancy in a tradition that springs from an individual refusal: "Here I stand; I can do no other; so help me God," Luther said staunchly at the conclusion of the Diet of Worms, or so legend will have it. And US Protestants face a religious culture that is increasingly driven by individual choice—of congregation, of music and worship preferences, of youth programs and Sunday school, even of pastor and denomination itself. Indeed, the very notion of a "denominated church" seems especially

---

15. Ratzinger, *Nature and Mission*, 51.

suited to a culture that praises self-reliance. The frontier, as Frederick Turner observed in a celebrated nineteenth-century essay, has defined the United States; every generation has sought a "new frontier." "The result," Turner concluded, in his masterful style, "is that to the frontier the American intellect owes its striking characteristics. That coarseness and strength combined with acuteness and inquisitiveness; that practical, inventive turn of mind, quick to find expedients; that masterful grasp of material things, lacking in the artistic but powerful to effect great ends; that restless, nervous energy; that dominant individualism, working for good and for evil, and withal that buoyancy and exuberance which comes with freedom—these are traits of the frontier, or traits called out elsewhere because of the existence of the frontier."[16] For Protestant theologians the virtues of the pioneer—a tough-mindedness, a fearless self-direction, a canny reliance on one's own resources—make communitarian ideals a cross-grained ideal. We will learn much from Ratzinger here, as we Americans in particular may feel in our cultural bones the *radicality* of a self, slain and broken open, in order to be alive, only in Christ, only in and for the neighbor.

We Protestants might find provocative and instructive, too, the topic of authority, which is well-rehearsed and entailed in Ratzinger's notion of the "larger I." For Ratzinger, as for John Henry Newman, a favorite of Ratzinger's youth, the teaching authority of the church, the magisterium, belongs to the very essence of the church, the "larger I." Now, it is part of the historical identity of the churches of the Reformation to reject a certain form of magisterium, the personal primacy and infallibility of the Roman pontiff, and his universal jurisdiction over the world's churches. To be sure, ecumenical talks have brought far greater precision and insight into this teaching of Roman primacy, and Protestants can only be grateful for a richer, less heated dialogue over hierarchy and episcopacy in the Western church. But beyond this, Benedict's resolute attention to the matter of authoritative teaching for the members of the body of Christ can only sharpen Protestant analyses of the place

---

16. Frederick Turner, "The Significance of the Frontier in American History," *Annual Report of the American Historical Association* (1893): 197–227 (here 227).

of dogma, Scripture, and creed within theology. Early in his vocation as prefect of the Congregation for the Doctrine of the Faith, Ratzinger addressed the neuralgic conflict of academic freedom in Catholic universities and faculties. His essay "On the Essence of the Academy and Its Freedom" reads as a digest of Ratzinger's history of the modern self, and the place of truth and right reason, within the freedom of cultural institutions. Here, Ratzinger's conviction that the new subject in Christ is at once individual and communal, broken open to transcendence, persuades him that authoritative truth must be the ground of freedom. "If truth purifies man from egotism and from the illusion of absolute autonomy, if it makes him obedient and gives him the courage to be humble, it thereby also teaches him to see through producibility as a parody of freedom and to unmask undisciplined chatter as a parody of dialogue. It is victorious over the tendency to mistake the absence of all ties for freedom. Thus, the truth is fruitful precisely by being loved for its own sake."[17]

Here Ratzinger ties together the objective elements of truth and goodness to the subjective dimensions of humility and obedience. In fact, he concludes that "the freedom of the truth belongs not merely accidentally but essentially in the context of worship, of cult."[18] This brief allusion to worship belies what is in fact a crimson thread throughout Ratzinger's work, the place of liturgy in Christian theology. The remade subjects that now live in Christ, and he in them, are seen most clearly in the sacrament of baptism. The church's rite is the objective enactment of the dying and rising self, the expansive awareness of corporate existence in the mystical body of Christ. (Ratzinger much admired de Lubac's essay in ecclesiology *Corpus Mysticum*.) "Because Christian conversion throws open the frontier between the 'I' and the 'not-I,' it can be bestowed upon one only by the 'not-I' and can never be achieved solely in the interiority of one's personal decision. It has a sacramental structure." This inner freedom is a gift of baptism, "an event involving the

---

17. Ratzinger, *Nature and Mission*, 39.
18. Ratzinger, *Nature and Mission*, 41.

Church."[19] A cardinal ideal of modern Protestant theology—the human self as gift and not achievement—emerges directly from Ratzinger's ecclesial subjectivity. The church in its sacramental grace draws the convert now into the depths, where the old self is drowned and put off, and then draw up into the new life, where Christ lives among and in us. Protestants who have long cherished an ideal of the immediate relation of the Christian to Almighty God might find this appeal to worship, to church, and to authority far too rich for their blood. But as the history of Protestant theology has shown, the appeal to holy Scripture as sole authority has not settled but rather engendered sharp-edged debates, and the unstable relation between early conciliar defini-tions—Nicaea, say, or Chalcedon—and the reception of these Symbols by Protestant theologians has made authority in modern dogmatics a complex and unfinished task. We may well find ourselves in agreement with Ratzinger's ringing conclusion to this essay: "To clarify the concept of freedom numbers among the crucial tasks of the present day—if we are about the preservation of man and of the world."[20]

Finally, we might consider more carefully the virtues that infuse this new subject: the cardinal virtue of reason and the theological graces of faith, hope, and love. In his ill-fated address to the University of Regensburg, his old alma mater, the new Pope Benedict took up the relation of faith and reason, and the "de-Hellenization" that threatens to tear these principles asunder. Benedict sees threats to rationality throughout the rise of a secular, emancipated Europe. In a lovely and unexpected turn, Benedict first indicts not the loss of faith, but rather the loss of *reason* in the modern and postmodern cultures of today's universities. His startling citation from a medieval polemic between a Christian ruler and a Persian scholar was intended to stress the pri-macy of reason; in a later footnote, he explicitly rejects the historical "polemic" against Islam.[21] His central aim: the human being exercises the gift of reason because God's very nature is rational, the *Logos* itself. Once

---

19. Ratzinger, *Nature and Mission*, 52.

20. Ratzinger, *Nature and Mission*, 41.

21. Benedict XVI, "Appendix II: The Regensburg Address," in Rowland, *Ratzinger's Faith*, 166–74 (here 168).

again we see Benedict's central commitment to theism as the ground of all virtues, all freedoms, all realisms. The exalted nature of the human being—the burst of rationality into the realm of animal nature—must put down roots into the soil of eternal reason, or lose its confidence in rationality altogether. Benedict sees such an unmooring in the European drive toward de-Hellenizing, a coarse rejection of the heritage of Attic philosophy and ethics from the culture of the West.

Several stages lead out of a thirteenth-century harmony of faith and reason into a present-day collapse of rationality as a universal, human given. Readers familiar with genealogies of the modern, beginning with the twentieth-century Thomist Jacques Maritain, will be surprised to find Descartes missing in the rogues gallery. In his encyclical *Spe Salvi*, Benedict rather fastens on Francis Bacon, the sixteenth-century author and naturalist. In Bacon, "a new era emerged. … It is the new correlation of experiment and method that enables man to arrive at an interpretation of nature in conformity with its laws and thus finally to achieve the 'triumph of art over nature.'"[22] Not logical relation or ontological truth characterizes rationality now, but rather the contingent, the random, the brute fact. Ecofeminists have pointed to Bacon as the first spokesman for a technical domination of nature; but Benedict puts this exemplar to other uses. For the pope, Bacon articulates a vision of "secular redemption," a mastery over the world that is given only by a joining of "science and praxis," not by faith in Jesus Christ. Thus Christian faith is reduced to a private sphere, a "preference," and has hopes only in a realm far removed from this earth; theology can no longer claim to reveal and guide the affairs of this world. Progress belongs to the pragmatic. In this way, at times unwittingly, and by slow but relentless steps, faith is decoupled from reason, and reason given an entirely secular air and empirical pedigree.

Benedict does not hesitate to rebuke Catholics for participating in this dismemberment. Indeed, in the first methodological chapter of *The Nature and Mission of Theology*, then Cardinal Ratzinger deplores the sundering of faith and reason into distinct spheres or planes; this is

---

22. Benedict XVI, *Spe Salvi: Saved in Hope* (San Francisco: Ignatius, 2007), 41.

"manual Thomism," and the *Communio* school argued forcefully for a profound intercommunion of faith and reason, grace and nature, not their ranked separation. But, all the same, Benedict's main targets remain Protestant theologians, from Luther forward. Benedict considers the sixteenth-century assault on scholasticism and metaphysics, all in the name of a revived return to Scripture, a dangerous severing of theology from rationality, *logos*, and a defiance of the providential aim to join the faith of Israel with the reasoned argument of the Greeks. Harnack, Ritschl, Barth: all are chided for their attempt to remove classical metaphysics from the inner citadel of doctrine. Those of us who consider these theologians, and their schools, fathers in the faith will want to study Benedict closely here. In what way can metaphysics be properly joined to scriptural exegesis, if at all? How is the providence of God understood in the development of doctrine in the early church, in the theologians of the Mediterranean basin? How can argument serve the search for understanding of the faith? How can acculturation of the gospel be realized should Hellenization and mission be joined in this way? These are central questions in Protestant dogmatics of the present day, and Benedict will prove a wise guide—even when his solutions cannot be adopted.

Benedict's fundamental aim in this revisionary historiography remains, however, theological and doctrinal. He seeks to anchor the human person in a profound interpenetration of faith, hope, and love, in which the greatest of these is love. The true progress of humanity, Benedict argues time and again, can come only by a deep moral transformation, the grounding of the human self in the God who is Love. There can be no "secular progress," in the strict sense of these terms. Rather, the God who is at once *Logos* and Love, and the telos of all faith and hope, must call humanity to himself and dwell within the human family. This is true, humane hope. Benedict in his first papal encyclical, *Deus Caritas Est*, speaks in a full-throated Augustinian voice. Here he seeks to overcome another popular divide in modern theology, that between *eros* and *agape*. Christian life properly is not all self-giving, nor is it "world denying" or contemptuous of the body; rather love seeks to encounter, to enjoy, to learn, and then to hold fast. "Love embraces the whole of existence in each of its dimensions, including the dimension of time."[23] The "divine madness" that is *eros* must be embraced in order to be purified, matured, strengthened: "It is neither the spirit alone nor the body alone that loves: it is man, the person, a unified creature composed of body and soul, who loves. Only when both dimensions are truly united, does man attain his full stature. Only thus is love—*eros*—able to mature and attain authentic grandeur."[24] Unmistakable is Benedict's instinct for the *whole*, the unified and mutually indwelling elements of thought and life. Such organic, articulated unity can find its source and goal only in God, who is infinite Love. The novelty of biblical faith can be found in its fearless proclamation of a LORD who is at once divine *eros* and *agape*: "The one God in whom Israel believes loves with a personal love. His love, moreover, is an elective love: among all the nations he chooses Israel and loves her—but he does so precisely with a view to healing the whole human race. God loves, and his love may certainly be called *eros*, yet is also totally *agape*."[25] (As the human subject is at once inner and outer, so the divine subject is at once ascending and descending Love.) The calling, judging, and healing of the new human subject by a loving God will bring the Christian into deepest communion with his or her neighbor, and beyond them, to the whole world. Christian faith for Benedict is again, at once, individual and corporate, deeply personal and institutional, a self awakening and a sacrament: it is the whole rational, believing self impelled on a journey to the One who in Christ loved the world to the very end.

All Christians will find Benedict's exhortation about love powerful and powerfully moving. Protestants who too have wrestled with distinctions that become oppositions will find in this pope a radical call for love that can only bring hope to a divided church and a world longing once again to hope and to love. This is the vision of a modern theologian, deeply troubled by the integuments of a secular age; but deeply

---

23. Benedict XVI, *Deus Caritas Est* (Vatican City: Libreria Editrice Vaticana, 2006), 9.
24. Benedict XVI, *Deus Caritas Est*, 8.
25. Benedict XVI, *Deus Caritas Est*, 13.

committed to, and in love with it too. We have much to learn from this Catholic student of Bonaventure, himself a "soul on a journey to God."

3

Faith, Hope, and Love

Joseph Ratzinger on the Theological Virtues

GREGG R. ALLISON

We live in a confusing age characterized by unbelief, despair, and self-centeredness. Accordingly, we owe a debt of gratitude to Benedict XVI, who brought a degree of settledness through his reminder and employment of the theological virtues of faith, hope, and love.[1] As theological virtues, they apply in a particular way to theologians engaged in the task of theology. This appreciative essay will sketch out Benedict's contribution to this important and relevant topic by first presenting his perspective on theology and the theological task, then setting forth his view on faith, hope, and love.

THEOLOGY AND THE THEOLOGICAL TASK

Theology is sui generis. Such is the case, in Benedict's perspective, because theology is "the understanding, *logos*-like (= rational, understanding-through-reason) discussion of God" and, thus, "a fundamental task of the Christian faith."[2] For those engaged in the task, four expectations come to the forefront: (1) to critically exam Christian traditions in light of reason to find the core of the Christian faith; (2) to provide an orientation and meaningful content for today so as to respond to the need for religion and transcendence; (3) to promote interreligious dialogue; and (4) to comfort

---

1. Faith, hope, and love are called the "theological virtues" as presented in the *Catechism of the Catholic Church* §§1812–29.
2. Joseph Ratzinger, *Introduction to Christianity*, trans. J. R. Foster (London: Search Press, 1969), 46.

souls.[3] While shouldering the burden of these expectations, Benedict the theologian takes theology in a more traditional direction.

For Benedict, the theological task is "to serve the knowledge of the truth of revelation and ... unity in the Church" by "pondering what God has said and taught before us."[4] Clearly, revelation is at the heart of theology.[5] Indeed, theology is rational reflection on God's revelation; it receives its content from revelation. As scholars and leaders in the past and present have phrased it, theology is "faith seeking understanding."[6]

This faith seeking understanding should never stand alone. Indeed, theology should be done in conjunction with philosophy. With this perspective, Benedict distances himself from Martin Luther and Karl Barth, whom he considers as standing in opposition to philosophy.[7] Whether or not this assessment of two of Protestantism's theological giants is correct, Benedict does not champion philosophy as supplying theology's content but as indicating the manner in which theology may proceed.[8]

Beyond its cooperation with philosophy, theology should be done in the context of the Roman Catholic Church, with particular reference to the magisterium.[9] Indeed, theology and the church are bound together, as is the theologian with the church. As Benedict riffs on Galatians 2:20: a Roman Catholic theologian has "been crucified with Christ" and thus has exchanged the old subject (the "I" who has been crucified with Christ) for another subject (the "I" who no longer lives as before but lives now by faith in Christ), and this swap comes by means of

3. Joseph Ratzinger, *The Nature and Mission of Theology: Essays to Orient Theology in Today's Debates,* trans. Adrian Walker (San Francisco: Ignatius, 1991), 7.

4. Ratzinger, *Nature and Mission,* 9, 104.

5. Benedict beautifully rehearsed "the peculiarity of the specifically Christian scandal ... the ineradicable positivity of Christianity. What I mean is this: Christian belief is not merely concerned ... with the eternal, which as the 'quite other' would remain completely outside the human world and time; on the contrary, it is much more concerned with God in history, with God as man. By thus seeming to bridge the gulf between eternal and temporal, between the visible and invisible, by making us meet God as a man, the eternal as the temporal, as one of us, it knows itself as revelation. Its claim to be revelation is indeed based on the fact that it has, so to speak, introduced the eternal into our world: 'No one has ever seen God; the only Son, who is in the bosom of the Father, he has made him known' (John 1:18)." Ratzinger, *Introduction to Christianity,* 27.

6. Ratzinger, *Nature and Mission,* 16, 103.

7. Ratzinger, *Nature and Mission,* 18–19.

8. Ratzinger, *Nature and Mission,* 20, 28–29.

9. Ratzinger, *Nature and Mission,* 46–47.

death. Such death is not a private, mystical experience; rather, it occurs within the church, within its sacramental structure, specifically by baptism. Indeed, the "I no longer live" defines the essence of baptism.[10] Accordingly, a theologian doing theology always involves the church.

The presuppositions of theology are four. First is faith.[11] Theology presupposes faith in the word of God and flows from a desire to know God in Jesus Christ.[12] Benedict emphasizes faith as expressed in baptism, which is entrance into the Roman Catholic Church.[13] Thus, for Benedict, faith is a gift from Christ to the church.[14]

The second presupposition of theology is reason.[15] Tying the first and second prerequisites together, "faith presupposes reason and

---

10. Ratzinger, *Nature and Mission,* 50–52.

11. Ratzinger, *Nature and Mission,* 55–56.

12. For Ratzinger, "the life of faith is a path which leads to the knowledge of and encounter with God. ... Faith, in fact, is an encounter with God who speaks and works in history and converts our daily life, transforming within us mentalities, value judgements, decisions and practical actions. Faith is not an illusion, a flight of fancy, a refuge or sentimentalism; rather it is total involvement in the whole of life." Benedict XVI, General Audience, November 14, 2012, http://w2.vatican.va/content/benedict-xvi/en/audiences/2012/documents/hf_ben-xvi_aud_20121114.html.

13. This perspective reflects the general view of Roman Catholic theology regarding faith: "But faith is more than an individual matter, a personal act, because no person can believe alone. Indeed, faith is received from others, specifically, from the Catholic Church: 'It is the Church that believes first, and so bears, nourishes, and sustains my faith.' Nowhere is the ecclesial nature of faith more evident than in the sacrament of Baptism. To the infant who is being baptized, the Church grants faith. To the adult who is ready to be baptized, the priest poses this question: 'What do you ask of God's Church?' The response: 'Faith.'" Gregg R. Allison, *Roman Catholic Theology and Practice: An Evangelical Assessment* (Wheaton: Crossway, 2014), 109. The citations are from the *Catechism of the Catholic Church,* §168. Cf. Benedict XVI, General Audience, October 31, 2012, http://w2.vatican.va/content/benedict-xvi/en/audiences/2012/documents/hf_ben-xvi_aud_20121031.html.

14. Cyril O'Regan, "Benedict the Augustinian," in *Explorations in the Theology of Benedict XVI,* ed. John C. Cavadini (Notre Dame, IN: University of Notre Dame Press, 2012), 24.

15. Benedict's papacy sat squarely in the context of the contemporary breakdown of the relationship between faith and reason. Quite often, then, he addressed the rise of natural sciences, the achievements of technology, and the Kantian notion of pure reason that limits knowledge to what is perceived. Such developments banish issues of God's existence, eternal life, and human purpose to the ash heap of meaninglessness; they deny that faith is a source of knowledge. Benedict ably challenged the dogmatic limitation of knowledge and reason to phenomena perceived by the senses. He underscored that such limitation of knowledge is without warrant and dismissed a truncated reason as irrational. For this general discussion, see Scott W. Hahn, *Covenant and Communion: The Biblical Theology of Pope Benedict XVI* (Grand Rapids: Brazos, 2009), 36–39. In short order I will mention Benedict's Regensburg address in some detail. For Benedict's perspective on the historical development of this phenomenon, see Ratzinger, *Introduction to Christianity,* 30–39.

perfects it, and reason, enlightened by faith, finds the strength to rise to knowledge of God and spiritual realities."[16] This reason, which is not pure reason but is purified by faith, is an essential component of theology.[17] Thomas Aquinas is "an effective model of harmony between faith and reason, dimensions of the human spirit that are completely fulfilled in the encounter and dialogue with one another."[18] For Benedict, a separation between faith and reason leads to disastrous consequences; he refers to them as "pathologies."[19] For example, faith without reason leads to fideism, reason without faith leads to nihilism, and pure reason (à la Kant) is nonexistent.[20]

Accordingly, for Benedict, reason is a prerequisite for theology, because human reason depends on and reflects divine reason, who is the eternal Word of God, the Logos (John 1:1–18).[21] Indeed, approaching theology with proper reason and faith leads to an understanding of

---

16. Benedict XVI, Angelus Address, St. Peter's Square, January 28, 2007, http://w2.vatican.va/content/benedict-xvi/en/angelus/2007/documents/hf_ben-xvi_ang_20070128.html.

17. Benedict XVI, *Deus Caritas Est,* §28.

18. Benedict XVI, Angelus Address.

19. O'Regan, "Benedict the Augustinian," 39.

20. Tracey Rowland, *Ratzinger's Faith: The Theology of Pope Benedict XVI* (Oxford: Oxford University Press, 2008), 5; Ratzinger, *Nature and Mission,* 102. In his brilliant Regensburg address, Benedict lamented the hegemony of the "canon of scientificity" that relegates the issue of God to the realm of the unscientific. He continued, "It must be observed that from this standpoint any attempt to maintain theology's claim to be 'scientific' would end up reducing Christianity to a mere fragment of its former self. But we must say more: if science as a whole is this and this alone, then it is man himself who ends up being reduced, for the specifically human questions about our origin and destiny, the questions raised by religion and ethics, then have no place within the purview of collective reason as defined by 'science,' so understood, and must thus be relegated to the realm of the subjective. The subject then decides, on the basis of his experiences, what he considers tenable in matters of religion, and the subjective 'conscience' becomes the sole arbiter of what is ethical. In this way, though, ethics and religion lose their power to create a community and become a completely personal matter. This is a dangerous state of affairs for humanity, as we see from the disturbing pathologies of religion and reason which necessarily erupt when reason is so reduced that questions of religion and ethics no longer concern it. Attempts to construct an ethic from the rules of evolution or from psychology and sociology, end up being simply inadequate." Benedict XVI, "Faith, Reason and the University: Memories and Reflections," September 12, 2006, https://w2.vatican.va/content/benedict-xvi/en/speeches/2006/september/documents/hf_ben-xvi_spe_20060912_university-regensburg.html.

21. Ratzinger, *Nature and Mission,* 103. Ratzinger opposes the "theologically neutral" variety of reason so prevalent in contemporary secular society. Rowland, *Ratzinger's Faith,* 46.

divine revelation.[22] "Reason knows that it has not been left to its own devices. It is preceded by a Word which, though logical and rational, does not originate from reason itself but has been granted it as a gift and, as such, always transcends it."[23]

The third presupposition of theology is conversion. For Benedict, "theology is based upon a new beginning in thought which is not the product of our own reflection but has its origin in the encounter with a Word which always precedes us. We call the act of accepting this new beginning 'conversion.' Because there is no theology without faith, there can be no theology without conversion."[24] He further explains that conversion may take on various forms, from an instantaneous event (e.g., the conversions of Augustine, Newman) to other manifestations. In any case, conversion involves both a turning from the old "I" (who has been crucified with Christ) to the new "I" (who no longer lives as before but lives now by faith in Christ).[25] By nurturing faith as real, personal, and certain, "converted" theologians may abound in creative theology.[26]

The fourth and final presupposition of theology is truth. Because truth—along with the first three presuppositions—is essential to theology, theology is distinguished from all other approaches as found in other systems of belief. (As explained earlier, theology is sui generis.)

> Theology, in the strict sense of the word, is an exclusively Christian phenomenon, which has no equivalent in other religions. These affirmations presuppose that faith regards the truth ... [and] that this truth becomes accessible only in the act of faith ... [and] that, once accepted, this truth illumines our whole being and, therefore, appeals to our intellect and even solicits our understanding. It is assumed that this truth addresses itself as such to reason and requires the activity of reason in order to become man's own possession and to deploy its full dynamism.

---

22. Benedict XVI, General Audience, November 21, 2012, http://w2.vatican.va/content/benedict-xvi/en/audiences/2012/documents/hf_ben-xvi_aud_20121121.html.

23. Ratzinger, *Nature and Mission*, 103–4.

24. Ratzinger, *Nature and Mission*, 57.

25. See the above discussion.

26. Ratzinger, *Nature and Mission*, 57.

... In this sense, rationality belongs to the essence of Christianity in a way which the other religions do not claim for themselves.[27]

This truth is revelation. It is the Word revealed. It is not truth such as a postulate of reason, nor is it a mere proposition; rather, truth is personal because it is about a Person—the Word—who is revealed through the written word. Indeed, Benedict described the "principal task" of a theologian: "to understand the text as it now stands, as a totality in itself with its own particular message. Whoever reads Scripture in faith as a Bible must make a further step. ... Faith gives us knowledge of something more than a hypothesis; it gives us the right to trust the revealed Word as such."[28]

Theology is to be characterized by faith, reason, conversion, and truth. What of the men and women who engage in the task of theology? Theologians are to be characterized by the three theological virtues of faith, hope, and love.

FAITH

Benedict defined faith as "the decision that at the very core of human existence there is a point which cannot be nourished and supported on the visible and tangible, which encounters and comes into contact with what cannot be seen and finds that it is a necessity for its own existence. Such an attitude is certainly to be attained only by what the language of the Bible calls 'reversal,' 'con-version.' ... Indeed belief *is* the con-version in which man discovers that he is following an illusion if he devotes himself only to the tangible."[29] As developed in the *Catechism of the Catholic Church*, such faith is characterized by the following elements:[30] Faith is a *grace*; specifically, it is "a gift of God, a supernatural virtue infused

27. Ratzinger, *Nature and Mission*, 56.

28. Joseph Cardinal Ratzinger, *Gospel, Catechesis, Catechism: Sidelights on* The Catechism of the Catholic Church (San Francisco: Ignatius, 1997), 67–68.

29. Ratzinger, *Introduction to Christianity*, 24–25; cf. Benedict XVI, General Audience, December 5, 2012, http://w2.vatican.va/content/benedict-xvi/en/audiences/2012/documents/hf_ben-xvi_aud_20121205.html. Though introduced above, the virtue of faith will be more fully developed in this section.

30. The following discussion is adapted from Allison, *Roman Catholic Theology and Practice*, 108–10.

by him."[31] Citing *Dei Verbum*, Benedict says, "Before this faith can be exercised, man must have the grace of God to move and assist him; he must have the interior help of the Holy Spirit, who moves the heart and converts it to God, who opens the eyes of the mind and 'makes it easy for all to accept and believe the truth.'"[32] And so faith is a *human act*: "the human intellect and will cooperate with divine grace."[33] As an authentic decision of people, faith "involves them and uplifts them in a gamble for life that is like an exodus, that is, a coming out of ourselves, from our own certainties, from our own mental framework, to entrust ourselves to the action of God who points out to us his way to achieve true human freedom."[34]

Faith is linked with *understanding*. Faith is not counter to reason but is intimately associated with it. Still, faith goes beyond reason to bring certainty, because it is grounded on the true word of God. In this regard, faith seeks understanding as believers grow in knowledge of God and his revelation. And faith is in accord with, not in conflict with, science—though it does stand opposed to scientism.[35] Additionally, faith is *free*; it cannot be coerced.[36] It is also *necessary*; it is a requirement for salvation.[37] Importantly, apart from truly exceptional situations, the sacrament of baptism is the site where saving grace and faith are to be found.[38]

> Our journey starts from Baptism, the sacrament that gives us the Holy Spirit, making us become children of God in Christ, and marks our entry into the community of faith, into the Church: one does not believe by oneself, without the prior intervention of the grace of the Holy Spirit, one does not believe alone, but

31. *Catechism of the Catholic Church* (henceforth, CCC), §153.
32. Cf. Benedict XVI, General Audience, October 24, 2012, http://w2.vatican.va/content/benedict-xvi/en/audiences/2012/documents/hf_ben-xvi_aud_20121024.html. The citation is from *Dei Verbum*, §5.
33. CCC §155.
34. General Audience, October 24, 2012.
35. CCC §156–59.
36. CCC §160.
37. CCC §161.
38. For the Roman Catholic view of the necessity of baptism and its exceptions, see CCC §§1257–61. For an evangelical assessment, see Allison, *Roman Catholic Theology and Practice*, 265–66 and 285–88.

together with one's brethren. As from Baptism every believer
is called to new life, and to make this confession of faith his or
her own, together with the brethren.[39]

Thus, for Benedict and Roman Catholics in general, salvation is appro-
priated sacramentally at baptism.[40]

Still, faith can be *lost*. Because it is a free gift of God, people can lose
faith through persistent sin, apathy, worldliness, neglect of the means
of grace, and more. So that this possibility does not become actual,
believers must nourish faith on the word of God and the sacraments.
Indeed, faith is not without effort; it requires "working through love"
while grounded in the church's faith.[41] Faith is a *beginning*, providing a
foretaste of the beatific vision, which is seeing God face-to-face. Rather
than a destination, faith the beginning of eternal life.[42] Finally, faith is
not placed in propositions about God and his ways, but *in the realities*
that they express. Specifically, divine revelation is both propositional,
including both written Scripture and orally transmitted tradition, and
personal, revealing God himself so that his people may have an intimate
relationship with him. Thus the faithful believe in the reality of God
who is made known through the doctrines of the faith.[43]

Benedict intimately links faith with written revelation. Indeed, he
presents a "hermeneutic of faith," which is a basic and essential disposition that theologians must adopt toward the study of Scripture.
Indeed, theology "must come to acknowledge this faith as a hermeneutic, the space for understanding, which does not do dogmatic violence
to the Bible, but precisely allows the solitary possibility for the Bible

---

39. Benedict XVI, General Audience, October 24, 2012.
40. Baptists and Reformed Christians disagree with the Roman Catholic view.
41. CCC §162. Protestants from a Reformed theological perspective, which embraces
the perseverance of the saints and assurance of salvation, dissent from this loss of faith/
salvation perspective. This Reformed view maintains that all genuine believers, not merely
those who profess faith, will continue in Christ firmly to the end. This perseverance
and, flowing from it, assurance of salvation, is never apart from ongoing faith (1 Pet 1:5)
"working through love" (Gal 5:6). Still, justification, which is by faith alone, is the divine
eschatological verdict that the ungodly (Rom 4:5) are "not guilty" but "righteous instead"
pronounced proleptically.
42. CCC §163.
43. CCC §170.

to be itself."[44] While generally appreciative of the insights of historical criticism, Benedict is wary of its potentially destructive approach to the Bible. Historical criticism's insistence on objectivity, even to the point of suspending belief in the content—particularly the supernatural elements—of Scripture, is wrong-headed and ultimately unfruitful. Instead, the posture of faith is proper, given the subject matter of the Bible. Thus theologians must adapt themselves rightly—faithfully—to the word revealed. Ratzinger says it this way:

> Faith is itself a way of knowing. Wanting to set it aside does not produce pure objectivity, but comprises a point of view which excludes a particular perspective while not wanting to take into account the accompanying conditions of the chosen point of view. If one takes into account, however, that the Sacred Scriptures come from God through a subject which lives continually—the pilgrim people of God—then it becomes clear rationally as well that this subject has something to say about the understanding of the book.[45]

Thus theologians are called to employ a "hermeneutic of faith" as they go about their task.

On the matter of faith's relationship to the other theological virtues, especially love, Benedict was deeply influenced by both Augustine and Bonaventure. For both of these ecclesial doctors, love was a crucial motive in the theological endeavor of faith seeking understanding. Benedict summarizes their view this way:

> Faith can wish to understand because it is moved by love for the One upon whom it has bestowed its consent. Love seeks understanding. It wishes to know ever better the one whom it loves. It "seeks his face," as Augustine never tires of repeating. Love

---

44. Joseph Ratzinger, "Biblical Interpretation in Crisis," *First Things*, April 26, 2008, https://www.firstthings.com/web-exclusives/2008/04/biblical-interpretation-in-crisis.
45. Joseph Ratzinger, "Relationship between Magisterium and Exegetes," Address to the Pontifical Biblical Commission, May 10, 2003, http://www.vatican.va/roman_curia/congregations/cfaith/pcb_documents/rc_con_cfaith_doc_20030510_ratzinger-comm-bible_en.html.

is the desire for intimate knowledge, so that the quest for intelligence can even be an inner requirement of love. Put another way, there is a coherence of love and truth which has important consequences for theology and philosophy. Christian faith can say of itself, I have found love. Yet love for Christ and of one's neighbor for Christ's sake can enjoy stability and consistency only if its deepest motivation is love for the truth.[46]

Theology, as faith seeking understanding, is properly motivated by love for the truth, indeed, love for the One who is the true God. This love prompts theologians as they properly seek understanding of the one true God to love him ever more deeply.

In his most extensive treatment of the meaning of faith,[47] which involves commenting on the *Catechism of the Catholic Church*, Benedict provides detailed answers to three key questions: What does one / the church believe? Who believes? How does one believe? He explains that "the *Catechism* displays the act of faith and the content of faith in their indivisible unity."[48]

In terms of "who believes," Benedict underscores the act of faith. As such, "faith is an orientation of our existence as a whole" that cannot be "realized unless all the energies of our existence go into maintaining. Faith is not a merely intellectual, or merely volitional, or merely emotional activity—it is all of these things together. It is an act of the whole self, of the whole person in his concentrated unity." While "a supremely personal act," faith does not curve in on itself but "transcends the self, the limits of the individual," opening up a person of faith to engage with others. Moreover, this personal act of faith liberates the faithful from themselves. "Faith is a perishing of the mere self and precisely

---

46. Ratzinger, *Nature and Mission*, 27.
47. Benedict XVI, "On the Meaning of Faith," in *The Essential Pope Benedict XVI: His Central Writings and Speeches*, ed. John F. Thornton and Susan B. Varenne (San Francisco: HarperOne, 2007), 211–16.
48. Benedict XVI, "On the Meaning of Faith," 212.

a resurrection of the true self."[49] This results in fellowship with God through Christ.

As for "what one believes," Benedict explains that at the core of the "essential content of faith" is "an encounter with the living God. God is, in the proper and ultimate sense, the content of our faith. Looked at in this way, the content of faith is absolutely simple: I believe in God."[50] Still, this is not mere theism, faith in a generic god, for true belief in God is mediated through Jesus Christ, who is both fully divine and fully human. As the only one who has seen the Father (John 1:18), Christ can reveal him so that the faithful may see God. "We could say that to believe is to be granted a share in Jesus' vision. He lets us see with him in faith what he has seen."[51] This revelation comes about by the Holy Spirit, through whom faith comes.

For Benedict, this act of faith unfolds the articles of faith. The reverse is also true: "this content of faith (*fides quae [creditur]*) bears directly on our life; it asks for a conversion of life that gives life to a new way of believing in God (*fides qua [creditur]*)."[52] This dynamic always takes place in, and is nurtured by, the Roman Catholic Church, which is "contained in the first movement of the act of faith itself. The church is not an institution extrinsically added to faith as an organizational framework for the common activities of believers. No, she is integral to the act of faith itself. The 'I believe' is always also 'We believe.'"[53] Within the community of faith, the act of faith "is a response to the triune God" that also embraces the incarnation, the hypostatic union, salvation history, the church, and all other items of faith, including creation, eternal life, sin, grace, the liturgy, the sacraments, prayer, and ethics. Indeed,

49. Benedict XVI, "On the Meaning of Faith," 212.
50. Benedict XVI, "On the Meaning of Faith," 213. Cf. Benedict XVI, General Audience, November 14, 2012.
51. Benedict XVI, "On the Meaning of Faith," 213.
52. Benedict XVI, General Audience, October 17, 2012, http://w2.vatican.va/content/benedict-xvi/en/audiences/2012/documents/hf_ben-xvi_aud_20121017.html.
53. Benedict XVI, "On the Meaning of Faith," 213. Elsewhere, Benedict insisted, "The institution [the Roman Catholic Church] is not merely a structure that can be changed or demolished at will, which would have nothing to do with the reality of faith as such." Benedict XVI, "The Ecclesiology of the Constitution on the Church: *Lumen Gentium*," in Thornton and Varenne, *The Essential Pope Benedict XVI*, 99.

Benedict appeals to the faithful to "get a glimpse of the intrinsic unity of the faith, which is not a multitude of propositions but a full and simple act whose simplicity contains the whole depth and breadth of being."[54]

Regarding "how one believes," Benedict appeals to Paul's affirmation "that faith is an obedience 'from the heart to the form of doctrine into which you were handed over' (Rom 6:17)."[55] In the expression "the form of doctrine" Benedict finds support for "the sacramental character of faith. We do not think up faith on our own. It comes not from us as an idea of ours but to us as a word from outside. It is, as it were, a word about the Word; we are 'handed over' into this Word."[56] Benedict links this "'handed over' into the Word" to the sacrament of baptism, "an immersion into water, symbolizing death." He thus returns to Paul's discussion (Gal 2:20) that the act of faith is the crucifixion of the old "I" and the resurrection of the new "I" who no longer lives as before but lives now by faith in Christ. This "destruction and renewal of the self" always occurs within the church, within its sacramental structure, specifically by baptism. Benedict draws out the implication: "The act of faith is unthinkable without the sacramental component."[57]

HOPE

Benedict relates hope to the other theological virtues of faith (along with reason) and love: "Hope encourages reason and gives it the strength to direct the will. It is already present in faith, indeed it is called forth by faith. Charity in truth feeds on hope and, at the same time, manifests it. As the absolutely gratuitous gift of God, hope bursts into our lives as something not due to us, something that transcends every law of justice. Gift by its nature goes beyond merit, its rule is that of superabundance."[58] Hope arises from faith and, given faith's close connection to reason, encourages reason. Love flourishes with hope and reveals

54. Benedict XVI, "On the Meaning of Faith," 214.
55. Benedict XVI, "On the Meaning of Faith," 214.
56. Benedict XVI, "On the Meaning of Faith," 214.
57. Benedict XVI, "On the Meaning of Faith," 214–15.
58. Benedict XVI, *Caritas in Veritate*, Encyclical Letter, June 29, 2009, §34, http://w2.vatican.va/content/benedict-xvi/en/encyclicals/documents/hf_ben-xvi_enc_20090629_caritas-in-veritate.html.

hope. Ultimately, however, hope is not grounded on faith and love, but it is itself a divine and gracious gift that eclipses all notion of payment for work done, reward for good accomplished, and merit for virtue demonstrated. Hope is particularly called forth in contexts of pain and suffering, persecution and devastation.

Benedict articulated the nature of hope in his second papal encyclical—*Spe Salvi* (2007), dedicated to the theme "in hope we were saved."[59] He closely connects faith with hope, opining that they "seem interchangeable" in Scripture (§2). If faith is the beginning of eternal life, "the one who hopes has been granted the gift of a new life" (§2). As to the question, "In what does this hope consist?" Benedict reverses Paul's description of nonbelievers as being "without hope and without God in the world" (Eph 2:12) to express his answer: to receive hope is "to come to come to know God" (§3). Hope and faith are deeply interrelated: "faith is the substance of things hoped for; the proof of things not seen" (Heb 11:1). But Benedict appeals to Aquinas for a better rendering of the first phrase: "faith is a *habitus*, that is, a stable disposition of the spirit, through which eternal life takes root in us and reason is led to consent to what it does not see" (§7).[60] Accordingly, what one hopes for is already present in the believer, "not yet visible in the external world ... but because of the fact that, as an initial and dynamic reality, we carry it with us, a certain perception of it has even now come into existence" (§7). Indeed, faith as hope "draws the future into the present, so that it is no longer simply a 'not yet'" (§7).

Importantly, hope is particularly operational in the midst of persecution. Relying on Hebrews 10:34–39, Benedict holds high the perseverance of Christians who, when their substance—life's normal, concrete security—was ripped away, stood on a better ground: the foundation of faith and hope. This freedom from the oscillating moorings of mere earthly existence led to their complete renunciation of themselves, even

---

59. Benedict XVI, Spe Salvi, Encyclical Letter, November 30, 2007, http://w2.vatican.va/content/benedict-xvi/en/encyclicals/documents/hf_ben-xvi_enc_20071130_spe-salvi.html. In-text parenthetical citations are to the section numbers of the encyclical under discussion.

60. His discussion of Thomas Aquinas is based on the *Summa Theologica*, II-II, q. 4, a. 1.

to the point of martyrdom. Such is hope (§§8–9). Benedict laments the contemporary transformation of faith and hope into arrogant self-effort fueled by human confidence in science, technology, unbounded reason, and absolute freedom: "faith in progress as such" (§17). However, these skills and values, which allegedly guarantee progress in and of themselves, stand in conflict with faith and the church (§18). Consequently, Benedict asserts that such progress—attempted apart from God—is ultimately futile: "man needs God, otherwise he remains without hope" (§23). Benedict offers three concrete "settings" in which to learn and practice hope: Prayer leads to hope and purifies it (§§32–34). Acting to foster human flourishing, and aiding those who are suffering, is hope in action (§§35–36). Faith in the last judgment, which is mocked and denied by many today, "is first and foremost hope" (§43). The fact that people often experience little or no justice in this life leads to faith and hope in eternal life, in which justice will be meted out. Thus, for Benedict, "the image of the Last Judgment is not primarily an image of terror, but an image of hope ... an image that evokes responsibility" and directs people's "gaze to the crucified and risen Christ" (§44).[61]

LOVE

Significantly, Benedict's first papal encyclical was *Deus Caritas Est* (2005): *God Is Love.* Some Catholic scholars see this writing as Benedict's remedy to Vatican Council II's *Gaudium et Spes* (1965), the Pastoral Constitution on the Church in the Modern World (especially

---

61. At this juncture, Benedict articulates traditional Roman Catholic eschatology of two eternal states and one temporary state: Hell, one of two permanent states, is for "people who have totally destroyed their desire for truth and readiness to love." Heaven, the other eternal state, is for "people who are utterly pure, completely permeated by God, and thus fully open to their neighbors" (*Spe Salvi,* §45). Purgatory, the one temporary state, is for "the great majority of people" in whose depth of being remains "an ultimate interior openness to truth, to love, to God. In the concrete choices of life, however, it is covered over by ever new compromises with evil" (§46). While affirming the two eternal destinies of hell and heaven (though disagreeing with Benedict on the grounds of access into these states), most Protestants will dissent from the Roman Catholic doctrine of purgatory and reject Benedict's support—1 Corinthians 3:12–15; 2 Maccabees 12:38–45; the communion of saints, whose prayers are offered for those in purgatory—for this doctrine. Still, for Roman Catholics, the existence of purgatory should prompt the faithful not to merely ask, "how can I save myself? but also to query "what can I do in order that others may be saved and that for them too the star of hope may arise?" (§§47–48).

§§15–17).[62] In its discussion of human dignity, Vatican II emphasized the intellect (along with industriousness), the conscience (along with the search for truth and solutions to besetting societal problems), and freedom (along with self-control and free choice) without any mention of love. Benedict, it is claimed, intended his initial encyclical to correct this lacuna, as human dignity is first and foremost grounded in the revelation that God is love.[63]

Benedict offers a sustained theology of love in *Deus Caritas Est*: Every expression of human love is "the response to the gift of love with which God draws near to us" (§1). Indeed, divine love—*agape*—and human love are intrinsically linked. Benedict decries *eros* in the sense of sinful erotic love that dehumanizes and is exclusively physical. Still, he skillfully explains that Christianity is not anti-body; after all, it is a human person—body and soul—who loves. Accordingly, when *eros* is about concrete matters of human existence, *eros* and *agape* are not antithetical but complementary.[64] It is only when *eros* is sinfully reduced to physicality, leading to a debasement of the body, that it is no longer compatible with divine love.

Building off the Hebrew words for love, Benedict underscores definitive love as concern and care for others; ready for renunciation and sacrifice, love seeks the good of others. Part and parcel of divine love is that it is a forgiving love. Benedict focuses on Jesus Christ as the incarnate love of God: by Christ's death on the cross, human beings can truly and concretely understand the revelation "God is love" (1 John 4:8). Nevertheless, nonsacramentalist Protestants will object to Benedict's assertion that "Jesus gave this act of oblation an enduring presence through his institution of the Eucharist at the Last Supper" (§13). As the Eucharist draws Catholics "into Jesus' act of self-oblation,"

62. Rowland, *Ratzinger's Faith*, 41.

63. Of course, Benedict is not the first to have this orientation. Indeed, his preference for the giant theologians Augustine and Bonaventure reflects and nourishes this emphasis on love. Rowland, *Ratzinger's Faith*, 149.

64. Indeed, Benedict calls attention to the fact that the prophets Hosea and Ezekiel "described God's passion for his people using boldly erotic images. God's relationship with Israel is described using the metaphors of betrothal and marriage; idolatry is thus adultery and prostitution" (*Deus Caritas Est*, §9).

they "enter into the very dynamic of his self-giving" and thus become united with Christ and with one another. Certainly, Protestants will appreciate Benedict's close connection of union with Christ and union with Christ's disciples, as well as his connection of the love of God with the love of others. But the corollary that *agape* becomes a term for the Eucharist, the bodily gift of God's love through which the divine work continues in and through his people, is problematic for a significant portion of Protestantism.

As to the concreteness of the divine love, Benedict wonders, "Can we love God without seeing him" (§16)? He grounds his positive answer in the fact that the love of God and the love of neighbor are inextricably linked. "One is so closely connected to the other that to say that we love God becomes a lie if we are closed to our neighbor or hate him altogether" (§16). We can love God without seeing him because we can love others. Moreover, God has become visible in Jesus Christ (John 14:9), so we can love God through the Son incarnate. Due also to the Christ-church interconnection—axiomatic for Roman Catholic ecclesiology—Benedict affirms the visibility of God "in his word, in the sacraments, and especially in the Eucharist" (§17).[65] Depending on their tradition, Protestants will react more negatively or positively to this notion of visibility.

Benedict emphasizes that the love demonstrated by the church is a manifestation of the shared love between the three persons of the Trinity (§19). Having concentrated on the Father and the Son, Benedict underscores the Holy Spirit, who was poured out on the day of Pentecost by those two. "The Spirit, in fact, is that interior power which harmonizes their [believers'] hearts with Christ's heart and moves them to love their brethren as Christ loved them. ... The Spirit is also the energy which transforms the heart of the ecclesial community, so that it becomes a witness before the world to the love of the Father, who wishes to make humanity a single family in his Son" (§19). Following traditional Trinitarian theology and pneumatology, reference to the Holy Spirit

---

65. For a discussion of the Christ-church interconnection, see Allison, *Roman Catholic Theology and Practice*, 56–66.

as the bond of love between the Father and the Son, and his names of "Love" and "Gift," would ground this discussion and carry it along.[66]

In the conclusion to his *Deus Caritas Est* (§§40–42), Benedict offers several outstanding examples of love. Because he gave half of his cloak to a poor man, Martin of Tours (d. 397) received a dream of Jesus wearing that cloak. The monastic movements, originating with Antony the Great (d. 356), have always featured hospitality, refuge, care of the sick, education, and other humanitarian initiatives. Francis of Assisi, Ignatius of Loyola, John Bosco, and Mother Teresa also make Benedict's list of "lasting models of social charity for all people of good will." Exceeding all these stellar examples is Mary: "As a believer who in faith thinks with God's thoughts and wills with God's will, she cannot fail to be a woman who loves."[67]

CONCLUSION

There is much to commend and appreciate about Benedict's understanding of theology and its virtues. He presents theology and its task as grounded on revelation, specifically Jesus Christ as revealed in sacred Scripture, which must be interpreted through a "hermeneutic of faith." He insists on faith as a stable and enduring posture that demands and engages with the totality of the theologian's life. This faith is not mere theism, a belief in some amorphous god. On the contrary, true belief in God is mediated through the Son of God incarnate, who is fully divine and fully human, and such belief is prompted by the gracious activity of the Holy Spirit. Benedict closely links faith and hope: hope's proper object is not some dream or self-effort but God himself and his promises. And Benedict roots Christian theology in the concreteness of love. As Tracey Rowland puts it, "Even though he is probably one of the most intellectual popes in history, for him Christianity is above all a matter of the heart. However, it is not thereby something soapy and

---

66. Catholic resources for this topic are many and readily available. A personal preference is Matthew Levering, *Engaging the Doctrine of the Holy Spirit: Love and Gift in the Trinity and the Church* (Grand Rapids: Baker Academic, 2016).

67. Most Protestants, while not surprised by it, will object to Benedict's focus on Mary.

saccharine. ... 'The very toughness of the adventure [of Christianity] is what makes it beautiful.'"[68]

As for concerns and critiques, as an evangelical theologian I am well aware of the fact that Roman Catholic theology and my own Protestant theology are significantly different theological systems grounded on different axioms (the Roman Catholic nature-grace interdependence and Christ-church interconnection; the Protestant principles of *sola Scriptura* and justification by grace alone through faith alone in Christ alone), different structures of authority, different ecclesiologies, and more. This leads me to be cautious. Certainly, I applaud and embrace the commonalities between Roman Catholicism and Protestantism. At the same time, I am aware that even when we use the same terms (e.g., grace, justification) and discuss the same theological concepts (e.g., the church, the sacraments), we may have significantly different ideas of what we are discussing.[69] With these caveats in place, I value the contribution of Benedict XVI and offer this appreciative essay on his development of the theological task and the theological virtues.

Because theologians treat revelation—the incarnate Word of God, Jesus Christ, and the inspired word of God, sacred Scripture—they must be the right kind of people. Specifically, they must be characterized by the three theological virtues of faith, hope, and love. Despairing of reliance on what is seen and believing in the reality of what is not seen, theologians must adopt a posture—even a hermeneutic—of *faith*. The subject matter of Scripture can only be known by faith, "for whoever would draw near to God must believe that he exists and that he rewards those who seek him" (Heb 11:6). Therefore theologians are duty- and love-bound to approach the entirety of their task—knowing and making known the Triune God—with faith.

68. Rowland, *Ratzinger's Faith*, 150. The citation is from Joseph Ratzinger, *Faith and the Future* (Chicago: Franciscan Herald Press, 1971), 75.
69. As a walk through the *Catechism of the Catholic Church* from an evangelical perspective, my *Roman Catholic Theology and Practice* underscores these commonalities and critiques these differences. On a more popular level, see Gregg Allison and Chris Castaldo, *The Unfinished Reformation: What Unites and Divides Catholics and Protestants after 500 Years* (Grand Rapids: Zondervan, 2016).

Through *hope*, theologians know God and enjoy the beginning of eternal life with the One who is the subject matter of their theological pursuits. While experiencing this intimate relationship with the Triune God and being thankful for it, theologians are quite aware that this "already" will one day yield to the "not yet"; thus they are called to and must wait patiently for the One who is still to come. This hope gets them through the suffering and heartache of their present existence. Indeed, they pursue the truth of God's revelation in his Word wherever it takes them. They withstand criticism of their theological musings and graciously respond when maligned. With the psalmist, they wonder and exclaim:

> Why are you cast down, O my soul,
> and why are you in turmoil within me?
> Hope in God; for I shall again praise him,
> my salvation and my God. (Ps 42:5–6)

Theologians nourish this virtue of hope by practicing concrete acts of love—praying, fostering human flourishing, and aiding those who suffer.

Because God is *love*, and because God takes the initiative to love them, theologians are able to love others. Indeed, their God-focused study must lead to them being other-focused. The love of God encountered in and fostered by their theological pursuits will certainly bear fruit in love for others. This love is concretely expressed as care and concern for others, requiring that they as theologians are self-giving and forgiving lovers. Even more, their theologizing itself is an act of love; their vocation is affection, for God and for those who are made in his image.

To conclude, I invite you to listen to Benedict XVI's treatment of the three virtues of faith, hope, and love joined together:

> Faith, hope and charity go together. Hope is practiced through
> the virtue of patience, which continues to do good even in
> the face of apparent failure, and through the virtue of humil-
> ity, which accepts God's mystery and trusts him even at times

of darkness. Faith tells us that God has given us his Son for our sakes and gives us the victorious certainty that it is really true: God is love! It thus transforms our impatience and our doubts into the sure hope that God holds the world in his hands and that, as the dramatic imagery at the end of the Book of Revelation points out, in spite of all darkness he ultimately triumphs in glory. Faith, which sees the love of God revealed in the pierced heart of Jesus on the Cross, gives rise to love. Love is the light—and in the end, the only light—that can always illuminate a world grown dim and give us the courage needed to keep living and working. Love is possible, and we are able to practice it because we are created in the image of God. To experience love and in this way to cause the light of God to enter into the world—this is the invitation I would like to extend.[70]

---

70. Benedict XVI, *Deus Caritas Est*, §39.

4

Expounding the Word of the Lord

Joseph Ratzinger on Revelation,
Tradition, and Biblical Interpretation

KEVIN J. VANHOOZER

There is much for evangelicals to appreciate in Joseph Ratzinger's engagement with questions of Scripture and its interpretation from 1965 to 2010. This is due in part to their common cause: as evangelicals represent a middle way between fundamentalist and modernist Christianity, so Ratzinger and other Catholics had to make their way between the fundamentalism of neo-scholasticism and the modernism of biblical criticism.[1] Vatican II, in which Ratzinger participated as an observer and commentator, was itself an attempt to bring the church into the present without forsaking its past.

The trajectory of Ratzinger's career is also telling, combining as it were two natures (academic; ecclesial) in one person: Joseph Ratzinger; Pope Benedict XVI.[2] He served as prefect of the Congregation for the Doctrine of the Faith (a theologian) and as president of the Pontifical Biblical Commission (an exegete). Moreover, as a reader of Scripture he unites both faith and reason. It is this integrated reading that is ultimately at stake, and at threat, in questions of biblical interpretation today.

---

1. Aidan Nichols describes modernism as the tendency to rely on historical-critical methods only in biblical interpretation, bypassing tradition and the history of interpretation. Aidan Nichols, *Catholic Thought Since the Enlightenment* (London: Gracewing, 1998), 84. In Tracey Rowland's words: "the Modernists wanted history without tradition, while the Roman School types wanted tradition without history." Tracey Rowland, *Ratzinger's Faith: The Theology of Pope Benedict XVI* (Oxford: Oxford University Press, 2008), 2.

2. I shall refer to him by the name he used as author of the work under present discussion. However, though the name may change, the essential position does not. His thinking on Scripture, tradition, and interpretation has remained fairly consistent from before Vatican II to his enthronement as pope.

The urgent question I raise here is whether Benedict's career does not merely parallel twentieth- and twenty-first-century evangelicalism but, in some ways, surpasses it. Benedict has called Roman Catholics to bridge what has become an ugly ditch between exegesis and theology. To the extent that he points the way beyond modernist biblical criticism to the promised land of theological interpretation, where the word of God is read with faith and reason by and for the people of God, past and present, he may have something to teach us.

In what follows we will examine (1) Ratzinger's understanding of the place of Scripture in the Roman Catholic pattern of theological authority—a pattern that begins with revelation and flows through tradition, always guided by the church's teaching office; and (2) his understanding of biblical interpretation in the academy and the church. Both parts will note areas of agreement and disagreement with evangelicals.[3]

SCRIPTURE IN THE PATTERN OF THEOLOGICAL AUTHORITY

Revelation

The young Joseph Ratzinger welcomed the opportunity Vatican II afforded to replace the older, propositional understanding of revelation characteristic of neo-scholasticism with something altogether more dynamic. In his 1967 commentary on *Dei Verbum* (Vatican II's document on revelation), he describes "how little intellectualism and doctrinalism are able to comprehend the nature of revelation."[4] Ratzinger approved of the new emphasis on revelation as *personal* rather than propositional, a dialogue whose purpose "is ultimately not information, but unity and transformation."[5]

---

3. In this sense, the present chapter may be seen as an updated version of Bernard Ramm's evaluation of pre-Vatican II theology in his *The Pattern of Religious Authority* (Grand Rapids: Eerdmans, 1957).
4. Joseph Ratzinger, "Revelation Itself," in *Commentary on the Documents of Vatican II*, ed. Herbert Vorgrimler (New York: Crossroad, 1989), 3:175.
5. Ratzinger, "Revelation Itself," 175.

Dei Verbum describes revelation not as a set of true statements but as God in self-communicative action: "It signifies a *reality* of which Scripture gives us *information* but that *is* not simply Scripture itself."[6] Scripture is a means and witness of revelation but is not itself identical with revelation. It is not the book that is revelation for Ratzinger, but the event of encountering God's Word in Scripture through faith. Revelation has its origin in God, and its destination in faith. This, for Ratzinger, is sufficient grounds for dismissing the principle of *sola Scriptura*: "Scripture is *not* revelation but ... is only a part of this greater reality."[7]

This "greater reality" that comes to be known in the event of revelation is nothing other than the living Christ: "He is revelation in the proper sense."[8] That Christ himself is God's revelation explains why revelation is an interpersonal event. Ratzinger insists on the element of faith, the reception of revelation. Strictly speaking, revelation includes the act of communicating (Word) *and* its reception (faith). The church—the assembly gathered by the Word—is in its coming together the place where the Word is again made flesh.[9] Here we might speak not of *expounding* the revelatory Word (the primary evangelical concern) as much as *expanding* it to include its right reception in the community of the faithful (Ratzinger's primary concern).

The early emphases in Ratzinger's writings on revelation become even more pronounced in the apostolic exhortation he issued in 2010 as Pope Benedict XVI, *Verbum Domini*. Though Benedict insists that the church "is born from and lives by" the word of God, this does not mean what Protestants mean in speaking of the church as a "creature of the word." Recall that, for Ratzinger, the "word" is first the eternal Word, God's only Son, the same Word who became flesh. This word was proclaimed by the apostles before it was written down. Benedict

---

6. Joseph Ratzinger, "The Question of the Concept of Tradition: A Provisional Response," in *God's Word: Scripture—Tradition—Office*, ed. Peter Hünermann and Thomas Söding, trans. Henry Taylor (San Francisco: Ignatius, 2005), 51.

7. Ratzinger, "Question of the Concept of Tradition," 53.

8. Ratzinger, "Question of the Concept of Tradition," 56.

9. "Her [the church's] form is the incarnate Word of God that is made flesh again and again by the Word of faith and, as flesh deigns again and again to become Word." Joseph Ratzinger, *Principles of Catholic Theology: Building Stones for a Fundamental Theology*, trans. Mary Frances McCarthy (San Francisco: Ignatius, 1987), 352.

says explicitly that "the Christian faith is not a 'religion of the book':
Christianity is the 'religion of the word of God.'"[10] And again: "The novelty of biblical revelation consists in the fact that God becomes known
through the dialogue which he desires to have with us."[11]

The word of God is expressed in human words thanks to the inspiration of the Holy Spirit, who also guarantees the truth of these words.
However, Benedict's explanation of verbal inspiration may strike evangelicals as odd: "As the word of God became flesh by the power of the
Holy Spirit in the womb of the Virgin Mary, so Sacred Scripture is
born from the womb of the Church by the power of the same Spirit."[12]
Moreover, revelation for Ratzinger appears to be secured not by verbal
inspiration alone, but also by illumination. The same Spirit who guided
its authors must also guide its faithful readers.

In sum, revelation is not propositional but interpersonal: the event
of receiving God's word in faith. Indeed, "Listening to God's Word is
the definitive principle of Catholic theology."[13] Revelation is not verbal—
the words on the pages of Scripture—but the personal encounter with
the living Word that accompanies the hearing or reading of those biblical words in faith. The notion of a faithful listening community—
the church—is thus built in to Ratzinger's concept of revelation. For
Ratzinger, it is impossible to speak of the word of God without also
speaking of the church's listening. The *verbum Dei is a verbum in ecclesia*.[14]

Tradition

Another name for the word the church receives is Tradition, and
Ratzinger is aware that the Roman Catholic way of conceiving the
Scripture-tradition relation is one of the key flash points with the
Protestant Reformers. His position has remained constant from his 1965

10. Benedict XVI, *Verbum Domini: The Word of the Lord* (Boston: Pauline Books &
Media, 2010), 14.
11. Benedict XVI, *Verbum Domini*, 11.
12. Benedict XVI, *Verbum Domini*, 32.
13. International *Theological Commission, Theology Today: Perspectives, Principles, and
Criteria* (Washington, DC: Catholic University of America Press, 2012), 5.
14. The first two parts of Benedict's *Verbum Domini* are *"Verbum Dei,"* which treats the
"God who speaks," and *"Verbum in Ecclesia,"* which treats the church that listens to and
receives the word.

essay "The Question of the Concept of Tradition" to his 2010 *Verbum Domini.*

Ratzinger is aware of the Protestant critique of the idea, often associated with the Council of Trent, that Scripture and tradition are two independent sources of revelation.[15] The Reformers were especially critical of the idea that, alongside the written Scriptures, the Roman Catholic Church also transmitted unwritten traditions, both doctrines and practices, under the authority of the church's teaching office or magisterium. *Sola Scriptura* was the Reformers' counter to the idea that the church's teaching could stand beside Scripture as equally authoritative. For Roman Catholics, the teaching office of the church guarantees the word's meaning, whereas Protestants deregulate the word: "It is ... in this reversal of the relations between word and office that the real opposition lies between the Catholic and Protestant conceptions of the Church, which would then coincide with the opposition between their concepts of tradition."[16]

Whereas the Council of Trent was concerned to defend its *traditions* (plural) from the Reformation critique that some Roman Catholic doctrines and practices were unbiblical accretions, the major concern of *Dei Verbum* (Vatican II's Dogmatic Constitution on Divine Revelation) was to emphasize *tradition* (singular), the Spirit-guided progress of the word in the church.[17] Ratzinger approves of the way *Dei Verbum* describes the relationship of Scripture and tradition not as two separate sources but as "a single sacred deposit of the word of God, which is entrusted to the

---

15. At Vatican II, there was a spirited attempt to reinterpret the infamous partim-partim formulation (that is, that revelation is passed on *partly* by Scripture, *partly* by tradition). Ratzinger—reflecting the conclusions of *Dei Verbum*—is happier speaking of the incompleteness of Scripture.

16. Ratzinger, "Question of the Concept of Tradition," 44.

17. Ratzinger did express regret that Vatican II did not wrestle with the question of criteria with which to discern legitimate from illegitimate tradition (Rowland, *Ratzinger's Faith*, 53).

Church."[18] Stated differently: the word of revelation remains present in history through both Scripture and tradition *insofar as these are received in faith by the (Roman Catholic) church*. The word of God (Scripture and tradition) is "not an independent reality floating above the Church, but rather is something the Lord passed on to the Church."[19]

Benedict wants to see the Scripture-tradition relation as a both-and, not an either-or: "The living Tradition is essential for enabling the Church to grow through time in the understanding of the truth revealed in the Scriptures."[20] Scripture and tradition are thus the central ingredients in the task of theology, namely, to seek "the full truth stored up in the mystery of Christ."[21] Benedict's is an expansive word-centered theology: the word of God is given in Scripture as an inspired testimony to revelation, and constitutes the supreme rule of faith "together with the Church's living Tradition."[22]

The Scripture-tradition relation forces one to think through the pattern of theological authority. Bernard Ramm provides a good summary of the Protestant view of the pattern: (1) Christ is the supreme content of Scripture and the supreme object of the Spirit's witness; (2) the Spirit is the chief witness to Christ and also inspired the Scriptures; (3) the Scriptures are inspired by the Spirit and witness supremely to Christ.[23] Conspicuous by their absence is any mention of tradition or the church. Ratzinger acknowledges the Protestant concern not to let the church overshadow the word, but then parries the Protestant thrust: "Can the

---

18. *Dei Verbum*, in *Vatican Council II*, vol. 1, *The Conciliar and Post Conciliar Documents*, ed. Austin Flannery, rev. ed. (Northport, NY: Costello, 1996), §10. The Council of Trent said that saving truth is contained "both in the written books and the unwritten traditions." Heiko Obermann designates this position as Tradition II (the "two-source" view), which he distinguishes from Tradition I (the "one-source" view), according to which tradition transmits the same revelatory content as Scripture. See Heiko A. Oberman, *Forerunners of the Reformation: The Shape of Late Medieval Thought* (New York: Holt, Rinehart & Winston, 1966), 58; see also John W. O'Malley, *What Happened at Vatican II* (Cambridge: Harvard University Press, 2008), 146–47, 227–28; Matthew Levering, *An Introduction to Vatican II as an Ongoing Theological Event* (Washington, DC: Catholic University of America Press, 2017), 33–44.
19. Ratzinger, "Question of the Concept of Tradition," 45.
20. Benedict XVI, *Verbum Domini*, 30.
21. *Dei Verbum*, §24.
22. Benedict, *Verbum Domini*, 32.
23. Adapted from Ramm, *The Pattern of Religious Authority*, 47.

word be set up as independent, without handing it over the arbitrariness of the exegete?"[24] In Ratzinger's Catholic pattern of authority, Christ hands over the word to the church. The church is the living tradition of God's word and, through its teaching office, the guarantor of right reception and interpretation.

Office

Ratzinger identifies the real nub of the debate between Protestants and Roman Catholics as not the sufficiency of Scripture but "the mode of presence of the revealed word among the faithful."[25] The Scripture-tradition debate remains insoluble unless and until we understand both as aspects of the larger issue of revelation, which "always and only becomes a reality where there is faith."[26] This is a most important point. Ratzinger never thinks of God's word in isolation from the community that hears and receives it. His is therefore an "expansive" word-centered theology, for implicit in "word" is the Spirit that accompanies it, the community that receives it, and the teaching office that guarantees it. It follows that we will never achieve clarity about either Scripture or tradition apart from a consideration of the church, the living locus of the word of God: "It is precisely in his Church ... that [Christ] is living and present: she is his body, in which his Spirit is at work."[27] Moreover, the church is itself made up of both sheep and shepherds, namely, the people of God and the bishops, together with the pope, who lead them.

The church receives revelation and tradition in faith. But what is the church? Evangelicals sometimes forget what their Protestant forebears knew well: the ascended Christ "gave ... the shepherds and teachers, to equip the saints for the work of ministry, for building up the body of Christ" (Eph 4:11–12).[28] For Ratzinger and Roman Catholics, bishops and the pope are part of the divinely given structure of the church, twin

---

24. Ratzinger, "Question of the Concept of Tradition," 46.
25. Ratzinger, "Question of the Concept of Tradition," 50.
26. Ratzinger, "Question of the Concept of Tradition," 52.
27. Ratzinger, "Question of the Concept of Tradition," 58.
28. For a Reformed theological account of the church's teaching office, see Michael Allen and Scott R. Swain, *Reformed Catholicity: The Promise of Retrieval for Theology and Biblical Interpretation* (Grand Rapids: Baker Academic, 2015), 102–3.

threads in the pattern of authority.[29] These offices play a decisive role in preserving the integrity of tradition, which is to say, where God's word has been *rightly* received.

Ratzinger notes that apostolic *succession* and apostolic *tradition* "were originally neighboring terms."[30] "Tradition" means what is handed down, and at the beginning of everything that is handed down "stands the fact that the Father gives away the Son to the world."[31] We see examples of this handing down in Scripture itself (1 Cor 15:3–4; 1 Tim 3:16). This mystery gets handed down in Scripture and tradition so that the faithful can receive revelation, which, as we have seen, is for Ratzinger not a static body of truths, but the personal presence of the living Christ. The real need for the teaching office becomes apparent when there is disagreement about which tradition is truly apostolic. In the second century, the gnostics claimed to possess a secret tradition handed down orally from the apostles. Before there was a written canon (as of yet the New Testament had not been formed), the church needed a criterion for discerning false from true tradition, and according to Ratzinger it found it in the apostolic tradition guaranteed by apostolic succession: "Before the New Testament itself became Scripture, it was faith that expounded 'Scripture' (that is, the Old Testament)."[32] Call it Ratzinger's rule: "The succession is the form of the tradition, and the tradition is the content of the succession."[33]

Apostolic succession is a kind of privileged paper trail: only those teachings that come from the apostles and their successors are deemed reliable. Ratzinger nicely turns the tables on easy Protestant stereotypes, insisting that the real purpose of apostolic succession is not to add to Scripture but to dispute the existence of "secret" nonapostolic traditions: "'Apostolic succession' is by its nature the living presence of the

---

29. "The Church appears ... not as a circle with a single center, but as an ellipse with two foci: primacy *and* episcopacy." Ratzinger, "Primacy, Episcopacy, and *Successio Apostolica*," in *God's Word*, 19.

30. Ratzinger, "Primacy, Episcopacy, and *Successio Apostolica*," 23.

31. Ratzinger, "Question of the Concept of Tradition," 63.

32. Ratzinger, "Primacy, Episcopacy, and *Successio Apostolica*," 26.

33. Ratzinger, "Primacy, Episcopacy, and *Successio Apostolica*," 28.

word in the personal form of witness."[34] In response to Protestants who still see apostolic succession as a second stream of revelation *alongside* Scripture, Ratzinger appeals to Jesus' high-priestly prayer for his apostles: "I do not ask for these only, but also for those who will believe in me through their word" (John 17:20). Ratzinger argues that "word" in this context does not mean exclusively the written word, for the New Testament was as yet not formed. Even in the early days of the church, then, its teaching office played a vital role.

There are many bishops in the Roman Catholic Church, but not all have inherited sees where there had once been an apostle or a local community of faith that had received letters from an apostle. Ratzinger argues that, among these privileged centers of apostolic witness, Rome stands paramount, for it lays claim to three apostles of its own: Peter, Paul, and John. The teaching office of the church includes both the college of bishops and the bishop of Rome, though only the see of Rome "represents the ultimate and genuine criterion of Catholicity."[35] In sum: the church is the living presence of the divine word, "and this presence is given concrete shape in those persons—the bishops—whose fundamental task is that of holding fast to the word and who are thus the personal form of the 'tradition.'"[36]

Does this mean that, for Ratzinger, revelation is also ongoing, as is the tradition of the church? It is an important question, for evangelicals affirm the finality of revelation in Scripture and the sufficiency of Scripture in attesting it. John Stott signals this evangelical conviction by highlighting the Greek term *hapax*: "once and for all," as in "the faith that was once for all delivered to the saints" (Jude 3).[37] According to Ratzinger, revelation does have its *hapax* character, insofar as Christ appeared in history, yet it "also has its constant 'today,' insofar as what

---

34. Ratzinger, "Primacy, Episcopacy, and *Successio Apostolica*," 30.

35. Ratzinger, "Primacy, Episcopacy, and Successio Apostolica," 33. Roman Catholics appeal to Luke 22:32 in support of Peter (and his successors) enjoying primacy. Jesus tells Peter that he has prayed that Peter's faith would not fail so that he could in turn strengthen his brothers (the apostles and their successors).

36. Ratzinger, "Primacy, Episcopacy, and *Successio Apostolica*," 35.

37. John Stott, *Evangelical Truth: A Personal Plea for Unity, Integrity, and Faithfulness*, rev. ed. (Downers Grove, IL: InterVarsity Press, 2003), 33.

once happened remains forever living and effective in the faith of the Church, and Christian faith never refers merely to what is past; rather, it refers equally to what is present and what is to come."[38] Evangelicals are concerned that such statements appeal to the church's ongoing reception of the Word as a warrant for developing new dogmas whose authority seems to stem more from the *sensus fidelium,* or the teaching office of the church, than from the text of Scripture itself (for example, the immaculate conception of Mary, made official in 1854). In this, evangelicals are merely echoing the Reformers' protest of what they took to be Rome's domestication of God's word to the teaching office of the church.

For evangelical Protestants, God's written word stands over, and sometimes in criticism of, the church. Continuing reformation of the church depends on Scripture's being the supreme authority of the church's faith and life, an independent criterion in light of which even the church's teaching office may be found wanting. For his part, Ratzinger thinks that Protestants have got it the wrong way around: "Office ... [is] the criterion for the word. It guarantees the word."[39] Ratzinger explicitly denies *sola Scriptura.* Scripture is never alone, he insists, because it is not the word of God apart from the community who receives it in faith. Referring to the Augsburg Confession (1530) in particular, Ratzinger complains, "Nothing is said about office."[40] However, for the reception to be deemed faithful, there must be an official means of guaranteeing authenticity, namely, episcopal succession and the magisterium.

Ratzinger acknowledges the Protestant challenge to Roman Catholics: "Can the word be handed over to the Church without having to fear that it will lose its own life and power under the shears of the Magisterium or amid the uncontrolled growth of the *sensus fidelium?*"[41] Yet Ratzinger wants Protestants to feel in turn the force of the Roman

---

38. Ratzinger, "Question of the Concept of Tradition," 86–87. Leonardo de Chirico, an Italian evangelical, contends that Roman Catholic theologians fail to maintain the distinction between "once for all" and "more and more": "Roman Catholic ecclesiology rests on the idea of the continuation of the incarnation of the Son of God in his mystical body, that is, the Church." Leonardo de Chirico, "The Blurring of Time Distinctions in Roman Catholicism," *Themelios* 29, no. 2 (2004): 41.

39. Ratzinger, "Question of the Concept of Tradition," 44.

40. Ratzinger, "Question of the Concept of Tradition," 44.

41. Ratzinger, "Question of the Concept of Tradition," 46.

Catholic counterchallenge: "Can the word be set up as independent without handing it over to the arbitrariness of the exegete, to be emptied in the disputes of historians, and thus to the complete loss of normative authority?"[42] This leads to the all-important issue to which Ratzinger dedicated much of his work: How can faith and reason work together in the particular matter of biblical interpretation?

SCRIPTURE AND INTERPRETATION

To this point, Ratzinger has more or less towed the line of Vatican II. In his capacity as president of the Pontifical Biblical Commission and later as pope, however, he has been more outspoken, particularly in calling for a more theological reading of the Bible. Pope Leo XIII's 1893 encyclical *Providentissimus Deus* reined in the perceived excesses of biblical criticism. However, some fifty years later, Pope Pius XII released an encyclical, *Divino Afflante Spiritu*, which encouraged Roman Catholic biblical scholars to employ the critical tools and methods of academic scholarship, which the pope suggested were themselves providential. Twenty years later, Vatican II attempted a habitable synthesis between patristic and modern modes of reading the Bible as the word of God in the words of human beings. Since that time, however, the "methodological spectrum of exegetical work has broadened in a way which could not have been envisioned" by Vatican II.[43] This leads to a final and contested question: Who has authority in matters of biblical interpretation?[44] What is arguably Ratzinger's most important contribution, not least for evangelicals, may be found just here, in his proposal for reading Scripture with faith and reason, as believing exegetes: simultaneously saints and scholars.

---

42. Ratzinger, "Question of the Concept of Tradition," 46.

43. Ratzinger, preface to *The Interpretation of the Bible in the Church*, ed. J. L. Houlden (London: SCM, 1995), 5.

44. For a more recent Protestant response to Roman Catholic challenges, see my *Biblical Authority after Babel: Retrieving the Solas in the Spirit of Mere Protestant Christianity* (Grand Rapids: Brazos, 2016).

The Erasmus Lecture (1988)

In 1988 Joseph Ratzinger delivered the Erasmus Lecture in New York City on the topic "Biblical Interpretation in Crisis." At the time, he was prefect of the Congregation for the Doctrine of the Faith, an arm of the Roman curia founded to defend the church from heresy but which today is responsible for promoting and safeguarding Catholic doctrine. Ratzinger's lecture was remarkable for two reasons: first, because he chose to speak not on doctrine but biblical interpretation; second, because he stayed for the conference that followed and engaged in dialogue with an ecumenical spectrum of biblical scholars and theologians. According to Richard John Neuhaus, Ratzinger belied the stereotype of someone who desires to control the conversation, choosing instead to dialogue as a form of church ministry.[45]

Ratzinger's Erasmus Lecture repays serious attention, even now, some thirty years later. The subtitle announces the nature of the crisis: "On the Question of the Foundations and Approaches of Exegesis Today." Evangelicals too have come to appreciate the centrality of biblical hermeneutics: even those who believe and celebrate the gospel have to interpret it. Evangelicals err in thinking that a high view of biblical authority translates into the right hermeneutic. Too often it does not. Indeed, this is one of the differences evangelicals had with the early fundamentalists. It is simply too easy to identify "what the Bible says" with what one's Bible teacher says.[46] One of the hallmarks of evangelicals is to affirm orthodoxy *and* engage modern learning, rather than insisting on the correctness of one's own interpretive tradition simply because it was one's own.

The crisis to which Ratzinger alludes in the title of his lecture pertains to the ways in which the historical-critical method and its offspring have complicated the project of biblical interpretation, making it so difficult that laypeople may feel they are entering a maze from which there

---

45. Richard John Neuhaus, foreword to *Biblical Interpretation in Crisis: The Ratzinger Conference on Bible and Church,* ed. Richard John Neuhaus (Grand Rapids: Eerdmans, 1989), ix. For a fuller account of the conference and the ensuing discussion, see the last chapter by Paul T. Stallsworth, "The Story of an Encounter," 102–90.

46. See further Kathleen C. Boone, *The Bible Tells Them So: The Discourse of Protestant Fundamentalism* (Albany: State University of New York Press, 1989).

is no return: "Abandon hope all ye who enter here!" But complexity is not the only problem. In addition, and more seriously, "Faith itself is not a component of this method, nor is God a factor to be dealt with in historical events."[47] Historical criticism leads, finally, to a situation where exegetes lose interest in theology, and theologians work with doctrines that are "as independent as possible from exegesis."[48]

Ratzinger identifies hermeneutics as the middle or mediating step that links the past meaning that is the object of the historical method and the pure literal sense that the average reader today understands. The challenge is to avoid on the one hand an arbitrary understanding that laypeople today might read into the text, and on the other a scholarly understanding that has nothing to do with faith. Once the historical-critical method has turned the past into something dead, Ratzinger asks, "who can reawaken it so that it can live and speak to me?"[49] At the time of his lecture in 1988, Ratzinger stated that "a truly convincing answer has yet to be formulated."[50] Ratzinger is not alone in speaking of a crisis in biblical interpretation. Brevard Childs's *Biblical Theology in Crisis*[51] makes a similar point as does, more recently, Michael Legaspi's *The Death of Scripture and the Rise of Biblical Studies.*[52]

Ratzinger is aware of newer hermeneutic approaches, such as Rudolf Bultmann's appropriation of Martin Heidegger's existentialist philosophy as a framework through which to hear the New Testament in today's terms. This is one strategy for making a past word present, yet Ratzinger is skeptical about what is *heard* in this conceptual translation:

---

47. Joseph Ratzinger, "Biblical Interpretation in Crisis: On the Question of the Foundations and Approaches of Exegesis Today," in Neuhaus, *Biblical Interpretation in Crisis*, 2.
48. Ratzinger, "Biblical Interpretation in Crisis," 3. Ratzinger cites Karl Rahner as an example of one who came to see theology as independent from exegesis (3n2).
49. Ratzinger, "Biblical Interpretation in Crisis," 4.
50. Ratzinger, "Biblical Interpretation in Crisis," 4. Ratzinger's call for a new synthesis has not gone unnoticed. Several Roman Catholic scholars are now trying to live out his call to unite historical-critical scholarship with theological interpretation. See, for example, Ignacio Carbajosa, *Faith, the Fount of Exegesis: The Interpretation of Scripture in Light of the History of Research on the Old Testament*, trans. Paul Stevenson (San Francisco: Ignatius, 2013).
51. Brevard Childs, *Biblical Theology in Crisis* (Philadelphia: Westminster, 1970).
52. Michael C. Legaspi, *The Death of Scripture and the Rise of Biblical Studies* (Oxford: Oxford University Press, 2011).

"In the end, are we listening to Jesus or to Heidegger with this approach to understanding?"[53] Ratzinger is also aware of forms of biblical criticism that move beyond trying to recover the past, such as materialist and feminist exegesis, yet he sees them as symptoms of how bad the crisis has become, for "they are no longer interested in ascertaining the truth, but only in whatever will serve their own particular agendas."[54] Something similar may be said of the various forms of ideology-critique, liberation, and postcolonial interpretation.

Interestingly, Ratzinger believes that evangelicals and Catholics alike face a similar challenge, namely, to preserve the undeniable contributions of the historical method—the attention to the original contexts and literary forms—while at the same time acknowledging its limitations and blind spots. Specifically, Ratzinger calls for a "criticism of criticism" that would acknowledge that the critical method does not yield scientific certainty or "assured results."[55] Ratzinger here appeals to, and applies, Heisenberg's "uncertainty principle" to the historical method: "Heisenberg has shown that the outcome of a given experiment is heavily influenced by the point of view of the observer."[56] It follows that biblical scholars can never simply reproduce the "as it actually happened" of history, as if criticism provided them with a detached "view from nowhere."[57] On the contrary, the history of biblical criticism tells us as much about the historical context *of the critics* as it does the biblical texts, for biblical commentaries invariably reflect the academic and social interests of the times in which they were written: "In the diachronic reading of exegesis, its philosophic presuppositions become quite apparent."[58] Ratzinger insists on the point: "At its core, the debate

53. Ratzinger, "Biblical Interpretation in Crisis," 4.
54. Ratzinger, "Biblical Interpretation in Crisis," 5.
55. Ratzinger, "Biblical Interpretation in Crisis," 6.
56. Ratzinger, "Biblical Interpretation in Crisis," 7. The German physicist Werner Heisenberg (1901–1976) introduced his Uncertainty Principle in 1927. It applies to quantum mechanics and states that one cannot ascertain both the momentum and the position of a particle (for example, an electron) at the same time, because the very act of observing the one affects the value of the other, thus introducing uncertainty into the equation.
57. This is Thomas Nagel's label for the idea that following critical procedures guarantees an objectivity that virtually erases one's particular situatedness and personal perspective. See Thomas Nagel, *The View from Nowhere* (Oxford: Oxford University Press, 1986).
58. Ratzinger, "Biblical Interpretation in Crisis," 8.

about modern exegesis is not a dispute among historians: it is rather a philosophical debate."[59]

Ratzinger concludes his Erasmus Lecture on a constructive note, with a section titled "Basic Elements of a New Synthesis." He calls, first, for an openness to the biblical text as a supernatural reality, a word from God: "Modern exegesis … completely relegated God to the incomprehensible, the otherworldly, and the inexpressible in order to be able to treat the biblical text itself as an entirely worldly reality according to natural-scientific methods."[60] Second, interpreters must be open to the possibility that the events behind the text may themselves form part of a unified redemptive history whose ultimate meaning is revealed only at the end of the sequence, namely, the event of Jesus Christ. Finally, Ratzinger calls for biblical interpreters to recognize that faith, rather than some philosophy or methodological naturalism, is a hermeneutic that does not do violence to the Bible but, on the contrary, offers the only possibility we have "for the Bible to be itself."[61]

Verbum Domini (2010)

Some twenty years later, Ratzinger, now Pope Benedict, returned to the question of biblical interpretation in his 2010 *Verbum Domini*, a response to a synod of bishops that met in Rome in 2008 to discuss the theme "The Word of God in the Life and Mission of the Church." The synod was in one sense an answer to Ratzinger's call for a new synthesis, and in another sense the culmination of a trend begun with Vatican II's *Dei Verbum* to make the reading, study, and interpretation of the Bible more central to the life of the church.[62] Benedict's response to the synod is structured in three parts: the word of God, the word in the church, the word to the world. He treats biblical interpretation in the first part, liturgy and catechesis in the second, and the church's

---

59. Ratzinger, "Biblical Interpretation in Crisis," 16. See also Joseph Ratzinger, *The Nature and Mission of Theology: Approaches to Understanding Its Role in the Light of Present Controversy*, trans. Adrian Walker (San Francisco: Ignatius, 1995), 13–29.
60. Ratzinger, "Biblical Interpretation in Crisis," 17.
61. Ratzinger, "Biblical Interpretation in Crisis," 23.
62. Benedict XVI, *Verbum Domini*, 4–5.

mission in the third. The location of biblical interpretation in the first part is telling: Benedict sees the church rather than the academy as the "primary setting" for biblical interpretation, for the primary task is to hear the revealed word *of God*.[63]

To insist that *"the primary setting for scriptural interpretation is the life of the church"*[64] ensures that faith serves as the fundamental hermeneutic. This applies especially to theologians, who must be purveyors not of their own ideas but of the Roman Catholic "trademark."[65] Put differently: theologians must speak not in their own name "but in the name of the common subject, the Church."[66] Everything begins by acknowledging Scripture for what it really is, the word of God in human words (1 Thess 2:13), but one can only acknowledge the Spirit who inspired Scripture if one reads it in the faith that the same Spirit bestows. While scholars can notice "interesting elements on the level of textual structure and form,"[67] a proper understanding of Scripture's subject matter requires faith.

The faith teaches that the Word was made flesh. That's why Benedict affirms the benefits of much modern biblical scholarship. Historical-critical exegesis in particular is indispensable, for it is tied to the historical fact of the incarnation: "The history of salvation is not mythology, but a true history, and it should thus be studied with the methods of serious historical research."[68] Benedict insists on maintaining the balance between the historically determined literal sense and the theologically determined spiritual sense, for the human words of the Bible are also the word of God.[69]

---

63. Benedict's *Verbum Domini* has been described as "one of the most detailed and explicit magisterial teachings on 'historical-critical exegesis' ever promulgated." Brant Pitre, *"Verbum Domini* and Historical-Critical Exegesis," in *Verbum Domini and the Complementarity of Exegesis and Theology,* ed. Scott Carl (Grand Rapids: Eerdmans, 2015), 26.

64. Benedict XVI, *Verbum Domini,* 46 (emphasis original).

65. "But not everyone is free to assert that what he says represents Catholic theology. Here there is a sort of 'trademark,' a historical identity which the Magisterium knows it is called to defend." Ratzinger, *Nature and Mission,* 8.

66. Ratzinger, *Nature and Mission,* 68.

67. Benedict XVI, *Verbum Domini,* 47.

68. Benedict XVI, Intervention in the Fourteenth General Congregation of the Synod, October 14, 2008, *Insegnamenti* 4, no. 2 (2008): 492, quoted in *Verbum Domini,* 50.

69. See further Pitre, *"Verbum Domini* and Historical-Critical Exegesis," 26–40.

How does one read the Bible in order to hear the divine authorial intention? Ratzinger affirms the three criteria suggested by *Dei Verbum*: (1) attend to the unity of the whole Scripture through canonical exegesis; (2) attend to the living tradition of the church; and (3) respect the analogy of faith. In sum: the new synthesis for which Ratzinger called in 1988 involves not supplanting grammatical-historical exegesis but in supplying it with a theological dimension.

Before exploring what is involved in this theological dimension, it will be helpful to bring Benedict's broader vision into focus. At all costs he wants to avoid a dualistic approach to Scripture in which biblical scholars read in one way and systematic theologians in another. In particular, Benedict wishes to prevent exegetes from reading the Bible as if it were "*a text belonging only to the past.*"[70] Such reading characterizes a secularized hermeneutic "based on the conviction that the Divine does not intervene in human history."[71] Benedict offers a pithy yet powerful formulation of this point: "Where exegesis is not theology, Scripture cannot be the soul of theology."[72]

The way forward involves a harmony of faith and reason such that exegetes should adopt no criteria that would rule out in advance God's self-communication in the human words of Scripture. As concerns the role of faith, Benedict is keen to retrieve the exegetical approach of the church fathers, including the spiritual sense. The spiritual sense is the meaning of the biblical texts when read "under the influence"—of the Holy Spirit, that is—in the context of the community of the faithful. To read the Bible in faith means to read it as one book. One cannot do this in terms of critical reason only, for viewed in historical terms, the Bible is not a single book. Moreover, to read the Bible as the word of God for the people of God includes listening to the interpretations that have emerged over time in the communion of saints. It is because the communion of saints is a living tradition that Scripture ultimately belongs not to the past, but to the church—yesterday, today, and forever.

---

70. Benedict, *Verbum Domini*, 54 (emphasis original).
71. Benedict, *Verbum Domini*, 55.
72. Benedict XVI, Intervention, 493–94.

Jesus of Nazareth (2007)

Benedict put many of his own recommendations into practice in his *Jesus of Nazareth*, a book-length attempt to answer Jesus' question to his disciples, "Who do you say that I am?" (Matt 16:15). The book aims to bridge the same ugly ditch that separates exegetes from theologians, only this time in a christological rather than hermeneutical register, where the dualism in question is that between the "Jesus of history" and the "Christ of faith." In particular, Benedict is disturbed by Rudolf Schnackenburg's dismal verdict about the scholar's ability to respond to Jesus' query: "A reliable view of the historical figure of Jesus of Nazareth through scientific effort with historical-critical methods can be only inadequately achieved."[73]

Benedict uses his foreword to *Jesus of Nazareth* to provide a sketch of his own method.[74] He again emphasizes the historical-critical method as an indispensable dimension of exegesis given the historical particularity of biblical faith: "And the word became flesh" (John 1:14). At the same time, he also repeats his call for exegetes to recognize the limits of the method. Historical interpretation cannot make the Word present, nor treat the diverse texts as "one" Bible, nor exhaust the task of hearing God's word in the human words. To read the Bible in the spirit in which it was written, one has to attend to its canonical form and its christological content.

For Benedict, biblical inspiration ultimately funds spiritual interpretation. Yes, we need to understand the historical context to understand the human words of Scripture, yet these words have a "deeper value," for their human authors do not speak as self-contained individuals, for themselves only. The human authors "are not autonomous writers in the modern sense; they form part of a collective subject, the 'People of God.' ... This subject is actually the deeper 'author' of the Scriptures."[75] This claim returns us to the way Ratzinger views the pattern of theological

---

73. Rudolf Schnackenburg, *Jesus in the Gospels: A Biblical Christology* (Louisville: Westminster John Knox, 2005), 316.
74. Benedict XVI, *Jesus of Nazareth*, vol. 1, *From the Baptism in the Jordan to the Transfiguration* (New York: Doubleday, 2007), xi–xxiv.
75. Benedict XVI, *From the Baptism in the Jordan to the Transfiguration*, xx–xxi.

authority: "The People of God—the Church—is the living subject of Scripture; it is in the Church that the words of the Bible are always in the present."[76] Benedict's view of Jesus of Nazareth thus goes beyond what purely historical-critical exegesis can say. The goal is "a properly theological interpretation of the Bible."[77]

CONCLUSION

In a presentation celebrating the one-hundredth anniversary of the Pontifical Biblical Commission, Cardinal Ratzinger refers to Moses gazing on the promised land "of an exegesis liberated from every shackle of magisterial surveillance."[78] Whereas exegetes in the first half of the twentieth century were barred from entry, Vatican II marks "the entrance into the Promise Land of exegetical freedom."[79] However, freedom with no boundaries risks destroying itself. The magisterium no longer imposes norms on exegetes, yet the text does, and tradition is faith's reception of divine revelation in and through the text of Scripture. There is no such thing as pure exegetical objectivity, and when biblical scholars pretend there is, they lose sight of the Bible's special and specific (theological) nature.

For Ratzinger, we might say, faith has its reasons that a purely critical reason cannot know. Faith receives the Christ presented in the Scriptures, but the Christ of the Scriptures is also the Jesus of history. Yet the full truth of the Jesus of history, the revelation of the Father, must be received in faith. Faith is a mode of knowing, and the critical attempt to set faith aside "does not produce pure objectivity, but sets up a cognitive standpoint that rules out a certain [theological] perspective."[80] Here it is important to recall Ratzinger's insistence that the church, the community of faith, is the "living presence" of the word, and that the church's bishops are the concrete corporate form of tradition. To read in

76. Benedict XVI, *From the Baptism in the Jordan to the Transfiguration*, xxi.
77. Benedict XVI, *From the Baptism in the Jordan to the Transfiguration*, xxiii.
78. Joseph Ratzinger, "Exegesis and the Magisterium of the Church," in *Opening Up the Scriptures: Joseph Ratzinger and the Foundations of Biblical Interpretation*, ed. José Granados, Carlos Granados, and Luis Sánchez-Navarro (Grand Rapids: Eerdmans, 2008), 128.
79. Ratzinger, "Exegesis and the Magisterium of the Church," 129.
80. Ratzinger, "Exegesis and the Magisterium of the Church," 135.

faith means, for Ratzinger, to read as a member of the church, a single reading subject.[81] Apart from the concrete reality of the church (that is, lived Roman tradition), Scripture becomes a victim of experts' disputes.

Differences between evangelicals and Roman Catholics of course remain. The most important concerns the pattern of interpretive authority and the catholicity of the church. For Benedict, Scripture, tradition, and the Roman magisterium always coincide, because they are guided by the same Spirit. By way of contrast, evangelicals acknowledge that, tragically, the church sometimes errs, both by misinterpreting what is said or by adding to what is not. Scripture therefore retains supreme authority over Roman tradition and interpretations. The Bible, not the college of bishops, is our ultimate authority. Moreover, evangelicals acknowledge the positive role of catholic tradition in biblical interpretation, but point out that Rome does not enjoy a monopoly on catholicity.[82]

Ratzinger's most enduring legacy may well be his attempt to make good on Vatican II's claim that "the study of the sacred page should be ... the very soul of theology."[83] At the same time, he also insists that exegetes "do not stand in some neutral area, above or outside the history of the Church ... [rather] the faith of the Church is a form of *sympathia* without which the Bible remains a closed book."[84] Indeed, Roman Catholic scholars, thanks to Ratzinger's leadership, may now be ahead of evangelicals as far as being intentional about not putting asunder what God has put together: exegesis and theology.[85] As one Catholic biblical scholar puts it, "Today it is starting to be an established fact for Catholic exegetes that the interpretive task must not stop

---

81. Ratzinger appeals to Gal 2:20 ("It is no longer I who live, but Christ who lives in me") in support of the claim that the church is not an abstract principle but a single and living (reading) subject (*Nature and Mission*, 51–52, 61).

82. For an expansion of this point, see my "A Mere Protestant Response," in Matthew Levering and Kevin Vanhoozer, *Was the Reformation a Mistake? Why Catholic Doctrine Is Not Unbiblical* (Grand Rapids: Zondervan, 2017), 191–231.

83. *Dei Verbum*, §24.

84. Ratzinger, "Biblical Interpretation in Crisis," 22–23.

85. See the essays in Carl, *Verbum Domini and the Complementarity of Exegesis and Theology*—particularly Pablo Gadenz, "Overcoming the Hiatus between Exegesis and Theology: Guidance and Examples from Pope Benedict XVI," 41–62.

with the historical-critical dimension but must go as far as theology."[86] In Benedict's words, "Where theology is not essentially the interpretation of the Church's Scripture, such a theology no longer has a foundation."[87] As an evangelical, I not only appreciate Ratzinger's exhortation to do theology biblically and to read the Bible theologically; I also say, "Amen."[88]

86. Carbajosa, Faith, The Fount of Exegesis, 249. However, Carbajosa does not see theology as a second step beyond exegesis, as if the text were not inspired by God, but rather as a second dimension, alongside the historical, in what ought to be a single exegesis.
87. Benedict XVI, Verbum Domini, 56.
88. The best book-length account of Benedict's way of relating Scripture, exegesis, hermeneutics, and theology is probably Scott W. Hahn, Covenant and Communion: The Biblical Theology of Pope Benedict XVI (Grand Rapids: Brazos, 2009). I am grateful to my PhD student Roy McDaniel and Todd Hains of Lexham Press for their helpful comments on an earlier draft.

5

"Behold the Man"

Joseph Ratzinger on Theological Anthropology

R. LUCAS STAMPS

Only the humanity of the Second Adam is the true humanity, only the humanity that endured the Cross brings the true man to light.[1]

—Joseph Ratzinger

The whole of Benedict XVI's theology has a certain anthropological orientation. To be sure, other central themes are no less prominent in Joseph Ratzinger's rich and textured theological program. Ecclesiology and Eucharist, liturgy and creed, Scripture and the fathers, and Christology and eschatology are among the more obvious candidates for a leitmotif. In a sense any of these will do, provided they are seen as gateways into the rich labyrinth of the Pope Emeritus's mature thought. But in each of these arenas, a strong case can be made that the nature and destiny of women and men as God's image bearers is never far from view. Perhaps the title of Ratzinger's book-length interview with journalist Peter Seewald best summarizes Ratzinger's theological vision: *God and the World*.[2] Ratzinger has always been zealous to preserve the central place of God himself in the church's theological and social teaching, but also with a view to the purpose and vocation of humanity as the crown of God's creation. A reader of Ratzinger's voluminous works searching for material along anthropological lines will surely not be disappointed. Ratzinger devotes explicit attention to the creation of humankind, the meaning of the *imago Dei*, the nature and

---

1. Joseph Ratzinger, *Dogma and Preaching: Applying Christian Doctrine to Daily Life*, trans. Michael J. Miller and Matthew J. O'Connell, ed. Michael J. Miller (San Francisco: Ignatius, 2011), 159.
2. Joseph Ratzinger, *God and the World: A Conversation with Peter Seewald*, trans. Henry Taylor (San Francisco: Ignatius, 2002).

consequences of the fall into sin, the constitution of humans as physical and spiritual creatures, the possibilities and parameters of human redemption in Christ, the implications of a biblical vision of humankind for societal and ethical dilemmas, and the ultimate destiny of humankind in union with God in the eschaton. These and other anthropological themes permeate Ratzinger's impressive corpus. The only challenge is attempting a synthesis of this capacious material.

This chapter cannot adequately address the full range of Benedict's theological anthropology. Instead, special attention will be given to Ratzinger's theology of the creation and the fall and to how he envisions the person of Christ himself as the key to understanding humanity's identity, redemption, and destiny.[3] As an orienting principle, I will note the distinctively Augustinian framework of Ratzinger's anthropology. Ratzinger's Augustinian, even pessimistic, understanding of humanity in this time between the times serves as a useful model for how the church in the West can navigate the unique challenges posed by our late modern and post-Christian world. For Ratzinger, true humanity is found in Jesus Christ, the second Adam, and in his passion and resurrection. The cross sets forth not only the gift of salvation but also the pattern of human vocation as the church awaits the final in-breaking of God's kingdom at the parousia. Thus, Pilate's proclamation is ironically true: *Ecce homo,* "Behold the man." In Christ, "we can discern what the human being, God's project, is, and thereby also our own status."[4]

CREATION

In 1981, Ratzinger delivered a series of Lenten homilies on the Genesis creation narratives that were eventually published as *"In the Beginning": A Catholic Understanding of the Story of Creation and the Fall.* He lamented that "the creation account is noticeably and nearly completely absent

---

3. According to Aidan Nichols, Ratzinger sees salvation history as a "the primary theological key to understanding Christian revelation." See Aidan Nichols, *The Thought of Pope Benedict XVI: An Introduction to the Theology of Joseph Ratzinger* (London: Burns & Oates, 2007), 34–35.

4. Joseph Ratzinger, *"In The Beginning": A Catholic Understanding of the Story of Creation and the Fall,* trans. Boniface Ramsey (Grand Rapids: Eerdmans, 1995), 57.

from catechesis, preaching, and even theology."[5] These lectures are a good place to begin our discussion of these most fundamental biblical and theological themes. Several anthropological issues emerge out of these succinct and pastoral addresses, which are supplemented by his other writings.

The Image of God

Ratzinger sees the creation of humankind as recorded in Genesis in a twofold sense. First, human beings are taken from the earth: Adam is formed from the "dust of the ground" (Gen 2:7 NIV). For Ratzinger, this earthy origin of humankind is both humbling and consoling. We are "only earth," but as such we are made from what the Genesis account identifies as "very good": the good earth made by the good Creator.[6] Ratzinger also draws out some of the ethical implications of humanity's common origin in the earth. "Emperor and beggar, master and slave are all ultimately one and the same person, taken from the earth and destined to return to the same earth." This egalitarianism of dust signals the "unity of the whole human race," and gives the lie to any "blood and soil" delusions of racial superiority.[7] "The Bible says a decisive 'no' to all racism and every human division."[8]

The second and decisive feature of humanity, however, lies in what distinguishes it from the rest of the created order: the *imago Dei*. God's image and likeness give humanity a heavenly character and destiny: "In the human being heaven and earth touch one another. ... Each human being is known and loved by God."[9] Ratzinger again teases out some of the ethical implications of this biblical teaching:

---

5. Ratzinger, "In the Beginning," ix.
6. Ratzinger, "In the Beginning," 43.
7. Ratzinger, "In the Beginning," 43.
8. Ratzinger, "In the Beginning," 44. See also Ratzinger's comment on the visit of the magi, who according to tradition hail from each known continent: "The black king is part and parcel of this: in the kingdom of Jesus Christ there are no distinctions of race and origin. In him and through him, humanity is united, without losing any of the richness of the variety." Benedict XVI, *Jesus of Nazareth*, vol. 3, *The Infancy Narratives*, trans. Philip J. Whitmore (New York: Image, 2012), 96.
9. Ratzinger, "In the Beginning," 44, 45.

Human life stands under God's special protection, because each human being, however wretched or exalted he or she may be, however sick or suffering, however good-for-nothing or important, whether born or unborn, whether incurably ill or radiant with health—each one bears God's breath in himself or herself, each one is God's image. This is the deepest reason for the inviolability of human dignity, and upon it is founded ultimately every civilization.[10]

The image is thus not some abstract feature of ancient Near Eastern religion but is a living doctrine that informs the church's social teaching on everything from abortion to inadequate health care to euthanasia.

But what is the essence of the *imago Dei* according to Ratzinger? He explicates this foundational anthropological doctrine along several lines. Foundationally, the image entails a representation of God and thus implies relationality: "Human beings cannot be closed in on themselves."[11] The image opens up humanity to relationship with God, whose own Trinitarian relations are the ground of all human relationality. This relationality is expressed, further, in the fact that humans are thinking and praying creatures: "They are most profoundly themselves when they discover their relation to their Creator."[12] But the *imago Dei* must also be understood in the definitive revelation of both God and humankind in the person of Jesus Christ. Christ is "the definitive human being, and creation is, at it were, a preliminary sketch that points to him."[13] Therefore, to bear the image of God means to be open to the possibility of brotherhood with Christ, the God-man. As such, bearing the image implies that humanity has yet to attain to the fullest expression of the image. Living with the consequences of the first Adam and yet caught

10. Ratzinger, *"In the Beginning,"* 45.
11. Ratzinger, *"In the Beginning,"* 47.
12. Ratzinger, *"In the Beginning,"* 48.
13. Ratzinger, *"In the Beginning,"* 48. Hence, Ratzinger serves as a helpful exemplar of the attempt to frame anthropology in christological terms. For more on christological anthropology from an evangelical perspective, see Marc Cortez, *Christological Anthropology in Historical Perspective: Ancient and Contemporary Approaches to Theological Anthropology* (Grand Rapids: Zondervan, 2016).

up in the work of the second Adam, human beings are "en route" and "oriented toward their future" when their true identity will be revealed.[14] Elsewhere, Ratzinger defines the image in terms of humankind's vocation to use their freedom to become one with the God who is pure freedom, pure relationality. The image, therefore, is not so much a static possession as it is a summons for humans to give themselves in love of God and neighbor.[15] When comparing Ratzinger's doctrine to the perennial debates about the image—substantive, relational, functional, christological—we find that Ratzinger opts for an all-inclusive teaching, but one that finds its center in Christ himself.

The Constitution of Human Persons

Given this twofold understanding of humankind's creation—of the dust and yet endowed with the image and likeness of God—it is unsurprising to find Ratzinger defending a certain kind of anthropological dualism. In his first papal encyclical, *Deus Caritas Est*, Benedict grounds the relationship between love (*eros*) and the divine in this twofold nature of humanity: "This is due first and foremost to the fact that man is a being made up of body and soul."[16] But Benedict's view should not be confused with some sort of sharp Cartesian separation of soul and body. He goes on to write, "Man is truly himself when his body and soul are intimately united; the challenge of *eros* can be said to be truly overcome when this unification is achieved."[17] A gnostic denigration of the body would be a betrayal of humanity's true identity: "Should he aspire to be pure spirit and to reject the flesh as pertaining to his animal nature alone, then spirit and body would both lose their dignity."[18] On the other hand, a purely physicalist understanding of human composition

---

14. Ratzinger, "*In the Beginning*," 49.
15. Joseph Ratzinger, "Freedom and Liberation: The Anthropological Vision of the Instruction *Libertatis Conscientia*," in *Joseph Ratzinger in* Communio, vol. 2, *Anthropology and Culture*, ed. David L. Schindler and Nicholas J. Healy (Grand Rapids: Eerdmans, 2013), 69.
16. Benedict XVI, *Deus Caritas Est*, Encyclical Letter, December 25, 2005, §5, https://w2.vatican.va/content/benedict-xvi/en/encyclicals/documents/hf_ben-xvi_enc_20051225_deus-caritas-est.html.
17. Benedict XVI, *Deus Caritas Est*, §5.
18. Benedict XVI, *Deus Caritas Est*, §5.

would result in a loss of intrinsic human "greatness." No, it is "neither the spirit alone nor the body alone that loves: it is the man, the person, a unified creature composed of body and soul, who loves. Only when both dimensions are truly united, does man attain his full stature. Only thus is love—eros—able to mature and attain its authentic grandeur."[19] Thus Ratzinger's theological anthropology can be categorized as "holistic dualism" or even "dualistic holism." A human being is neither pure spirit nor mere matter but is (ordinarily) a psychosomatic whole.[20]

Ratzinger's eschatology also bears out this holistic perspective. Ratzinger teaches the traditional two-stage understanding of personal eschatology: (1) an intermediate state when, upon death, the soul is temporarily separated from the body and (2) a final resurrection from the dead at the eschaton. Pointing to the parable of the rich man and Lazarus, Ratzinger speaks of this intermediate state as either a state of immediate punishment for the wicked or else a "provisional form of bliss" for the redeemed.[21] Naturally he also makes room for the doctrine of purgatory for those in need of purifying before entering into the bliss of heaven, but he seems to admit more than one possible interpretation of what this "time" of purgation might mean.[22] Its duration cannot be measured by ordinary worldly time, and its decisive element is an encounter with the risen Christ himself. In any case, the final state involves a transcending of any "temporary" state and a reconstitution of full humanity in the resurrection.[23]

Ratzinger also takes up the important but thorny issues surrounding the definition of "personhood." In an important 1990 essay in *Communio*, "Concerning the Notion of Person in Theology," Ratzinger suggests that the Christian faith essentially invented the notion of personhood on

---

19. Benedict XVI, *Deus Caritas Est*, §5.

20. I say "ordinarily" in order to make room for Ratzinger's understanding on the disembodied intermediate state, which is to be treated presently.

21. Benedict XVI, *Spe Salvi*, Encyclical Letter, November 30, 2007, §45, https://w2.vatican.va/content/benedict-xvi/en/encyclicals/documents/hf_ben-xvi_enc_20071130_spe-salvi.html.

22. Benedict XVI, *Spe Salvi*, §§47–48.

23. For more on Benedict's eschatology, see *Joseph Ratzinger, Eschatology: Death and Eternal Life*, trans. Michael Waldstein and Aidan Nichols (Washington, DC: Catholic University of America Press, 1988).

the back of its Trinitarian and christological controversies. Tracing the concept from Tertullian and the "prosopographic exegesis" of the earliest Christians through the great controversies of the fourth and fifth centuries, Ratzinger suggests that Christian theologians have not always appreciated the important insights this tradition suggests. Rather than beginning from a generic notion of personhood, as Boethius and later Thomas Aquinas did, Christian theologians ought to begin from a more basic Trinitarian and christological foundation. The great debates over the Trinity and the incarnation yielded an understanding of person as *pure relation*. The Son is not a distinct substance from the Father but shares in all things alike with the Father and Spirit as regards the divine essence. Neither is there anything accidental in the divine persons, since God is pure being, pure actuality. Instead, what distinguishes the divine persons is precisely their relations to one another, spelled out in the traditional relations of origin. So between the Aristotelian concepts of substance and accidents stands a "third specific fundamental category" of relation.[24] This, for Ratzinger, is the great Christian advance over antiquity vis-à-vis the notion of personhood. This same category was carried over into the christological developments of the fifth century and beyond. The Son of God assumes a true and complete human nature (including a human soul and will) but does not assume a distinct human person. Christ remains only one person, the person of the divine Son. And yet this formulation takes nothing away from Christ's true humanity. This is precisely where Ratzinger finds the Boethian understanding of personhood in terms of *substance* most lacking. Following Richard of St. Victor (rather than St. Thomas, who saw the incarnation as a grand exception to the Boethian rule), Ratzinger suggests that the concept of person should be understood at the level of *existence*, not *essence*.[25] In short, Ratzinger suggests that this relational understanding of person should be carried over from its Trinitarian and christological origins and applied more generally to the category itself. This yields

24. Joseph Ratzinger, "Concerning the Notion of Person in Theology," in Schindler and Healy, *Anthropology and Culture*, 108.
25. Ratzinger, "Concerning the Notion of Person in Theology," 113.

an understanding of human personhood, exemplified in the incarnate Son himself, that highlights mutual relatedness, "openness" to the other. The Christian concept of person thus "adds the idea of 'we' to the idea of 'I' and 'you.'"[26]

Creation and Evolution

Benedict also discusses the relationship between the biblical accounts of creation and the claims of evolutionary science. This issue highlights a theme that would later appear in one of the pope's most widely publicized (and most controversial) addresses: his Regensburg lecture of September 2006. There, Benedict gave an apology for the integration of philosophy into the fabric of Christian theology—for the integration of faith and reason. While he rejects the "canon of scientificity," according to which all human inquiry must bow to scientific criteria with the result that faith is reduced to mere subjectivity, Benedict does not oppose science itself.[27] Instead, he encourages an engagement with "the whole breadth of reason, and not the denial of its grandeur."[28] But this engagement must be open to questions regarding the ground of rationality, which naturally enough, Benedict sees in the *Logos* of God.

When addressing the question of evolution, Ratzinger summarizes his position succinctly: "We cannot say: creation *or* evolution, inasmuch as these two things respond to two different realities. The story of the dust of the earth and the breath of God ... does not in fact explain how persons came to be but rather what they are."[29] On the other hand, evolution "seeks to understand and describe biological developments. But in so doing it cannot explain where the 'project' of human persons comes from, nor their inner origin, nor their particular nature." So in the end,

---

26. Ratzinger, "Concerning the Notion of Person in Theology," 116. Ratzinger builds his critique of Enlightenment individualism on this basic theological foundation.

27. Benedict XVI, "Faith, Reason and the University: Memories and Reflections," University of Regensburg, September 12, 2006, http://w2.vatican.va/content/benedict-xvi/en/speeches/2006/september/documents/hf_ben-xvi_spe_20060912_university-regensburg.html. See also Benedict XVI, "Appendix II: The Regensburg Address," in Tracey Rowland, *Ratzinger's Faith: The Theology of Pope Benedict XVI* (Oxford: Oxford University Press, 2008), 166–74.

28. Benedict XVI, "Faith, Reason and the University."

29. Ratzinger, *"In the Beginning,"* 50.

"we are faced here with two complementary—rather than mutually exclusive—realities."[30] Ratzinger seeks the reconciliation of these two complementary stories in dialogue with the noted atheistic scientist Jacques Monod, who is forced to admit the sheer unlikelihood of the origin of life and the emergence of the human person. But where Monod must fall back on pure chance, Ratzinger puts forward the benevolent will of God. Humanity is not the result of "haphazard mistakes" but is willed by God himself as a "divine project" and "the fruit of divine love.[31] In other words, Ratzinger wants to put the question of creation and evolution in a completely different light, namely, the question of meaning and purpose. For Ratzinger, evolution is "situated on the phenomenological level and deals with the actually occurring individual forms in the world, whereas the belief in creation moves on the ontological level, inquires into what is behind individual things [and] marvels at the miracle of being itself."[32] Evolution is concerned with why there is this thing and not another; creation is concerned with the question of why there is anything at all. The special creation of humanity is to be found in the arising of spirit, which is the goal of creation's developmental process, with matter as "the prehistory of spirit." Elsewhere, Ratzinger seems to cast doubt on the notion of macroevolution (the development of one species into another), even as he states the undeniability of microevolution (adaptations within a species).[33] In any event, Ratzinger does not wall off the belief in creation from the findings of science. This willingness to incorporate some version of evolutionary theory into his doctrine of creation evidences Ratzinger's broader project of integrating faith and reason. Here too we see the Augustinian Ratzinger willing to plunder the Egyptians and to seek truth wherever it may be found.[34]

30. Ratzinger, *"In the Beginning,"* 50.
31. Ratzinger, *"In the Beginning,"* 56, 57. For more on Ratzinger's understanding of creation and evolution, see Ratzinger, *Dogma and Preaching,* 131–42.
32. Ratzinger, *Dogma and Preaching,* 133.
33. Joseph Ratzinger, *Truth and Tolerance: Christian Belief and World Religions,* trans. Henry Taylor (San Francisco: Ignatius, 2004), 179–80.
34. It is noteworthy that Augustine himself tended toward nonliteral interpretations of the days of creation. It is also worth noting that many (though not all) evangelicals may balk at Ratzinger's synthesis of the biblical teaching

THE FALL

Ratzinger's sober view of humanity's potential in a fallen world is perhaps his most distinctive contribution to theological anthropology in the postconciliar era. Here we see some separation from his predecessor, Pope John Paul II. While the two popes both carried forward a similar conservative agenda, Karol Wojtyła's papacy was characterized by a noted optimism in the church's renewal efforts. He often spoke of a "new springtime" of renewal and evangelization, an optimism no doubt shaped by the unique historical events that marked his inspiring career. Benedict, on the other hand, has tended to be more circumspect about the prospects for widespread cultural transformation. In another interview with Seewald, in 1996, Ratzinger warned that "maybe we are facing a new and different kind of epoch in the church's history, where Christianity will again be characterized more by the mustard seed, where it will exist in small, seemingly insignificant groups that nonetheless live an intense struggle against evil and bring good into the world—that let God in."[35] While the wedge should not be driven too sharply between the two popes, there seems to be a marked difference in tone between John Paul's "new springtime" and Benedict's smaller, purer, struggling church. Also here we see once again Ratzinger's indebtedness to Augustine, whose doctrine of sin has served to temper Ratzinger's expectations for cultural transformation. Ratzinger's lifelong opposition to ideologies (shaped by his early experience with National Socialism) is also of a piece with this Augustinian hamartiology.

Adam in the Garden

Ratzinger understands the biblical narrative of the fall in terms of its literary archetypes: the garden represents the good world that God has made, not as a threat to humans but as a gift to them; and the serpent, an image taken, according to Ratzinger, from Eastern fertility

---

with evolution. For an introduction to the evangelical perspectives taken on this issue, see J. P. Moreland and John Mark Reynolds, eds., *Three Views on Creation and Evolution* (Grand Rapids: Zondervan, 1999).

35. Joseph Ratzinger, *Salt of the Earth: The Church at the End of the Millennium; An Interview with Peter Seewald*, trans. Adrian Walker (San Francisco: Ignatius, 1996), 16.

cults, which represented the threat that the original readers of Genesis faced to abandon the covenant of the Lord.[36] The tempter appeals not to outright atheism, but instead to "an apparently completely reasonable request for information."[37] The temptation is not a denial of God's existence but of his goodness. "The first thing is not the denial of God but rather about his covenant, about the community of faith, prayer, the commandments—all of which are the context for living God's covenant."[38] The temptation to immediate pleasure, to a perversion of human freedom, remains with us. Art and technology, for example, can provide positive opportunities for humans to enjoy and deploy God's good gifts, but when they are severed from God's lordship, they can be twisted into self-destruction. Ratzinger understands the original temptation, which in various ways continues to confront all humanity, as a temptation to deny our limitations, which amounts to a denial of our creatureliness. Thus the story of the fall serves as a powerful object lesson that sin distorts our freedom and pulls us away from God and from our own good: "Sin is, in its essence, a renunciation of the truth."[39] In Ratzinger's understanding of humanity's fallen state, we might even be forgiven for hearing echoes from another German Augustinian, who wrote of humanity's condition *incurvatus in se*.[40]

Original Sin

When Ratzinger treats the doctrine of original sin, he acknowledges that this time-tested Christian doctrine faces severe headwinds in a culture of individualism and isolation: "According to our way of thinking guilt

---

36. Ratzinger, "In the Beginning," 64–65. Thus Ratzinger appears to take a relatively late date for the final composition of the Pentateuch. This interpretation demonstrates the lengths to which Ratzinger is willing to go in incorporating the insights of biblical criticism, without undercutting the basic thrust of Scripture as a theological book.
37. Ratzinger, "In the Beginning," 66.
38. Ratzinger, "In the Beginning," 66–67.
39. Ratzinger, "In the Beginning," 71.
40. Indeed, to Protestant ears, Ratzinger often sounds very close to affirming a Reformation understanding of the consequences of sin and of the radical need for the doctrines of grace that it introduces. But, of course, the principal disagreements of the Reformation remain, which can be seen especially when Benedict describes his fulsome understanding of saving faith in *Spe Salvi*, §7.

can only be something very personal."[41] But the relational understanding he defends with regard to the *imago Dei* is carried over to the doctrine of sin as well. "It must once again be stressed that no human being is closed in upon himself or herself and that no one can live of or for himself or herself alone. … Human beings are relational, and they possess their lives—themselves—only by way of relationship."[42] Sin is a "rejection of this relationality because it wants to make the human being a god."[43]

But relationality is an indelible component of the created order. So even with sin, no human decision remains in isolation. Adam stands at the origin of humankind, and so his fateful decision to distort his freedom into self-denial is passed on to his posterity. "Sin begets sin … therefore all the sins of history are interlinked."[44] Every human is brought forth into a state of sin due to Adam's first sin. This hamartiological reality has as its obverse a soteriological need: "Human beings alone cannot save themselves. Their innate error is precisely that they want to do this by themselves." Thus Ratzinger follows the entire Western tradition in siding with Augustine against any form of Pelagian self-salvation.[45] Since the problem of sin has severely damaged the matrix of human relationships, the solution to sin cannot arise from within humanity: "Only the Creator himself can be our Savior."[46] The incarnation and passion of Christ function as God's "contrary movement" against the powerful pull of sin.[47] Only the Creator-made-creature can reach into the abyss of our self-inflicted misery and raise us up out of it. "I believe," Ratzinger

---

41. Ratzinger, *"In the Beginning,"* 72.
42. Ratzinger, *"In the Beginning,"* 72.
43. Ratzinger, *"In the Beginning,"* 73.
44. Ratzinger, *"In the Beginning,"* 72.
45. Thomas Rausch sees Ratzinger's anthropology influenced on this point not just by Augustinianism but also by a kind of Platonic idealism undergirding it. "Thus, from an anthropological perspective, Ratzinger typically argues that the human person is oriented not to some interior depth but to the God who comes from without. … Only the Lord can effect our conversion, breaking our resistance to the powers that enslave us and enabling us to believe." Thomas P. Rausch, *Pope Benedict XVI: An Introduction to His Theological Vision* (New York, Paulist, 2009), 45.
46. Ratzinger, *"In the Beginning,"* 74.
47. Ratzinger, *God and the World*, 86.

tells Seewald, "that we should therefore never read the Genesis story without keeping in mind at the same time the story of Christ."[48]

But how exactly is Adam's sin transmitted to his posterity and on what moral basis? In answer to this question, Augustine famously appeals to the notion that all humanity is constituted as a singular whole in the person of Adam. "And what man became, not when he was created, but when he sinned and was punished: this he propagated, so far as the origin of sin and death are concerned."[49] Without necessarily negating this Augustinian understanding, Ratzinger answers the conundrum by appeal to the category of sanctifying grace. The original sin resulted in a loss of grace for all humanity. This lack of grace is not merely some external environmental factor but reaches into human moral constitution as well, and especially into our relatedness to God and our fellow human beings. "It is this disordered relationship, this world of disordered relationships, into which we are born."[50] Hence, humans are born with a need for the restoration of grace, which can only be effected by the Creator himself. Here again anthropology must return to Christology, to the true man, Jesus Christ. Just as humanity's creation must be framed in terms of Christ's person, so too the doctrine of sin. Only the God-man can rescue fallen humanity from their internal and relational disorder.

Humanity in a Fallen World

Perhaps the most telling aspect of Ratzinger's doctrine of sin is the way in which this Augustinian framework is applied to specific contemporary dilemmas. As noted above, Ratzinger seems less optimistic than his immediate predecessor that the church of the late modern world should expect a spiritual renewal on a wide scale. There is continuity between the two popes when it comes to the mission of the church to the world: to guard faithfully the deposit of faith, to commemorate its mysteries, and to present its claims to every human soul and every human society.

48. Ratzinger, God and the World, 86.
49. Augustine, The City of God against the Pagans, ed. R. W. Dyson (Cambridge: Cambridge University Press, 1998), 13.3.
50. Ratzinger, God and the World, 89.

But Ratzinger's prefecture at the Congregation for the Doctrine of the Faith and his papacy were characterized by a somewhat more adversarial posture against the evils and dangers that confront the contemporary church. Again, the church must be prepared to survive a waning period in its cultural influence as a smaller, purer community on the margins.

A consistent theme throughout Ratzinger's long career, perhaps shaped by his early years under the Third Reich, has been his opposition to all totalizing ideologies.[51] During his professorate at Tübingen in the 1960s, Ratzinger witnessed some of the more radical elements of the Marxist movement that was gaining ascendency among both students and professors in many European universities. He saw these trends as a threat to church's theological integrity—the deconstruction of the Christian message and its conversion into a political philosophy. Later as prefect, he became a fierce critic of the various liberation theologies that sought a fusion of Catholic social teaching and Marxism, while at the same time showing appreciation for what these theologies get right, namely, the church's call to love. In his voluminous writings (including his papal encyclicals), Ratzinger is often engaged in a kind of a prophetic confrontation with the dangers of late modernity: philosophical and ethical relativism, the dehumanizing potential of technology, the casualties of the sexual revolution, and the empty promises of political utopianism.[52]

But we should not cast Ratzinger's theological posture toward the modern world in purely negative terms. With John Paul II, Ratzinger sought to forge a conservative (not necessarily traditionalist) interpretation of the Second Vatican Council that avoided the dangers of premodern repristination, on the one hand, and (post)modern innovation on the other. Ratzinger was willing to incorporate some of the claims of evolutionary science into his theology of creation, as we have seen. And while his exegetical method is predominantly concerned with

51. In his appreciative but fairly critical treatment of Ratzinger's theology, Rausch reflects on what role the Nazi years had on Ratzinger's theological development and contrasts how his response differed from another German theologian, Johann Baptist Metz, who opted for a more Marxist approach. Rausch, *Pope Benedict XVI*, 14–15.

52. On these and other themes, see the many incisive essays in *Anthropology and Culture* and *Dogma and Preaching*.

theological interpretation (in dialogue with the fathers especially), he has shown a willingness to incorporate the findings of the critical scholarship of the Bible as well.[53] While he warns against the inherent dangers of technology (especially life-destroying biotechnology and other exploitative uses of technology), he can also praise the pursuit of technology as a worthy expression of the cultural mandate: "Technology, in this sense, is a response to God's command to till and to keep the land (cf. Gen 2:15)."[54] In his final papal encyclical, and the one most devoted to social doctrine, *Caritas in Veritate*, Benedict posits a framework for economic development that accounts for humanity's fallen condition and that avoids any pretense to utopia. But his framework is also seriously engaged with the various proposals on offer today, incorporating both markets and social welfare, both subsidiarity and solidarity, both local and global solutions. Benedict's economic philosophy can hardly be confused with Marxism, but neither can it be confused with a purely reactionary, status quo capitalism. His proposals seek a more comprehensive and multifaceted approach, one sensitive to humanity's capacity for evil and exploitation but also open to humanity's potential and possibility for genuine development.

Still Benedict is incredulous about human attempts to bring about the kingdom of God on earth through their own efforts. Marx's error lay precisely in his loss of the doctrine of sin: "He forgot that man always remains man. He forgot man and he forgot man's freedom. He forgot that freedom always remains also freedom for evil."[55] Materialism—whether Marxist or capitalist—cannot provide a lasting ground for human hope.

---

53. For more on Ratzinger's theological and exegetical method, see Benedict XVI, *Jesus of Nazareth*, vol. 1, *From the Baptism in the Jordan to the Transfiguration*, trans. Adrian J. Walker (San Francisco: Ignatius, 2008), xv–xxiv; Joseph Ratzinger, "Biblical Interpretation in Crisis: On the Question of the Foundations and Approaches of Exegesis Today," in *Biblical Interpretation in Crisis: The Ratzinger Conference on Bible and Church*, ed. Richard John Neuhaus (Grand Rapids: Eerdmans, 1989), 1–23. See also Ignacio Carbajosa, *Faith, the Fount of Exegesis: The Interpretation of Scripture in the Light of the History of Research on the Old Testament*, trans. Paul Stevenson (San Francisco: Ignatius, 2011). Carbajosa is self-consciously building on Benedict's call to engage interpretation on "both methodological levels, the historical-critical and the theological."

54. Benedict XVI, *Caritas in Veritate*, Encyclical Letter, June 29, 2009, §69, https://w2.vatican.va/content/benedict-xvi/en/encyclicals/documents/hf_ben-xvi_enc_20090629_caritas-in-veritate.html.

55. Benedict XVI, *Spe Salvi*, §21.

Only God can bring about the kingdom: "Certainly we cannot 'build' the Kingdom of God by our own efforts—what we build will always be the kingdom of man with all the limitations proper to our human nature. The Kingdom of God is a gift, and precisely because of this, it is great and beautiful, and constitutes the response to our hope."[56] This Augustinian perspective on the limits of our efforts should shape our expectations but never cause us to flag in our commitments: "We can try to limit suffering, to fight against it, but we cannot eliminate it."[57] Again, only the work of God can bring about the kingdom. This is why Benedict is so eager to give pride of place to the incarnate God in his understanding of humanity's destiny. Hope—true hope—can only be secured if we have certainty of the divine love even in and beyond death.[58]

Ratzinger's early response to the student movements of the 1960s can be seen as a summary of his mature thought on this point as well: Marxism had taken "biblical hope as its basis but inverted it by keeping the religious ardor but eliminating God and replacing him with the political activity of man."[59] The "youth movement" had enthusiasm for the scholastic mantra *gratia praesupponit naturam* (grace presupposes nature), even if they misunderstood it original context and intent. For his part, Ratzinger prefers a more Bonaventurian (and Augustinian) perspective: *gratia perficit naturam* (grace perfects nature). Grace does indeed presuppose nature as an ontological object; neither sin nor salvation erases our creatureliness. But grace also assumes a "second nature" in humans—one that we have acquired by sin and its self-destructive habits. Hence, humanity retains its inherent dignity, but after the fall it is so distorted that it stands in desperate need of a gracious intervention that is, indeed, *super*natural.[60]

---

56. Benedict XVI, *Spe Salvi*, §35.

57. Benedict XVI, *Spe Salvi*, §37.

58. On the themes of hope and hope beyond death, see Joseph Ratzinger, "Beyond Death" and "On Hope," in Schindler and Healy, *Anthropology and Culture*, 1–16 and 28–41, respectively. See also, of course, *Spe Salvi*.

59. Cited in Rausch, *Pope Benedict XVI*, 7.

60. For Ratzinger's treatment of these themes, see his essay "*Gratia Praesupponit Naturam*: Grace Presupposes Nature," in *Dogma and Preaching*, 143–61.

CONCLUSION

The key to understanding Ratzinger's anthropology is to be found in the true man, the last Adam, Jesus Christ. Humanity's true identity is only disclosed in Jesus, the archetypal human being. God's assumption of humanity in Christ reveals not only the worth and dignity of every human being in the eyes of God but also the gift and calling of redemption that gives humanity its purpose.[61] Only in the ignominy of the cross can we see, not just the divine love, but also the worth of the human and the glory of our destiny. Further, humanity's plight can only be solved by divine action in the person and work of Jesus. Original sin is not merely an official church dogma but also an undeniable datum of human experience. Its presence should temper any hopes for establishing God's reign by dint of moral or social effort, even as it gives us ample motivation to pursue justice as far as it may be accomplished before the final in-breaking of God's kingdom. The true Christian hope lies not in political or social action but in the incarnation, passion, resurrection, and return of the God-man. In the meantime, the church may have to bear witness to this gospel from the margins, Ratzinger warns, but it does so with its final hope secured in the kingdom of Christ.

We close with Ratzinger's treatment of Pilate's pronouncement, *Ecce homo*, since it summarizes well the key themes we have highlighted concerning Ratzinger's Christocentric anthropology and the hope that it offers to fallen and suffering humanity:

> "Ecce homo"—the expression spontaneously takes on a depth of meaning that reaches far beyond this moment in history. In Jesus, it is man himself that is manifested. In him is displayed the suffering of all who are subjected to violence, all of the downtrodden. His suffering mirrors the inhumanity of worldly power, which so ruthlessly crushes the powerless. In him is reflected

---

61. Indeed, each individual is created and loved by God precisely as an individual. See Ratzinger's evocative discussion of Ps 119:73 ("Your hands have made and fashioned me") in Benedict XVI, *A School of Prayer: The Saints Show Us How to Pray*, trans. L'Osservatore Romano (San Francisco: Ignatius, 2016), 213–14.

what we call "sin": this is what happens when man turns his back upon God and takes control over the world into our own hands.

There is another side to all this, though: Jesus' innermost dignity cannot be taken away from him. The hidden God remains present within him. Even the man subjected to violence and vilification remains the image of God. Ever since Jesus submitted to violence, it has been the wounded, the victims of violence, who have been the image of the God who chose to suffer for us. So Jesus in the throes of his Passion is an image of hope: God is on the side of those who suffer.[62]

---

62. Benedict XVI, *Jesus of Nazareth*, vol. 2, *Holy Week: From the Entrance into Jerusalem to the Resurrection*, trans. Philip J. Whitmore (San Francisco: Ignatius, 2011), 199–200.

6

Learning Jesus' Prayer

Joseph Ratzinger on Christology

CHRISTOPHER R. J. HOLMES

We have much to learn from Benedict XVI's christological vision. Most important, I think, is its "spiritual" character. In the bulk of this chapter I unfold this. I also consider what non-Catholics (such as myself) have to learn from Benedict, but also what Benedict could learn from Reformed Protestants such as myself. In so doing, I take up Benedict's Gospels trilogy, *Jesus of Nazareth*, and his remarkable text *Behold the Pierced One*.

PRAYER AND CHRISTOLOGICAL INQUIRY

What does Benedict mean by a "spiritual Christology"? "Spiritual Christology" has two dimensions. First, it concerns Jesus himself; second, those who do Christology. Regarding the first dimension, Benedict writes that "according to Luke, we see who Jesus is if we see him at prayer." Or, as Herbert McCabe puts it, Jesus "is sheer prayer."[1] Indeed, "the entire person of Jesus is contained in his prayer."[2] Prayer is the key to Christ. Why? In prayer Jesus expresses his filial relationship to the Father: "His whole being is at home in this relationship."[3] In prayer, Jesus beholds the Father. His prayer, anchoring at it does his words and deeds, shows us who he is, the Father's only beloved. Jesus' prayer is Christology's home.

Jesus' whole being is prayer. He is prayer. His prayer expresses the basic creedal truth that he is "of one substance with the Father." Prayer is the most

---

1. Herbert McCabe, OP, *God Matters* (Springfield, IL: Templegate, 1991), 220.
2. Joseph Ratzinger, *Behold the Pierced One: An Approach to Spiritual Christology,* trans. Graham Harrison (San Francisco: Ignatius, 1986), 19–20.
3. Ratzinger, *Pierced One*, 21.

direct way into understanding his person, meaning that his prayer reiterates his origin, his being from the Father in the Holy Spirit. Jesus prays as he does because he is from God, and Jesus gives the Spirit "without measure" because of his heavenly origin (John 3:34). Jesus' prayer is the entry point into the metaphysics of his person and of the divine life in general.

In taking Jesus' prayer seriously, Benedict takes Scripture seriously. Benedict's Christology is deeply scriptural. Scripture is the prime source for him. Scripture generates theological claims regarding Christ. It would thus not be too far off the mark to describe Benedict as a kind of *sola Scriptura* Catholic, meaning that for Benedict Scripture is generative in an immediate and normative sense. To be sure, Benedict takes tradition seriously, and it is a mediate source for christological reflection. Only Scripture, however, is an immediate source.[4] Scripture is the voice of the living Lord.

Benedict argues that one receives Jesus inasmuch as one prays. Christological inquiry is the fruit of prayer. In other words, Jesus yields his meaning *for us* insofar as we pray. This is something we must pause to think deeply about. What A. N. Williams calls the "personal dimension" is immensely important for Benedict.[5] Christology is self-involving, a matter of the mortification and vivification of our minds.

Christological knowledge is spiritual knowledge—"the Lord is the Spirit" (2 Cor 3:17). Knowing Jesus Christ is directly related to what sorts of persons we are. The more spiritual we are, the more we may be said to know him. If we are not the right sorts of persons, or on our way to becoming right sorts of persons, then we will be unable to know him, let alone love him. Knowledge of Jesus Christ "insists upon the relevance of the state of the knower: as the knower goes, so goes the knower's knowing."[6]

---

4. In making this point, I am indebted to A. N. Williams's treatment of Scripture's generative character. See *The Architecture of Theology: Structure, System, and Ratio* (Oxford: Oxford University Press, 2011), 7.

5. Williams, *Architecture*, 29.

6. Williams, *Architecture*, 28.

We must be his disciples, follow after him, if we are to know him. His origin, his being from the Father, is inaccessible without "the personal dimension."[7] Benedict cannot conceive of christological inquiry devoid of sanctifying faith. Inquiry is itself a fruit of faith and prayer, of the heart and mind being made whole. Put differently, our hearts must be in the right place. Part of what makes Benedict's efforts so edifying is the extent to which he encourages the reader to "seek the things that are above, where Christ is" (Col 3:1). Unless we love him, we cannot know him, and knowing is born in faith, hope, and love.

Though Benedict does not bring out the ecclesial character of such knowing in any great depth, at least as far as his trilogy is concerned, it is nonetheless assumed. We learn to pray in church, in the community that calls out "our Father." This is a community gathered around and by the preached word and sacrament. Accordingly, Christology is not best suited to academia, where often—though not always—methodological naturalism prevails. Christological inquiry's home is where people are learning to pray, where they are encouraged to pray, "Lord Jesus Christ, Son of the living God, have mercy upon me, a sinner." Modern academic culture, in its pursuit of objectivity, has often discouraged, implicitly and explicitly, such calling. Indeed, calling out to Christ is not superfluous to Christology but is its basic principle of intelligibility. We must believe in him and need him if we are to see him—with the eyes of the heart—as he is.

It is to this dimension of Christology that I wish Karl Barth would have given greater scrutiny. Perhaps because of his fear of subjectivism, Barth does not always encourage talk of the "personal dimension." Though I cannot pursue this point in any extended fashion, Benedict (unlike Barth) argues that consideration of this dimension is intrinsic to theological knowledge. Theological knowledge does not simply rely on prayer; stronger than that, it is born of prayer. Accordingly, theology is not simply meditation through thought; stronger than that, it is meditation through prayer, which is the highest manner of beholding available to us in this life. The object of knowledge—the living Lord

7. Williams, *Architecture*, 29.

Jesus Christ himself—is known in prayer. Not the university classroom so much as the kneeler in the church is Christology's home. There is, to be sure, a place for the university classroom, but it is subservient to the church, epistemologically speaking, as the place where people learn to call on Jesus' Father as "our Father." The kind of "neutrality" that the classroom—at least in ostensibly pluralistic and secular settings assumes—is indifferent to the spiritual condition of the knower. Is the knower praying? Does she read Scripture in a community nourished by word and sacrament? Is the knower growing in faith, hope, and love? The classroom in a naturalistic setting does not require such questions, intrinsic though they are to christological inquiry.

CHRISTOLOGICAL PILGRIMAGE

Benedict's Christology thus assumes an ascetical shape, a pilgrimage whose form is prayer. Jesus' being one with the Father and Spirit—the very significance of this—is yielded in prayer. We have access in one Spirit to the Father of lights, whose light we see in his Son, our Lord. Christology cannot be reduced to prayer, for Benedict, but its *significance* is found in prayer. The telos of Christology is to join with Jesus in his prayer, that we may in him fulfill the greatest commandment—"You shall love the Lord your God" and "your neighbor as yourself" (Matt 22:37, 39). We may love the Lord our God with all that we are when we allow his Son to love his Father through us. Because Jesus Christ is God, he unites us in the Spirit to our God and Father, enabling us to obey the greatest commandment. And so we love and trust the gospel.

Consideration of prayer's relationship to Christology is foundational to Christology itself. One enters into the truth that is Jesus Christ by praying, indeed by praise and confession as the most basic modes of knowing Christ. The conciliar formulations that we cherish from the fourth century unfold the first principles of his person. They are not misguided attempts to comprehend what is incomprehensible; rather, they gesture toward what enables him to save as he does—his oneness with the Father (and Son). When conciliar Christology is understood as an attempt to apprehend, we see how compatible it is with prayer.

Prayer, too, is a mode of apprehending—not comprehending—what we love. Benedict recognizes the epistemological import of prayer. We pray so that we might apprehend, and having apprehended we pray, for we recognize that there is nothing better than to seek his face.

Christology, on Benedict's terms, which I wholly endorse, is a relational undertaking. We cannot discuss Jesus Christ without discussing what we say he is—the Savior of the world. Our relationship to him—who we say he is—is not separable from our description of his person. This distinguishes christological doctrine from the doctrine that stands upstream of it, namely, the doctrine of God. The doctrine of God—the what and who of God—demands, for example, that we mention God's aseity, that it is possible to speak of God as one independent of all that is not God. God has life in and of himself without reference to other things. Whereas with Christology, the relational import is far more immediate: Jesus is the Savior of the world. Jesus Christ—the Son of God—does a new thing in time that agrees with who he has always been: he saves sinners. Accordingly, we cannot describe Jesus Christ as anything less than the world's Savior, our Savior. This is not to negate the Son's aseity, for the life he is and has is common to the Father and the Spirit, independent of us, world without end. Rather, the point is simply that Christology has this relational dimension—from the start as it were.

What also renders Benedict's efforts most edifying is his desire to address us as he unfolds the mystery of Christ. We are confronted in his christological writings as those who need to pray. We need to pray in order to do Christology. If we are to speak of him as he is, we must speak of ourselves as those who are saved, being saved, and as those who will be saved by his life, death, resurrection, ascension, and session. A way of life—a life of love, the love to which Peter (and we in him) are called in John 21:1–19—grounds a basic set of beliefs regarding the metaphysics of his person. Prayer establishes sets of truths regarding his person and work. Though Benedict does not tell us how prayer underwrites Christology, he is insistent that it must. Again, though Benedict does not deploy a doctrine like that of sanctification with respect to the development of christological confessional statements, it is assumed. Benedict assumes that liturgy is, following Williams's astute words, "relevant to doctrinal development."[8] The church catholic believes as it does because it has prayed as it has. Benedict understands doctrinal development—culminating with the conciliar formulations—to be complementary to liturgical practice.

For Benedict, spiritual Christology has as its correlate a spiritual people. We must pray in order to do Christology well. Jesus, who is "sheer prayer," may only be apprehended in prayer. Without prayer, we cannot progress in theological understanding. Prayer evokes an "eye of love" and encourages the "faculty of beholding."[9] Without love, we can neither behold Jesus Christ nor receive him. "Christology," Benedict writes, "is born of prayer or not at all."[10]

JESUS' PRAYER

We must step back for a moment and reflect on the significance of what Benedict is arguing. First, most significant to Jesus' identity is neither his words nor his deeds but his prayer, which encapsulates both. His words and deeds proceed from his filial relationship with his Father, our Father, as expressed in prayer. Second, christological inquiry may never be detached from confession. The church's confession of Jesus only yields "its meaning within prayer."[11] Without prayer on our part, we miss "the source of his preaching and action," which is his prayer.[12] Divorced from prayer, christological inquiry seeks after knowledge, but when undergirded by prayer, it seeks knowledge's highest form, beholding. Benedict would have us behold Jesus Christ. Benedict's Christology points, as Jesus does, toward "purity of heart ... what enables us to see."[13]

What Benedict has, I think, made clear is that knowledge of Jesus Christ is prayerful knowledge; knowledge of him comes through prayer. Scripture's patterning of Jesus Christ, his person and work, is intelligible

8. Williams, *Architecture*, 85.
9. Ratzinger, *Pierced One*, 27.
10. Ratzinger, *Pierced One*, 46.
11. Ratzinger, *Pierced One*, 19.
12. Benedict XVI, *Jesus of Nazareth: From the Baptism in the Jordan to the Transfiguration*, trans. Adrian J. Walker (New York: Doubleday, 2007), 182.
13. Benedict XVI, *From the Baptism in the Jordan to the Transfiguration*, 325.

in and via prayer. This is Christology's task: to bring us before the face of Jesus Christ, and we are brought before that face insofar as we pray. Our prayer is the source of our knowledge, just as "Jesus' prayer [is] as the source of his action."[14] Or, as Williams says of theology in general, "To articulate theology is at least potentially, or in some instances, to pray."[15] Prayer is the source of all that Jesus does, and it is where christological understanding is also nourished. As Benedict says, Jesus' "very nature contains direction and norm," and the direction he supplies is found in prayer. When we pray, we become "inwardly one with this direction."[16] Benedict's brilliance is to remind us of what catholic Christianity has always reminded us of, namely, that our understanding of who Jesus Christ "is cannot be separated from our understanding of how we go about understanding" Jesus Christ.[17]

Benedict teaches us that understanding is, ultimately, found in "the way of the Cross."[18] The cross, as a seat of prayer and understanding, is where Scripture locates us. We read "with the suffering Christ, and so it must ever be."[19] Indeed, prayer's locus is the cross. "The messianic age is first and foremost the age of the Cross."[20] Just as the cross interprets what kind of Messiah he is, so too does the cross contextualize our prayer for understanding. When we pray, we open ourselves up to a kenotic way of knowing. This is a way in which all of our preconceived ideas fall away. It is about proceeding with open hands. This is, to be frank, a gesture toward martyrdom. "Martyrdom," says Benedict, "can be overcome only in prayer."[21] The prayer that overcomes martyrdom is again one of open hands, to die with hands outstretched that we might be received with Christ into his kingdom.

---

14. Benedict XVI, *From the Baptism in the Jordan to the Transfiguration*, 182.
15. Williams, *Architecture*, 159.
16. Benedict XVI, *From the Baptism in the Jordan to the Transfiguration*, 204.
17. Williams, *Architecture*, 135. Though Williams says this of "God," the same is true of Jesus Christ.
18. Benedict XVI, *From the Baptism in the Jordan to the Transfiguration*, 299.
19. Benedict XVI, *From the Baptism in the Jordan to the Transfiguration*, 313.
20. Benedict XVI, *From the Baptism in the Jordan to the Transfiguration*, 315.
21. Benedict XVI, *From the Baptism in the Jordan to the Transfiguration*, 154.

Another way to put this is that Christology is, for Benedict, profoundly participatory, indeed, and as I have implied, ascetical. We learn of Jesus Christ by praying, via the mortification and vivification of the flesh. When we join with "the women who are constantly opening the door to the Lord and accompanying him to the Cross," we experience with them "the Risen One."[22] This one transforms our sight so that we may see him as he is and so experience "a decisive re-orientation toward a new manner of human existence."[23] It is within the realm of piety that the developed metaphysical (fourth-century) form of the person of Christ is known. Yes, we believe, and in believing, trusting, and receiving him as he is, we know him who is "for us and our salvation," and accept that he is *homoousios* with the Father.

When the heart of Christology is Jesus' prayer, and when we undertake that christological study in prayer, we read Scripture differently. Accordingly, we do not look behind the gospel narratives to find the "historical" Jesus. Instead, we read as those "guided by the hermeneutic of faith."[24] A "hermeneutic of faith" is, not surprisingly, christological through and through. Such a hermeneutic recognizes Jesus as the center of Scripture, and "learns from him how to understand the Bible as a unity."[25] The upshot of this is, for Benedict, a distinct lack of suspicion: "I trust the Gospels."[26]

Significantly, prayerful reception of the Gospels does not make him indifferent to history. The history that the Gospels record "took place here on this earth."[27] But they are not of this earth, and cannot therefore be understood in an earthly way, that is, without prayer. The historical Jesus, the Jesus of the Synoptics and John, is one and the same, and he is, as has been said, pure prayer. He is his prayer, though that does not mean Benedict dispenses with the historical-critical

---

22. Benedict XVI, *Jesus of Nazareth*, vol. 2, *Holy Week: From the Entrance into Jerusalem to the Resurrection*, trans. Philip J. Whitmore (San Francisco: Ignatius, 2011), 263.
23. Benedict XVI, *Jesus of Nazareth*, vol. 3, *The Infancy Narratives*, trans. Philip J. Whitmore (New York: Image, 2012), 11.
24. Benedict XVI, *Holy Week*, xvii.
25. Benedict XVI, *From the Baptism in the Jordan to the Transfiguration*, xix.
26. Benedict XVI, *From the Baptism in the Jordan to the Transfiguration*, xxi.
27. Benedict XVI, *From the Baptism in the Jordan to the Transfiguration*, xv.

method in discerning the character of Jesus' prayer. Benedict writes, "The historico-critical method and other modern scientific methods are important for an understanding of Holy Scripture and tradition. Their value, however, depends on the hermeneutical (philosophical) context in which they are applied."[28] The historical-critical method must be applied in faith and in a prayerful spirit.

The relationship between the historical-critical method and faith is similar to the relationship between reason and faith. Of the latter, Benedict notes, "Without reason, faith would not be truly human; without faith, reason has neither a path nor a guiding light."[29] The hermeneutic of faith, of prayerful trust, does not dispense with historical-critical insights. The latter reminds us of the humanity of these narratives. However, we do not receive these human testimonies without faith. Faith receives them in prayer following Jesus' prayer. Indeed, Christian faith discerns in prayer "those aspects of the historical-critical method that are of continuing value."[30] Principally, this boils down to "what the respective authors intended to convey through their text in their own day."[31] This is where the historical task begins and ends. The historical task ends there because it is utterly ill-equipped to ask "the second question posed by good exegesis ... : is what I read here true? Does it concern me?"[32]

Just so, Benedict decisively reorients the historical task. The historical task simply prepares me (the reader) to seek the truth of what is written. It is a tool in discerning the truth. Historical criticism thus has very real limits. It is not ecumenical dogma's enemy, but it is clearly subservient to it. Accordingly, the Gospel narratives encourage ecumenical dogma. The narratives describe one whose "presence is not spatial, but divine."[33] Dogma describes, with the help of Greek metaphysical idioms, his presence as divine. He is divine because he is one with the Father,

---

28. Ratzinger, *Pierced One*, 42.
29. Ratzinger, *Pierced One*, 43.
30. Benedict XVI, *Holy Week*, xiv.
31. Benedict XVI, *Infancy Narratives*, xi.
32. Benedict XVI, *Infancy Narratives*, xi.
33. Benedict XVI, *Holy Week*, 283.

homoousios. In arguing so, Benedict presents a most helpful account of the relationship between dogma and the narratives. The narratives, in particular, their articulation of Jesus' origin, illuminate, Benedict avers, "what came later, and conversely the developed form of christological faith helped to make sense of that origin. Thus did Christology develop."[34] Jesus' divine origin interprets what came later, and what came later in terms of the tradition helps us to appreciate what is in Scripture. Importantly, Benedict's account of the relationship between the narratives and dogma emphasizes the dogmatic character of the narratives themselves. The narratives do not resist what came later as if that were some kind of imposition. Instead, his origin, again, illuminates conciliar formulations, even as those formulations clarify what came before. Conciliar Christology is a fruit of Jesus' divine presence.

At this point, we gain insight into the Catholic shape of Benedict's vision. Benedict draws on the tradition (Greek and Latin) in a generous way, simply because that tradition, guided as it is by the Spirit, helps us see the "decisive reorientation" that Jesus has achieved.[35] Tradition does not better the Scriptures; it is not an improvement on them. The Scriptures are exemplary for all time. Tradition does not seek to define what cannot be defined but rather simply points us to what is there in the Scriptures.

A REMARKABLE VISION

What have we (non-Catholics) to learn from this remarkable vision from the outstanding servant of the gospel? Much. Perhaps counterintuitively, Benedict helps us to "learn how to listen to the voice of creation."[36] Creation is not mute. Creation speaks. It speaks not of itself but of God, and in speaking of God, it speaks of Christ. "Creation, interpreted by the Scriptures, speaks to humanity again."[37] Benedict's consideration of creation's voice as complementary to Christ is crucial to his vision. The reason that the Scriptures speak as they do and that creation speaks as

---

34. Benedict XVI, *Infancy Narratives,* 54.
35. Benedict XVI, *Infancy Narratives,* 11.
36. Ratzinger, *Pierced One,* 114.
37. Benedict XVI, *Infancy Narratives,* 106.

it does is because of God. God is a loquacious God. Though creation needs Scripture if its voice is to be heard properly, it, like Scripture itself, has a voice, and its voice is compatible with God's.

Many "modern" Christians think that creation, to say nothing of Scripture, is mute. They somehow need to be made to speak. Benedict's account is a powerful endorsement of the created order as having a voice, declaring as it were God's goodness and power. God's voice does not dispense with, say, Matthew's voice. The Lord does not compete with "the trees of the field" as they "clap their hands" (Isa 55:12). Instead, Matthew's recollection of "real history, theologically thought through and interpreted, helps us to understand the mystery of Jesus more clearly."[38]

The appeal, in part, of Benedict's spiritual Christology is that it does not force you to choose between Matthew's recollection and God, between creation's voice and Christ. Matthew and creation—in particular, created things like eucharistic bread and wine—speak as they do because God delights in "transubstantiating all earthly reality."[39] That Matthew's recollection is the word of the Lord is parallel to a deep christological truth. Discussing "the ontological *union* of two faculties of will," Benedict notes that they "remain independent within the unity of the Person." If such is the case, we have a useful insight for understanding how what is human and what is divine are not collapsed. Instead, the union of the Gospel narratives with the voice of the Lord himself is not a threat to their independence but shows "at the existential level, there is a communion (*koinonia*) of the two wills."[40] There exists a communion between Matthew's recollection and the one recollected, the voice of Christ and the voice of creation, all of which heralds God's transubstantiation of "all earthly reality."[41]

The promise of Benedict's Christology aligns in some respects with another great leader of the church catholic, Karl Barth. Section 69 of Barth's *Church Dogmatics* IV.3.I describes eloquently the radiance of the

---

38. Ratzinger, *Pierced One,* 119.
39. Ratzinger, *Pierced One,* 89.
40. Ratzinger, *Pierced One,* 92.
41. Ratzinger, *Pierced One,* 86.

resurrected and ascended Christ whose voice is luminous and clear, and is to be found in the Scriptures. Benedict, like Barth, recognizes "that Jesus himself is the living Torah, the complete Word of God."[42] It is the Son who speaks here, who draws the Gospel writers' voices to himself. He subsumes them into himself, transforming them in such a way that their voice is his.

CONCLUSION

Having said something about what non-Catholics may take from Benedict, what might Benedict take from a Prayer Book Anglican such as myself? Not surprisingly, I am wary of Benedict's elevation of the Eucharist above the preached word. Benedict has much to say about the Eucharist as "necessary for salvation. The necessity of the Eucharist is identical with the necessity of the Church and vice versa."[43] That confidence seems to me to be somewhat misplaced. The Eucharist is where we are sealed in the gospel promises proclaimed on the basis of Scripture. Eucharist does not hang in the air, but is downstream of the proclamation of the word. The Eucharist is necessary, but its necessity derives from the word. Not simply the Eucharist alone but also the preached word are "the foundation, day by day, of both community and vocation."[44]

The other point that I would like to raise is in regard to idolatry. Benedict has many helpful things to say about how "the Son creates communion between God and man and thus also makes possible a new communion among human beings." Yes, the Lord Jesus does make enemies into friends, establishing thereby "a new communion among human beings."[45] What I think also needs to be said is that Jesus' power to establish a new community is very often revealed over and against us who continue (even within the church) to prefer gods of our own making. The community is very often hostile to its Lord, its members

---

42. Benedict XVI, *From the Baptism in the Jordan to the Transfiguration*, 317.
43. Ratzinger, *Pierced One*, 93.
44. Ratzinger, *Pierced One*, 100.
45. Ratzinger, *Pierced One*, 93.

unwilling and unable "to be heaven to each other."[46] Ecclesiology should be "Israel-like." Benedict's spiritual Christology sponsors an ecclesiology that is in my view a bit too confident. Christ does not so much call us "to discover him in others and thus to be heaven to each other" as to bear witness to him as heaven come to earth, and to call others to be his witnesses too.[47]

That said, and to conclude, there is much here that is of profound worth and value. I am deeply taken by Benedict's spiritual awareness. He understands that unfolding the person and work of Christ requires us to become different sorts of persons. We are required to become those who pray, who seek him, who receive him as their Savior. Prayer is the key to entering, epistemologically speaking, into Christology, not only in terms of Scripture but in terms of the conciliar tradition as well. Prayer is the key to remaining christologically minded. The only Jesus we receive in the Scriptures is one who is "making all things new" (Rev 21:5).

---

46. Ratzinger, *Pierced One*, 128.
47. Ratzinger, *Pierced One*, 128.

7

"Behold the Handmaid of the Lord"

Joseph Ratzinger on Mary

TIM PERRY

Having been thinking and writing about the Blessed Virgin Mary from within a Protestant confession since 2004, I am routinely asked *when* I will become a Catholic. My routine answer is this: "There is only one reason, finally, to become Catholic: one is convinced that the Roman Church is what she claims to be; there is only one reason, finally, not to do so: one is not so convinced." While I do believe this is an honest and appropriate answer—it is, after all, a simple theological comment on the equally true but less satisfying "I don't know; not yet, anyway"—it seldom satisfies my questioners. Often, they follow with this: But what about Mary?

Far more than debates about the nature of the magisterium or the papacy, about sacraments or justification, it seems that Mary is the focal point of my questioners' concerns. This is hardly surprising; for while Mary did not figure a great deal in the first generation of the Reformation, or even the second, by the third, she had taken center stage. By then many Protestants had come to see in her the embodiment of all that was perceived to be at stake in the Reformation: a soteriology that combined faith and works; a view of revelation that held Scripture and tradition to be of equal value; and a piety that set up another Redeemer alongside Jesus.

Without dismissing any of the legitimate theological worries expressed above, I want to move in a different direction: instead of a polemical reading, I wish to consider "But what about Mary?" as asking whether there is anything in Marian thought from which contemporary committed Protestants can learn, and further, just what is at stake in seeking an answer. The purpose will be not so much to attack Catholicism or defend Reformation worries as it will be to see whether a close reading of Catholic texts can lead Protestants into a deeper and richer understanding not only of shared concerns but also of our own heritage.

Like the other essayists in this volume, my conversation partner is the Pope Emeritus, Benedict XVI. Ferreting out answers proceeds in three steps. In the first, I consider the context that decisively shaped Benedict's Marian reflections: the Second Vatican Council's document on the Blessed Virgin[1] and Pope Paul VI's instructions regarding its implementation (*Marialis Cultus*).[2] I then move to Benedict's own work; organized around his slim, early volume, *Daughter Zion*,[3] this section shall attempt a fairly full picture, directing readers to other writings in the notes. And finally, I will offer some tentative conclusions. In short, I will argue that, yes, Protestants do have much to learn from Catholic Marian belief and that the stakes are high, especially at this point in our common journey toward the Father's house.

THE CONTEXT

The document that became *Lumen Gentium* chapter 8 was born in controversy. In the run-up to the Second Vatican Council, Marian maximalist bishops hoped to see a document that would build on the previous century's flowering of Marian devotion, and perhaps even enshrine a new title—Mediatrix of all Graces—or a new definition—co-redemptrix. On the other, Marian minimalists wanted to see Marian doctrine and devotion more closely tied to holy Scripture and to the fathers and Marian piety more closely attuned to the Eucharist as the source and summit of the church's life. Thus, the first question the bishops

1. *Lumen Gentium*, Dogmatic Constitution on the Church, Vatican II, November 21, 1964, §8, "The Blessed Virgin Mary, Mother of God, In the Mystery of Christ and the Church," http://www.vatican.va/archive/hist_councils/ii_vatican_council/documents/vat-ii_const_19641121_lumen-gentium_en.html. Cited hereafter as *LG* and paragraph number.
2. Paul VI, *Marialis Cultus*, Apostolic Exhortation, February 2, 1974, http://w2.vatican.va/content/paul-vi/en/apost_exhortations/documents/hf_p-vi_exh_19740202_marialis-cultus.html. Cited hereafter as *MC* and paragraph number.
3. Joseph Ratzinger, *Daughter Zion: Meditations on the Church's Marian Belief*, trans. John M. McDermott, SJ (San Francisco: Ignatius, 1983). I shall cite the author's name as it appears on the text I use.

addressed had not so much to do with content as place: Where would the document on Mary go? Would it be independent (as the maximalists desired), or brought within the document on the church (the position of the minimalists)? In the closest vote of any taken in the council, the bishops decided that Marian reflection belonged within the larger document on the church. The final document, approved unanimously, thus appears as *Lumen Gentium* chapter 8. There is no new Marian title enshrined, no new definition offered, and it is deliberately attentive to biblical and patristic thought.[4]

Indeed, from the outset, the document's humility is clear. Far from intending to be a full accounting of Marian doctrine and devotion, or to break new ground, its aim is simply to describe the role of Mary in the plan of salvation (part 1) and in the life of the people of God (parts 2–4).[5] Mary, insists part 1, is no mere accident of history; her role is both typologically foreshadowed and prophetically announced in the Old Testament.[6] She is daughter Zion, in whom faithful Israel's vocation to bring God's blessing to the world is fulfilled; she is new Eve, who by her obedience undoes the disobedience of the first. Indeed, this is but the biblical working out of God's predestination. Mary is "present" as the mother of the Redeemer in the primordial divine decision to redeem. One of Adam's children, she is also first among the redeemed and redeemed in a singular way: she was preserved from original sin. This exalted status is then unfolded in the narration of the Gospel story: the annunciation and visitation, the virginal conception and birth; the childhood and temple stories; her presence at significant moments in Jesus' ministry up to the cross; and ending with her presence at Pentecost and her assumption into heaven and exaltation as Queen.[7]

Turning from the plan of salvation, the rest of the document unpacks Mary's role among the people of God, beginning with her place in the

---

4. LG §54. A fuller accounting of the debate and its results can be found in Tim Perry and Daniel Kendall, SJ, *The Blessed Virgin Mary* (Grand Rapids: Eerdmans, 2013), 62–65, and Tim Perry, *Mary for Evangelicals* (Downers Grove, IL: IVP Academic, 2006), 245–47.
5. LG §54.
6. LG §55–56.
7. LG §§57–59.

church. Here, the unique position of Mary as a mediator is assumed rather than argued. At issue is not whether Mary mediates but how. The council affirms that her mediation is subordinate to, grounded in, and rendered possible only by the unique mediation of her Son, the one mediator between God and humanity. Biblically it is seen in her cooperation with God in the virginal conception, her perseverance through the earthly ministry of Christ; it continues even now in her maternal care for all Christ's brothers and sisters, who are, in the order of grace, her own children.[8] It is in her role as virgin and mother to the faithful, further, that Mary is to be seen as a type of the church who is herself a virgin and mother, striving for the salvation of all her children and, as even now assumed into heaven, offers a present glimpse of what is as yet the church's future.[9] This eschatological note is repeated in the document's final section.[10]

Part 3 deals with Marian devotion only briefly. It is prophetically announced by Mary herself ("all generations will call me blessed,") and has been officially sanctioned in the term Mother of God since the Council of Ephesus (431). Given that devotion varies greatly due to time and place and creativity, very little regulation is offered here beyond the insistence that Marian devotional practice be governed by "sound doctrine"; that in and through such practices, the Son is known, loved, glorified, and obeyed; and that such devotions do not scandalize separated brothers and sisters, but invite a greater imitation of Marian virtues among the faithful.

In part because of part 3's brevity, Paul VI issued an Apostolic Exhortation in February of 1974, to spell out more concretely how Marian devotional reform and renewal ought to take place. Known as *Marialis Cultus*, the document falls into three parts. The first lays a framework for reforms by reviewing the Marian feasts of the liturgical year.[11] The guidelines themselves are found in part 2.[12] Generally,

---

8. LG §§60–61.
9. LG §§62–65.
10. LG §§68–69.
11. MC §§1–23.
12. MC §§24–39.

renewed and reformed Marian devotion is to be subordinate to the worship due the Blessed Trinity alone;[13] it is to especially accentuate the work of the Holy Spirit in the accomplishment of salvation;[14] and it is to remind the faithful of Mary's preeminent place *within* the church.[15] Specifically, it will carry biblical content in biblical language.[16] Far from being an alternative to corporate worship, Marian devotion will flow from and lead back to the Eucharist.[17] Finally, it will strive to keep ecumenical concerns in view and recognize its own cultural and psychosocial limitations.[18] Part 3, finally applies these guidelines specifically to the Angelus and the Rosary. Both Marian devotions are affirmed for the ways in which they invite the faithful to contemplate the mysteries of the incarnation and the events of the gospel. The Angelus, however, is to be distinguished from cultural accretions that are not part of its essential core; while the Rosary is to be propagated in a way that is natural, neither too "one-sided" nor "exclusive."[19]

Benedict XVI was the last pope to have attended the Second Vatican Council, and along with his predecessor, Pope St. John Paul II, was instrumental in interpreting and implementing its conclusions across the church for thirty years. These documents provide four interpretive keys with which to unlock Benedict's own Marian reflections.

First, the documents are, well, *Catholic*. This might seem obvious, but it is worth pointing out since, for some at least, Vatican II represents a jettisoning of much that had been taken as settled Catholic tradition. However true this estimation is, one will not find a rejection of the Marian dogmas in the council fathers or Pope Paul VI. On the contrary, the modern dogmas of the immaculate conception and assumption, along with the celebration of Mary's heavenly coronation, are blended almost seamlessly into the scriptural record. Whether or not one agrees with this position, there is something noteworthy at work

---

13. MC §§25.
14. MC §§26–27.
15. MC §§28.
16. MC §§29–30.
17. MC §§31–32.
18. MC §§33–37.
19. MC §§40–55.

here. The dogmas are reexpressed quite forcefully not as authorized by the magisterial authority of Popes Pius IX and XII (though this is certainly not denied!) as much as on the witness of the Scriptures and the fathers on whom those popes relied in making their respective declarations. Papal infallibility seems to be understood not as an infallibility of invention but rather as one of preservation in development. Doctrinal development may well say more, but it will never say other than what has already been said.[20]

Second, the council fathers and Pope Paul VI clearly recognize that certain Marian devotional expressions needed to be curtailed. The Marian century—beginning in 1854 with the promulgation of the immaculate conception and reaching its zenith in 1950 with the promulgation of her assumption—sometimes placed Marian devotion on a parallel track, unconnected to the eucharistic celebration of the people of God. This, in turn, all too often had the unhappy effect of placing Mary outside and above the church. While the modern dogmas ought not, will not, and cannot be weakened, the devotions that flow therefrom had to be channeled back into the banks provided by the Eucharist and the worship of the Blessed Trinity. If such correctives lessen the offense that some Marian excesses provoke among other Christians and help Catholics come to see the inevitable cultural and psychosocial limitations of Marian practices (as, indeed, all pious practices), so much the better.

Third, Marian doctrine and devotion are rightly cast in and bear the content of biblical language. Subsuming Marian devotion under the guidance of Scripture and church will be the key task for post–Vatican II Marian reflection. This is not to say that the Scriptures will be twisted so as to "find" prooftexts for the modern dogmas therein, but rather that the Bible and the Eucharist will ground and guide subsequent reflection thereon. It will be the task of subsequent theologians to show that when the whole of Scripture is read—including especially typological and prophetic readings of the Old Testament and not merely the opening

---

20. This reading of doctrinal development places the council more in line with John Henry Newman (1801–1890) than with G. W. F Hegel (1770–1831).

chapters of Matthew, Luke, and Acts—the modern dogmas can in fact be found latent and waiting for a full unfolding in the mind of the church.

Finally, noteworthy in these documents is the maternal link between Christology, ecclesiology, and eschatology. Mary, as she is found in the Scriptures and beyond, discloses the inner essence of the church. The church's own self understanding is typified and illumined by Mary's role as Virgin and Mother. There is a biblical intuition here that, however unfamiliar it may be to modern Protestants, needs to be heard. Mary as a symbolic portrayal of the people of God is certainly found in the Gospel of John, may well be present in Luke, and is overwhelming in Revelation 12. As such, Mary is a sign of eschatological hope that, whatever struggles the people of God face at present, their future is assured.

Going forward, then, we will watch for *fidelity* to received Marian belief, *modesty* in contemporary reflection, *bibliocentricity* of its articulation, and the primacy of Mary's *maternity* throughout.

THE CONTENT

Daughter Zion is a primer on Marian belief offered to Christians after a period of Marian devotional decline following the Second Vatican Council.[21] Offered first as a series of lectures and then as a slim book, it intends to address two interrelated questions: What remains of the church's Marian belief? and, What ought not to be lost?[22]

Mary in the Bible

The opening (and most important) chapter sets the biblical question front and center. Following the Second Vatican Council, many Catholics saw Marian reflection divorced from Marian practice, with the Bible playing a central role by its absence. The paucity of Marian material

---

21. This is in no way an indictment of the council! As we shall see, Ratzinger stands quite consciously within its parameters, and those elaborated in *Marialis Cultus*. For Ratzinger's thoughts on the place and purpose of Marian belief in Christian theology and the ongoing importance of Marian piety after Vatican II, see Joseph Ratzinger, "Thoughts on the Place of Marian Doctrine and Piety in Faith and Theology as a Whole," in Hans Urs von Balthasar and Joseph Cardinal Ratzinger, *Mary: The Church at the Source*, trans. Adrian Walker (San Francisco: Ignatius, 2005), 19–36, esp. 19–24.

22. Ratzinger, *Daughter Zion*, 7–8.

in the New Testament simply does not support the traditional Marian edifice; beyond the barest affirmation of the virgin birth, neither does it have purchase in the creeds. The vacuum has been filled by scholarship relishing in the allegedly pagan roots of Mariology—Diana or Artemis, the Great Mother, the pre-Christian use of the term *theotokos* (Mother of God). The result? Some Marian devotions have simply withered for lack of reflection while other doctrinally questionable practices have been allowed to flourish unchecked. Neither silence with respect to the tradition nor "mere tolerance" of unorthodox Marian proliferation will do, Ratzinger says. Both extremes need to be brought within the orbit of *biblical* Marian reflection.[23]

Protestant readers may well be startled to find that Ratzinger then turns to the Old Testament to begin. But his reasoning is clear. If the Marian material in the Gospels and elsewhere is shot through with Old Testament allusion (and it clearly is), then we will read that material rightly provided we are aware of the bases in the first testament on which it stands.[24] He begins with the "Old Testament's deeply anchored theology of woman,"[25] in which God does not have a divine consort, but instead takes as his bride his people. The prophets especially are unrelenting in their opposition to a female consort for God and to the fertility cults to which such theologies give rise. This is not to say, however, that they are misogynistic. On the contrary, the prophetic faith "gives to woman, in its own way, an indispensable place in its own model of belief and life, corresponding to marriage on a human level."[26] Where

---

23. Ratzinger, *Daughter Zion*, 10–11.

24. Ratzinger, *Daughter Zion*, 31–37. This biblical methodology is spelled out further in Ratzinger's introductory essay to Pope St. John Paul's *Redemptoris Mater*, which may be summarized as follows: Scripture is to be read as *one* book. In the midst of its diversity and even conflict, the reader is to listen for the one unifying voice and Scripture is to be read as a testimony for the present. It is not trapped in his historical-cultural location, but is a living document that speaks directly to today. See Joseph Ratzinger, "The Sign of the Woman," in *Mary: God's Yes to Man* (John Paul's Encyclical Redemptoris Mater) (San Francisco: Ignatius, 1987), 10–11.

25. Ratzinger, *Daughter Zion*, 13; Ratzinger, "The Sign of the Woman," 16–18.

26. Ratzinger, *Daughter Zion*, 14–15. This, rather than prooftexting from Mark or Ephesians or Romans, is where Christian theology of marriage ought to begin and where, significantly, reflections on virginity find their root also.

then do the people of God find themselves in the Old Testament's theology of woman?

First of all in Eve, who, created from Adam's rib, is his perfect complement. The sexes both together in their mutuality and each in their individuality are the image and likeness of God. While both sexes fall into sin, the fall and continued dignity of the woman is uniquely hers: she offers the fruit that is linked to death and "is nonetheless from now on the keeper of the seal of life and the antithesis of death."[27] Second, in the great mothers, Sarah, Rachel, and Hannah. Infertile women who are in the end truly blessed. They embody the "reversal of values" that is taken up and proclaimed in the Magnificat, the very same reversal of values that is at the core of the Sermon on the Mount.[28] They also provide in embryo the theology of virginity—earthly infertility becomes true fertility—which will come to full expression in the New Testament. Third, in the women-saviors of the Bible: Esther and Judith (who in turn is modeled after Jael). They embody Israel defeated and exiled and Israel resilient and hopeful. "It is significant that the woman always figures in Israel's thought and belief not as a priestess, but as prophetess and judge-savior."[29]

In the Old Testament, Israel is "interpreted simultaneously as woman, virgin [that is, infertile], beloved, wife and mother." The great women of Israel allow readers to glimpse Israel herself and further, fourth, allow them to read God's covenant with Israel as a marriage covenant in which the woman is a wife and at the same time a virgin awaiting the consummation of the marriage, who is infertile and yet bears children, who is no goddess, but is the creature God has chosen as his own.[30] The climax of the Old Testament's theology of woman, however, comes finally in its fifth element: the people of God are to find themselves in *Sophia*. Wisdom. Ratzinger affirms the christological import of the term, agreeing that the primary referent is to the Logos or Word begotten from eternity who became incarnate as Jesus of Nazareth.

27. Ratzinger, *Daughter Zion*, 17.
28. Ratzinger, *Daughter Zion*, 18–19.
29. Ratzinger, *Daughter Zion*, 20.
30. Ratzinger, *Daughter Zion*, 21–24.

He argues, however, that *Sophia* has a double referent. Emerging from God's creating and electing grace, she is also the creation's affirmative response to God's love.[31]

The theology of woman is, in Ratzinger's view, essential to a biblically informed faith. As Eve, the barren mother, the judge-savior, the covenant spouse, and Wisdom, the woman is essential material for the self-understanding of the people of God. Even as the people's hope is similarly typologically expressed, it bends toward a concrete personal name in the figure of Jesus Christ, so the people themselves, "provisionally personified," are also given a name: Mary.[32] Only a return to the Scriptures will provide traditional Marian doctrine the heft it needs to ground Marian devotion; only such a return will rein in neo-pagan speculation and the severing of Marian devotion from any kind of orthodox mooring; only such a return will prevent the severe adumbration of the faith as a whole.[33]

The Marian Belief of the Church

The remaining three lectures build on this Old Testament foundation, considering the New Testament content of the Marian belief of the church: Mary as virgin mother, her freedom from Adam's sin, and her bodily assumption into heaven.[34] Let us consider each in turn.

---

31. Ratzinger, *Daughter Zion*, 25–27.
32. Ratzinger, *Daughter Zion*, 28.
33. Ratzinger, *Daughter Zion*, 28–29. Here it is worth quoting him at length: "To deny or reject the feminine aspect in belief, or more concretely, the Marian aspect, leads finally to the negation of creation and the invalidation of grace. It leads to a picture of God's omnipotence that reduces the creature to a mere masquerade and that also completely fails to understand the God of the Bible, who is characterized as being the creature and the God of the covenant—the God for whom the beloved's punishment and rejection themselves become the passion of love, the cross."
34. I do not offer comment below on any aspect of Marian piety. Readers interested in the biblical roots of Marian devotion may with to consult Joseph Ratzinger, "'Hail, Full of Grace': Elements of Marian Piety according to the Bible," in Balthasar and Ratzinger, *Mary: The Church at the Source*, 61–79. Ratzinger's own warm Marian piety is glimpsed throughout the talks gathered in Joseph Ratzinger, *Teaching and Learning the Love of God: Being A Priest Today*, trans. Michael J. Miller (San Francisco: Ignatius, 2017), and in Benedict XVI, "The Praying Presence of Mary," in *Prayer* (Huntington, IN: Our Sunday Visitor, 2013), 175–80.

Mary the Virgin Mother

Ratzinger opens with a brief survey of relevant biblical texts concerning Mary's unique motherhood, notably, Galatians 4:4, 21–31, the genealogies and infancy narratives of Matthew and Luke, and an excursus on John 1:13.[35] Our focus, however, is on his theological unpacking of these texts. What is at issue in Mary's virginal maternity? First, it underscores the uniqueness of Jesus as the true Adam. In Christ, God has begun again, bringing forth fruit from barren Israel (Isa 54:1) not within history, but as a gracious interruption of it. Precisely as a virgin "Mary, the barren, blessed one, becomes a sign of grace, the sign of what is truly fruitful and salvific: the ready openness which submits itself to God's will."[36] Relatedly, it highlights Jesus' unique filial status: whereas John, modeling the call to Jeremiah, receives his vocation prior to his birth and is thus a prophet, Jesus' existence is through the Spirit and is not merely the prophet, but is indeed the Son.[37] Precisely to become fruitful, Mary submits to barrenness. In her fiat, she completes the barren-woman motif of the Old Testament and is the beginning of Christian reflection on virginity.[38]

---

35. Ratzinger, *Daughter Zion*, 38–47. The essays in Benedict XVI, *Jesus of Nazareth*, vol. 3, *The Infancy Narratives*, trans. Philip J. Whitmore (London: Bloomsbury, 2012) amplify his remarks here; see also Joseph Ratzinger, "Et Incarnatus Est du Spiritu Sancto ex Maria Virgine," in Balthasar and Ratzinger, *Mary: The Church at the Source*, 81–95. For Mary's place in the opening scenes of Acts, see Benedict XVI, "Praying Presence of Mary," 175–80.

36. Ratzinger, *Daughter Zion*, 48.

37. Ratzinger, *Daughter Zion*, 48–49.

38. Ratzinger, *Daughter Zion*, 49–52. The remainder of the essay takes up the problem of history. Are the accounts of Matthew and Luke reliable as history? Though Ratzinger's argument is dated (being delivered first in 1975), the major issues have not changed and his conclusion is still cogent. The *real* issue is not so much *what* happened as the philosophical question of *how* God relates to the world. One will argue against a historical reading of the text insofar as one is already committed to a philosophical naturalism that rules out miracles a priori. The theological results of such a move are disastrous, rendering us incapable of giving Christian answers to the fundamental questions of God, humanity, and their relationship. If God has not acted in history then Christian reflection is but another example alongside many of the "cultivation of the self." See also Joseph Ratzinger, *Introduction to Christianity*, trans. J. R. Foster, rev. ed. (San Francisco: Ignatius, 2004), 272–80. See also my remarks in a similar vein in *Mary for Evangelicals*, 274–80. Ratzinger does not take up perpetual virginity in detail in these lectures, but it is glimpsed here.

Freedom from Adam's Sin

From Mary's maternity, which traditional Protestants would broadly affirm, Ratzinger then moves to defend the two modern dogmas that they would not. The immaculate conception, if it is to stand, must address two charges: not only is it unattested in the record of revelation; it opposes what is, namely, the universal need for grace. For both Protestants and Catholics, Ratzinger's response will be quite surprising: both objections are themselves insufficiently biblical! Beginning with the second objection, Ratzinger wonders whether there is not a biblical warrant for thinking of grace as preservation from sin alongside grace as rescue therefrom and points us to the Old Testament notion of the holy remnant and argues that as the crucible of the people of God, Mary is its fulfilment. Here I quote him at length:

> As the holy remnant Mary signifies that in herself Old and New Covenants really are one. She is entirely a Jewess, a child of Israel, of the Old Covenant, and as such is a child of the full covenant, entirely a Christian: Mother of the Word. She is the New Covenant in the Old Covenant; she is the New Covenant *as* the Old Covenant, *as* Israel: thus no one can comprehend her mission or her person if the unity of the Old and New Testaments collapses. Because she is entirely response, correspondence ... she cannot be understood where grace seems to be in opposition to response, the real response of the creature, appears to be a denial of grace; for a word that never arrived, a grace that remained solely at God's disposal without becoming a response to him would be no grace at all, but just a futile game. The essence of woman was already defined in Eve: to be the complement that exists entirely in its derivation from the other, and nevertheless remains its complement. Here this essence reaches its acme: pure derivation from God and at the same time the most complete creaturely complement—a creature that has become response.

Mary is not merely the crucible for the people of God, but especially the people conceived as the holy remnant: she is saved precisely in her preservation from "bowing the knee to Baal," and as such can, as a creature, freely and entirely respond to the gracious initiative of God.[39]

It is thus *possible* to conceive of grace as preservation and to conceive of Mary as *the* fulfillment of such grace. But is not this a biblical assemblage after the fact? Can this reading itself be biblically justified? To begin, Ratzinger counters that original sin is itself biblically difficult to nail down; the key text, Romans 5, is itself an exercise in Old Testament typological reading. It is not so much a biblical "fact" as it is a "typological identification of every single man with man as such, with average man, with man from the beginning on. ... It has been identified in a theological (reflex) manner through typological Scriptural exegesis."[40] Why not read Mary in the same (typological) way? If she is the people of God, the one in whom both faithful Israel and the church are best seen, why not see the descriptions of the church as holy, immaculate, without spot, and so on, as applying in a unique way to her? If the church is, in her eschatological reality, an immaculate bride, then this reality is foreshadowed in Mary, the church's church.[41]

What, finally, does the immaculate conception mean? What theological weight is it intended to bear? Far from being merely historical or chronological, the dogma finds its worth first in its explication of original sin. Namely, original sin is *not* natural to being human, but is "a statement about a relationship that can be meaningfully formulated in the context of the God-man relation."[42] That is to say, original sin is not something to be found in isolated examination but is the "collapse" of what humans are in divine intent and in actual being. As a result, Mary's preservation therefrom is not so much her elevation above humanity; rather, it means she is truly human. The entirety of her humanity is given over to God from the first moment of conception such that, in her dispossession, she becomes truly herself; in her virginity, she becomes the "mother of all the living." Second, and following therefrom, the immaculate conception "reflects ultimately faith's certitude that there really is a holy Church—as a person and in a person. In this sense it expresses the Church's certitude of salvation."[43] What is glimpsed in Mary is the reality of the church and the hope of every believer.

The Bodily Assumption into Heavenly Glory

Ratzinger opens his defense of the bodily assumption by ceding ground: it cannot be defended in historical terms; it is a "theological, not an historical, affirmation." The dogma, in other words, is to be understood as a theological working out of veneration, "a most solemn form of hymnology."[44] As such, it refers to Mary as having fully entered into the joy that awaits all the redeemed; among the saints, she is the saintliest.[45] But, the objector asks, the Bible?! As a species of veneration, the assumption is justified by the visitation (esp. Luke 1:45, 48) and is built on Jesus' insistence in Mark 12 that because God *is* Life, all those who are in him are in some way *alive*. None of this, however, requires that Mary's heavenly glory be conceived in bodily terms, as the assumption does. There are here two points to consider. First, Eve represents the "ambiguity of biological becoming." Birth happens always under the sign of death. Mary, on the other hand, is the new Eve; she gives birth to life in the fullest way. Her maternity "is a bursting forth of life that casts off dying and leaves it behind once and for all."[46] Second, in Mary immaculately conceived, grace does not exist alongside sin and death but is pure and uninterrupted. She is entirely "Yes" to God. Death, therefore, as the judgment on sin is absent from her.[47] Finally, the assumption also and most importantly is to be read ecclesiologically. As the one who is *most* alive to God among all the saints, Mary is the fulfillment of the hope of

---

43. Ratzinger, *Daughter Zion*, 70–71.
44. Ratzinger, *Daughter Zion*, 73.
45. The holiness or saintliness that is unique to Mary is the ground for the unique mediation among the saints that she offers. See Ratzinger, "Sign of the Woman," 30–37.
46. Ratzinger, *Daughter Zion*, 78.
47. Here, however, a curious phrase is added: Death is foreign to Mary "even if the somatic end is present" (*Daughter Zion*, 79). I understand Ratzinger here to be echoing Pope Pius XII in *Munificentissimus Deus*, who refused to say whether Mary physically died or not. The wording of the dogma is deliberately ambiguous on this point.

all the baptized as expressed in Colossians 3:3 and Ephesians 2:6: the baptized will be raised up and seated with Christ. She is "not merely the Church's *promised* certitude of salvation but its *bodily* certitude also."[48]

Although this is far from a fully developed Mariology, as Ratzinger himself insists, the four themes arising from the Second Vatican Council and *Marialis Cultus* are plain. First, the future pope writes as a convinced Catholic. There are no calls to revisit *Ineffabilis Deus* (1854) or *Munificentissimus Deus* (1950) at all, let alone those (large) parts (e.g., the anathemas) that fall outside the scope of papal infallibility and could at least in theory be reconsidered. And yet, in contrast both to Pius IX and Pius XII and certainly to his great predecessor, Pope St. John Paul II, Ratzinger's Marian statements here are noteworthy for their modesty.[49] While there is ample room for devotional intensity to live within Ratzinger's parameters, the spirit of the work breathes humility that, though refusing to cede ground to opponents, works very hard to avoid unnecessary ecumenical provocation. Of particular interest is Ratzinger's insistence on returning to the biblical text, especially the text of the Old Testament, to buttress and to amplify his claims. Critics may well make the charge of question-begging (that is, he finds in the Bible that which he already believes for other reasons), but there is no doubt that he is well aware of the biblical challenges to Marian belief and is prepared to meet them in the pages of holy Scripture itself. Last, it is clear that for Ratzinger, everything stands or falls on Mary's virginal maternity as a matter of fidelity to Scripture, to tradition, indeed, to the basic truth of the gospel. If it falls, then the rest is irrelevant at best. On this point, we may repurpose Paul's remarks on the resurrection of Jesus: if Christ be not born of the Virgin (*natus ex virgine*), our faith is in vain.[50]

---

48. Ratzinger, *Daughter Zion*, 80–81.

49. Pope St. John Paul II, of course, was no mere repeater of nineteenth-century exaltation that wrapped "Marian privileges" in "great honorary titles." *Redemptoris Mater* (1987) is a more modest, more biblical document than previous ones. Nevertheless, it cannot be argued that in terms of Marian piety, Pope St. John Paul is easily the equal of Popes Pius IX and XII. The Pope Emeritus, on the other hand, is not. See Ratzinger, "Sign of the Woman," 20–21, for remarks on his predecessor's Marian humility.

50. On this point, ironically enough, Ratzinger sounds very much like Karl Barth.

CONCLUSION

At last we can turn to the questions posed at the outset. What has Ratzinger's Marian work to teach a convinced Protestant (as I am)? And just what is at stake in heeding his lessons? Before tackling the questions in order, I draw attention to the first question. I do not ask what the Pope Emeritus can teach me about Mary (though he does); nor do I propose that traditionally minded Protestants follow him in accepting his articulation of the modern dogmas. As I alluded to above, the problem with Mary from the third generation of the Reformation was not Mary, but the way in which central Reformational concerns came to be articulated in and through her. So now, following Ratzinger into Mary invites reflection not so much about the Mother of God as about central issues bound up in our common reflection on her.

The first of these has to do with holy Scripture, and namely, how to read it. It is my experience having grown up in the Wesleyan Church and served in the Anglican Church of Canada that at the parish level most Protestant Christians—clergy and laity, regardless of where they might plot themselves along the traditional liberal-radical continuum—don't really know how to read the Old Testament. It is regarded as a puzzling combination of bizarre liturgical rules that don't apply anymore, horrifyingly bloodthirsty stories best passed over in silence, some religiously quaint "Grimm's fairy tales" to amuse children in Sunday school or to be mined for sermon illustrations, and prophetic ethics. Only the latter is worth sustained reflection today. Ratzinger's slim volume reminds us that if we would take not only Mary but also the gospel—indeed, the New Testament itself—seriously, we need our reading imaginations reinvigorated. We need to learn how to read the Old Testament as *Christian Scripture*, and that means typologically and prophetically. Ratzinger reads the Old Testament with the fathers and finds there, as the old dictum asserts, the New Testament concealed. This in turn allows him to plumb the depths of the riches of the New Testament, for he has examined the whole cloth thread by prophetic and typological thread.

With respect to Mary, his challenge to Protestants is just this: once we recover a typological and prophetic scriptural imagination, we will begin to see the Old Testament at work in the depictions of Matthew, Luke, John, and the Revelator. And that means, in our own christological and ecclesiological reflections, we will need to say *something* about Mary. We may not go all the way with our Catholic friends. We can and ought to make the argument that much of Roman Marian belief seems to supplant the humanity of Jesus in the Christian imagination. But we will no longer be able to say, simply, that since the Bible is silent, so are we. For the Scriptures, as Ratzinger helps us to see, are not silent. Not at all.

Also, Ratzinger helps Protestants to recover the importance of the *natus ex virgine*. Traditional Protestants, of course, are quite adept at arguing over the "happened-ness" of the event whether as a matter of right exegesis or as history or some combination of the two. Apart from the all too predictable "Was Mary *really* a virgin?" breathlessness that suffuses Advent and Christmas documentaries on CNN, History, Fox News, and elsewhere, however, I wager we don't think about it much. Ratzinger invites us to reflect deeply on the biblical portrayal, to ask what theological weight it bears, to accord it a status that it holds *in the Scriptures themselves*. Specifically, he invites traditional Protestants to reconsider the doctrine as a sign of the uniqueness of Jesus: As one whose very existence depends on the miraculous intervention of the Holy Spirit, he truly is the second Adam created from the passive humanity of his mother even as the first was formed from the dust of the ground. Jesus is *the* interruption of grace. Second, he invites us to reflect on the *natus ex virgine* insofar as it informs the mystery of salvation. As adopted by God the Father, born again by the Spirit, believers themselves are the recipients of sheer grace. Like our elder brother, we are "children born not of natural descent, nor of human decision or a husband's will, but born of God" (John 1:13 NIV). A right and robust understanding of the doctrine precludes any notion of Pelagianism. Whatever cooperation with grace takes place in sanctification, that itself rests on a sheer gift without which we are lost.

At the same time, Ratzinger's deep immersion in Mary's virginal maternity ought to prompt traditional Protestants, especially in contemporary North America, to consider whether we have denigrated celibacy as a Christian vocation as worthy as marriage. Ratzinger insists that Mary's fruitfulness-in-virginity is the fulfillment of the Old Testament daughter Zion motif (a sign of the church as virgin espoused to God), as such she also illumines, for example, St. Paul's reflections on celibacy in 1 Corinthians 7. Celibates are, in their celibacy, freed from the concerns of their spouses in order to devote themselves more fully to the needs of the people of God. As such, they are living anticipations of the kingdom, where the saints neither give nor are given in marriage, for that which marriage signed (the union of Christ with his church) will have come in its fullness.

Last, Ratzinger's reflections on Mary, precisely because they are so very biblical, function to link Christology, ecclesiology, and eschatology.[51] Precisely *as* the Lord's mother in the Gospels of Luke and John (Christology), Mary is a symbolic expression of God's people, the church (ecclesiology). In some way she models the church on her pilgrimage here on earth and in so doing helps us to understand ourselves. When she appears in Revelation 12 as the people of God (it is simply impossible to divest this passage of Marian resonance, though some have tried), she discloses the church's eschatological and apocalyptic identity as that communion pursued by the enemy, protected in the wilderness by God, awaiting her final deliverance.

These are four possible avenues of reflection that Ratzinger's Marian work invites traditional Protestants to pursue. Certainly, more could be added—especially anthropology and gender—which may potentially upend the complementarian and egalitarian debates altogether. But we cannot build a full list here. These are enough to suggest that, without diminishing Reformational concerns, we have much to learn from the Pope Emeritus when he writes about the Blessed Mother of the Lord.

---

51. On the distinctively Marian notes in Christian eschatology, see Ratzinger, "Sign of the Woman," 27–30.

8

Undiminished, Transcendent, and Relevant

Joseph Ratzinger's Teaching on the Trinity

FRED SANDERS

It is curious that the doctrine of the Trinity is not a conspicuous element in the theology of Joseph Ratzinger. He has written no books and only a few essays directly focusing on the theological locus of the Triune God. Of course Trinitarian theology is never far beneath the surface of anything he wrote, but it is only occasionally on the surface. When we name the main characteristics of his thought, we rightly say that he is centered on the doctrine of the church, on the fundamental theology of revelation, on the theology of the liturgy, on intellectual culture, and, most centrally, on Jesus Christ. If we tried to list "Trinitarian" alongside "Christocentric," "ecclesiological," and "liturgical," we would no longer be saying what characterizes his main theological performances (as these other three adjectives certainly do). If we speak of Ratzinger's Trinitarianism, we are instead naming a central Christian doctrine that cannot ever be absent from the thought of any faithful and well-grounded theologian. I am looking into Ratzinger's work to see where he chooses to bring this doctrine to the surface, what he chooses to emphasize when he does so, and how he handles it in relation to his most characteristic interests.[1] Ratzinger definitely operates with a powerful set of Trinitarian commitments, and I would like to point out the most significant difference they made for the shape of his thought.

---

1. On the unsystematic character of Ratzinger's oeuvre, Tracey Rowland notes that "one does not find in his publications the presentation of a totally original theological synthesis, but rather a series of seminal interventions in theological debates thrown up by pastoral crises." Tracey Rowland, *Benedict XVI: A Guide for the Perplexed* (London: T&T Clark, 2010), 1. I am treating Ratzinger's trinitarianism as just such an intervention to a crisis.

ON NOT DIMINISHING THE TRINITY

Ratzinger's approach to the doctrine of the Trinity makes the most sense when we consider as broadly as possible what he thought was at stake in Christian witness in the modern world. Ratzinger was motivated by a sense that modern theology was in danger of trading away all that was best in the heritage of Christian doctrine. On his view, the danger was not that modern theology would accidentally do this in one fell swoop; it was that an entire series of trade-offs, carried out one after another along a definite trajectory, would result in the loss of faith's reality. Writing in 1968 in the preface to his *Introduction to Christianity*, Ratzinger said that "the theological movement of the last decade" had to remind thoughtful people of an old German folk tale, the story of Hans im Glück.[2] In the story, Hans is given a large lump of gold, but finding it hard to carry, gladly trades it for a horse. This horse he then trades for a less troublesome animal, and then trades a pig for a goose and so on, until he works his way down to his final trade, in which a scissor-sharpener convinces him to accept a whetstone. When Hans accidentally drops the whetstone into the river, he reasons that he hasn't lost much and simply returns home, glad to be entirely free of obligations at last. "How long his intoxication lasted, how somber the moment of awakening from the illusion of his supposed liberation," Ratzinger notes, is left "to the imagination of the reader." But for his part, Ratzinger makes clear how the story works as a parable of modern Christianity:

> The worried Christian of today is often bothered by questions like these: has our theology in the last few years not taken in many ways a similar path? Has it not gradually watered down the demands of faith, which had been found all too demanding, always only so little that nothing important seemed to be lost, yet always so much that it was soon possible to venture the next

2. Since the story, part of the Grimm collection, is not as well known outside of Germany, the English translators of *Introduction to Christianity* rendered "Hans im Glück" as "Lucky Jack." But they didn't get very much in the bargain; "Lucky Jack" is more euphonious English but is not a household name. For the German, see Benedict XVI, *Gesammelte Schriften: Einführung in das Christentum: Bekenntnis—Taufe—Nachfolge* (Freiburg: Herder, 2014), 31.

step? And will poor [Hans], the Christian who trustfully let himself be led from exchange to exchange, from interpretation to interpretation, not really soon hold in his hand, instead of the gold with which he began, only a whetstone which he can be confidently recommended to throw away?"[3]

There is something playful in the way Ratzinger makes his point: he uses a folk tale, allows that "such questions are unfair if they are posed in too general terms," and admits that "it is simply not correct to assert that 'modern theology' as a whole has taken a path of this sort." But he is in earnest when he warns that in the theological developments of midcentury Roman Catholicism, "there is widespread support for a trend which does indeed lead from gold to whetstone."[4]

It is easy enough to picture how this movement of diminishment, from gold to whetstone to the threat of a final splash, made itself felt in doctrines about the church and salvation, and certainly in ethics, and it is easy to recall Ratzinger's responses to those shifts. But how did it apply to the doctrine of the Trinity? How did this movement of diminishment make itself apparent in the way theologians under its influence spoke of the Triune God in the twentieth century?

The primary way that Christian confession of the Trinity was diminished in the twentieth century was by the loss of transcendence, and specifically the loss of a sense of God's transcendence over history. The deep interest of modern theology in the reality of history repeatedly distracted theologians from the eternal triune life in itself. Theologians often drew the doctrine down so close to human experience and historical development that they ended by entirely submerging the triunity of God into the history of salvation.[5] In many cases, this movement

3. Joseph Ratzinger, *Introduction to Christianity*, trans. J. R. Foster (San Francisco: Ignatius, 1990), 11.

4. Ratzinger, *Introduction to Christianity*, 11. The motif of happily trading away a fortune for something worthless places Hans im Glück in type 1415 in the Aarne-Thompson typology of folk tales.

5. I have told a longer, more complex version of this story in Fred Sanders, *The Image of the Immanent Trinity: Rahner's Rule and the Theological Interpretation of Scripture* (New York: Peter Lang, 2004). In what follows I am only offering a brief sketch of some aspects most relevant to Ratzinger's work.

remained only a kind of tone or attitude, suggesting that any talk of God in himself was irrelevant and inert, but that the real action was in the history of salvation. But often enough the movement went further, from gold to whetstone, in explicit denial that the Trinity has any internal or immanent life. Ratzinger rightly sensed that the tendency of much modern Trinitarianism was reductionist and in danger of being merely historicist. The style of Trinitarianism he deployed was designed to arrest that downward movement, using all the resources at his command to do so.

To catch the tone and tendency of the kind of diminished Trinitarianism that worried Ratzinger, we can take a glance at the best-selling book *On Being a Christian*, by Hans Küng.[6] In *On Being a Christian*, Küng presents a contemporary reinterpretation of the Christian message in light of a series of modern challenges, including a variety of humanisms, world religions, the scientific worldview, and secularity at large. The book was controversial because of the deflationary approach it took to Christian claims; in it Küng rehearsed the grand, classical statements of Christian soteriology and then notoriously asked, "but does a reasonable man today want to become God?" After all, "our problem today is not the deification but the humanization of man."[7] In a project of this kind, the topic of the Trinity is bound to come up rather late in the game. When it does come up, in the section on the church, it is treated in a peculiar way. Küng's overriding concern is to ensure that the church's doctrine of the Trinity be read as a statement about this world, about human experience, and about our encounter with the reality of God. Put negatively, his goal is to ensure that the doctrine of the Trinity not be taken as a statement about God in himself. In the course of his discussion, Küng acknowledges that the New Testament includes "numerous three-numbered, triadic formulas" that are theologically important, but warns that they must be understood in "their originally non-mythological sense" rather than as statements corresponding

6. Hans Küng, *On Being a Christian*, trans. Edward Quinn (New York: Doubleday, 1976). German original: *Christ Sein* (Munich: Piper, 1974).
7. Küng, *On Being a Christian*, 442.

to a view of God as three distinct persons.[8] Unfortunately, it is precisely in this latter sense that they were in fact understood in the course of doctrinal history: "The theological teaching which in fact emerged out of all this, of the immanent divine triunity ('Trinity'), attempting with the aid of Hellenistic terms to conceive Father, Son and Spirit in true diversity and undivided unity, has its own problems and unfortunately is scarcely understood by modern man."[9]

The alternative to such mythological and speculative Trinitarianism, for Küng, is to understand the Christian doctrine of the Trinity as a doctrine about salvation rather than about God. This, he claims, was the original intent of the New Testament statements that were the impetus for the doctrine:

> Even in John's Gospel none of the statements about Father, Son and Spirit or on God as spirit, light and love are ontological statements about God in himself and his innermost nature, about the static, self-sustaining essence of a triune God. In the whole of the New Testament such statements are concerned with the manner of God's revelation: his dynamic activity in history, the relationship of God to man and man's relationship to God. The triadic formulas of the New Testament are meant to express, not an "immanent" but an "economic" theology of the Trinity, not an inner-divine (immanent) essential triunity in itself but a salvation-historical (economic) unity of Father, Son and Spirit in their encounter with us.[10]

By using here the technical language of immanent and economic, Küng is alluding to the scholarly discussion about the relation between the eternal triune being of God and the historical manifestation of God as Father, Son, and Spirit in the history of salvation. Karl Rahner had inaugurated a new phase of this long discussion in his thesis that "the

---

8. Küng, *On Being a Christian*, 472.
9. Küng, *On Being a Christian*, 472.
10. Küng, *On Being a Christian*, 475.

economic Trinity is the immanent Trinity and vice versa."[11] By saying that the New Testament expresses an economic Trinity rather than an immanent Trinity, Küng is not only doing descriptive New Testament theology, but also setting up the prescriptive systematic claim that what Christian theology today ought to concern itself with is not a teaching about God in himself, but a teaching about the mysterious depths of salvation and its history. By interpreting Rahner's axiomatic statement about the economic and immanent Trinity in this way, Küng was adopting a particularly radicalizing reading of the axiom. Walter Kasper would later warn that this was neither the right way to interpret Rahner's axiom, nor was it theologically advisable: "The axiom is being completely misunderstood when it is turned into a pretext for pushing the immanent Trinity more or less out of the picture and limiting oneself more or less to consideration of the Trinity in the economy of salvation."[12] Kasper makes it clear that he has Küng's influential misinterpretation in mind when he gives this warning;[13] and indeed the downgrading of Trinitarianism to a description of salvation history is a way of pushing the Triune God "more or less out of the picture."

GOD AND HISTORY

While Christian faith obviously desires a doctrine of the Trinity that is engaged with salvation history, the kind of radical reorientation of the doctrine of the Trinity away from the doctrine of God and toward the doctrine of salvation represented by Küng's deflationary account is a move from the otherworldly to the this-worldly. It represents precisely the kind of gold-for-horse exchange that drew Ratzinger's concern. At

---

11. Karl Rahner, *The Trinity*, trans. Joseph Donceel (New York: Crossroad, 1997), 21. This argument by Rahner goes back as far as 1960, because this volume had its origin as Rahner's contribution to the massive, multiauthor *Mysterium Salutis* project. It was originally published there as "Der Dreifaltige Gott als Transzendenter Urgrund der Heilsgeschichte," in *Mysterium Salutis: Grundriss Heilsgeschichtlicher Dogmatik*, vol. 2, *Die Heilsgeschichte vor Christus*, ed. Johannes Feiner and Magnus Löhrer (Einsiedeln: Benziger, 1967), 317–97, here 328.
12. Walter Kasper, *The God of Jesus Christ*, trans. Matthew J. O'Connell (New York: Crossroad, 1984), 276.
13. In his endnote to this judgment, Kasper points not to *On Being a Christian* but to a slightly later book: "This tendency can be seen in H. Küng, *Does God Exist? An Answer for Today* (NY 1980), 699ff."

each successive trade, Hans im Glück is well able to rationalize the exchange; and for his part Küng makes a very strong appeal to the Christian desire for a relevant, engaged, and practical Trinitarianism for the modern age. Negatively, he warns that "we must always remember that the Trinity was not originally an object of theoretical speculation." Positively, "it was the object of the profession of faith and of the act of praise (doxology)." That is, "diagramatically, it could be said: God the Father 'above' me, Jesus as the Son and brother 'beside' me, the Spirit of God and Jesus Christ 'in' me."[14] This last way of putting it is particularly happy. But what could be charitably understood as a helpful nudge toward aligning Trinitarianism with salvation history instead shows itself to be part of the logic of diminishment and decline when it ends in the disjunctive counsel to divert our attention from God to history.

If every attempt to engage God and history were necessarily a diminishing of the doctrine of God, Christian theology as such would be in deep trouble. The Christian faith is inalienably historical, and its message must move ineluctably toward the good news of a God who intervenes in history. If every attempt to confess this were a problem, twentieth-century Roman Catholic theology in particular would have to be judged to be off track in one of its primary agendas, and Ratzinger's own theology would be a major part of the problem, because Ratzinger, along with Catholic theologians generally, was committed to engaging with history, especially following the direction of Vatican II. The important group of Roman Catholic theologians behind the multiauthor *Mysterium Salutis* project, for example, included divergent figures who would later align with the journals *Concilium* and *Communio* respectively. Yet all of them could agree that the task of thinking through the content of the Christian faith comprehensively in terms of salvation history (the titular mystery of salvation) was the central theological challenge of the twentieth century. The editors of these volumes explicitly described one of their aims as rightly relating God and history:

---

14. Küng, *On Being a Christian*, 476.

As the Greek fathers say, and as is shown especially in trinitarian theology, there is no talk about God in his inner threefold
life, and therefore no *theologia* in the strong sense of the word,
without reference to the *oikonomia*, the self-opening of the triune
God in salvation history. And without the depth dimension of
theologia, all talk about the *oikonomia* and salvation history
becomes admittedly flat and merely foreground. What Barth
said of evangelical theology holds also for Catholic: "The subject of evangelical theology is God in the history of his acts."[15]

But it is important to note how carefully balanced this brief programmatic statement is: just as on the one hand the Christian doctrine of God
must be worked out in terms of God's historical actions, so on the other
hand the history of salvation must be placed against the background of
a "depth dimension" that confesses the eternal, ontological priority of
God's own life. To lose that depth of divine being in itself would be to
unmoor salvation history from the reality in which it must be anchored,
rendering it "flat and merely foreground." When the Christian commitment to salvation history is developed in partnership with sustained
attention to the being of God, which transcends all history (including
salvation history), the Christian message is enriched and immeasur-
ably deepened. When, on the other hand, attention to salvation history
is developed in partnership with running polemic against speculation,
contemplation, and the irrelevance of theologizing about God in himself, the Christian message is diminished and traded away for something lesser. Ratzinger's own theology is characterized by attention to
the particulars of salvation history; especially in its Christocentrism it
is committed to expounding the message of God with us.[16] But instead
of engaging in polemic against speculation, Ratzinger's Trinitarianism

---

15. Johannes Feiner and Magnus Löhrer, "Einleitung," in *Mysterium Salutis: Grundriss Heilsgeschichtlicher Dogmatik*, vol. 1, *Die Grundlagen Heilsgeschichtlicher Dogmatik*, ed. Johannes Feiner and Magnus Löhrer (Zurich: Benziger, 1965), xxx. My translation.
16. Tracey Rowland, introducing Ratzinger's theology, surveys the critical fronts of modern Roman Catholic theology and identifies "the most fundamental and far-reaching" one to be "that of presenting a Catholic understanding of the mediation of history in the realm of ontology." Rowland, *Guide for the Perplexed*, 1.

constantly looks upward from salvation history to the mysterious depths of the eternal divine life.

Küng's one-sided approach to the doctrine of the Trinity proved to be increasingly influential. He had already said, at this early date, that "the New Testament is not concerned with God in himself, but with God for us, as he has acted on us through Jesus himself in the Spirit, on which the reality of our salvation depends."[17] The tone he adopted would be taken up at greater length and with much more attention to the details and dynamics of Trinitarianism by thinkers like Catherine Mowry LaCugna, whose 1991 book *God for Us: The Trinity and Christian Life* begins with the claim that "the life of God—precisely because God is triune—does not belong to God alone" and ends by saying that "the doctrine of the Trinity is not ultimately a teaching about 'God' but a teaching about God's life with us and our life with each other."[18] Such statements are capable of sympathetic interpretation; if we take them to presuppose a high view of a transcendent God who has a life in himself, which he graciously opens up to include a life with us, we can hear in them a gospel that does justice to God's own being and to God's serious involvement in salvation history. But Ratzinger's Trinitarianism refuses to leave this transcendence as a presupposition. Instead his Trinitarianism is concerned to make explicit the transcendence that must ground the engagement. In particular, Ratzinger was jealous to keep God from being subsumed within a thoroughly historicized ontology.

THE RELEVANCE OF THE TRANSCENDENT TRINITY

"The Church makes a man a Christian by pronouncing the name of the triune God," Ratzinger wrote in 1976.[19] While acknowledging that this "faith in the triune God" is what the church "considers the most decisive

---

17. Küng, *On Being a Christian*, 475–76.
18. Catherine Mowry LaCugna, *God for Us: The Trinity and Christian Life* (San Francisco: HarperSanFrancisco, 1991), 1 and 228. LaCugna's 1979 Fordham dissertation was on Hans Küng's theological method.
19. Joseph Ratzinger, *The God of Jesus Christ: Meditations on the Triune God*, trans. Brian McNeil (San Francisco: Ignatius, 2008). Original German edition: *Der Gott Jesu Christi: Betrachtungen uber den Dreieinigen Gott* (Munich: Kosel-Verlag, 1976), 25.

element of the Christian existence," Ratzinger admits that for Christians in the modern West, the invocation of the ancient formula can seem disappointing. "It is so far removed from our life. It is so useless and so incomprehensible. If some brief formula must be used, then we expect something attractive and exciting, something that immediately strikes us as important for man and for his life." Here Ratzinger feints in the direction of admitting the irrelevance of classical Christian Trinitarianism. But it is only a feint: in fact, he goes on to affirm, this apparent uselessness, remoteness, and incomprehensibility is the leading edge of the good news we need to hear. The first good word of the gospel is that the Christian faith is not about us, but about God. "Christianity is not oriented to our own hopes, fears, and needs, but to God, to his sovereignty and power."[20] Ratzinger uses the oddness and apparent irrelevance of the church's teaching on the Trinity as a way of making that point. It is a doctrine about a God who is above us, independent of us, and fully alive without us:

> We must learn anew to take God as our starting point when we seek to understand the Christian existence. This existence is belief in his love and faith that he is Father, Son, and Holy Spirit—for it is only thus that the affirmation that he is "love" becomes meaningful. If he is not love in himself, he is not love at all. But if he is love in himself, he must be "I" and "Thou," and this means that he must be triune.[21]

Ratzinger thus signals his awareness that we long for a God who is relevant to our own needs and desires, but leverages that awareness to evoke in us an even deeper longing. The deeper longing is for a God who is truly God, so that when we learn that such a God is turned toward us in love, we can properly appreciate the significance of the turning. By awakening our desire for a relevant doctrine of the Trinity and then warning us against a premature rush to relevance, Ratzinger seeks to secure the stability and grandeur of the classical doctrine of God and

---

20. Ratzinger, *God of Jesus Christ*, 26.
21. Ratzinger, *God of Jesus Christ*, 36.

also the intimacy of that God's salvation-historical commitment to us. Instead of playing off God-in-himself against God-for-us, Ratzinger makes it clear that he intends to confess both.

With these commitments in place, Ratzinger can go quite far in the direction of locating the doctrine of God within the horizon of salvation history. He waves off the possibility that the doctrine of the Trinity was created to serve speculative needs: "The doctrine of the Trinity did not arise out of speculation about God, out of an attempt by philosophical thinking to explain to itself what the fount of all being was like; it developed out of the effort to digest historical experiences."[22] Ratzinger goes on to spell out the historical experiences the early church was taking into account. They include the epochal transition from the Old Testament revelation to the New, which begins with recognition of God as the Father of Israel and the maker of the world, and comes to include the confession of Jesus Christ as the man who simply is God's presence. This is followed finally by a third, the experience of the Spirit, the presence of God in us, in our innermost being."[23] These revelations, or rather this single, extended, coordinated revelatory event, is simply given to us as God's chosen way of making himself known. It is a "sheer matter of fact" posited in divine self-revelation, and "the Christian faith first comes to deal with God in this triple shape in the course of its historical development."[24] Ratzinger grounds the doctrine of the Trinity in history in the sense that the eternally Triune God freely chose to make himself known as triune by manifesting himself as such over the course of history. The central point is the revelation of an antecedent and transcendent reality: "God is as he *shows* himself; God does not show himself in a way in which he is not. On this assertion rests the Christian relation with God; in it is grounded the doctrine of the Trinity; indeed, it is this doctrine."[25] God's self-revelation is a historical phenomenon grounded in the divine faithfulness and God's will to be known truly.

---

22. Ratzinger, *Introduction to Christianity*, 114–15.
23. Ratzinger, *Introduction to Christianity*, 115.
24. Ratzinger, *Introduction to Christianity*, 115.
25. Ratzinger, *Introduction to Christianity*, 117.

But the divine triunity is not confined to its historical revelation, and Ratzinger has always been quite alert to the danger of reducing Trinitarian theology to history. His characteristic way of writing about the Trinity is to exercise a careful balance, confessing God's engagement with history and his transcendence over it. The crucial reasons can be seen most clearly in a section of his *Introduction to Christianity* where he considers the heretical alternatives to orthodox trinitarianism. Having surveyed a number of erroneous views, Ratzinger settles on modalistic monarchianism as the heresy exerting the most pressure on Christian confession in the modern world. Ratzinger treats all of the heresies as earnest attempts to interpret the historical revelation of God in Christ and the Spirit. He identifies what is true in them before focusing on the crucial error that they introduce, and finally for clarity of instruction he returns to the "guiding motives" of orthodox Trinitarianism that must be affirmed in the face of these heresies. The guiding motive that comes into direct conflict with monarchianism is something Ratzinger describes, strikingly, as "striving to give the story of God's dealings with man its proper seriousness." To take God's self-revelatory acts in history seriously means that what we see is what we get:

> This means that when God appears as Son, who says "You" to the Father, it is not a play produced for man, it is not a masked ball on the stage of human history, but the expression of reality. The idea of a divine show had been canvassed in the ancient Church by the Monarchians.[26]

The three persons who interact in the course of salvation history really are, in some ultimately serious way, three persons in the unity of the one God. They are not three roles played over the course of history by a God who may or may not be unipersonal or impersonal or something else besides what he shows himself to be for us and our salvation.

It is this initial, revelatory seriousness that monarchianism fails to achieve. Certainly it "takes seriously the God who meets us, the God who comes towards us first as Creator and Father, then, Christ, as Son

---

26. Ratzinger, *Introduction to Christianity*, 117.

and Redeemer, and finally as Holy Spirit."[27] In that sense, the monarchian error gives history its due, recognizing the three central manifestations of God. But it ends up giving it more than its due, because while it engages with history, it never succeeds in engaging with God. The three figures it identifies in salvation history "are regarded only as masks of God which tell us something about ourselves but nothing about God himself." By showing us only God-for-us, the monarchian account leaves God-in-himself above the historical fray after all, which paradoxically leaves us trapped in a history without God, theologizing about merely historical phenomena. "Tempting as such an approach seems," Ratzinger warns, "in the end it leads back to a situation in which man is only circling round in himself and not penetrating to God's own reality."[28]

As an analysis of the significance of an early heresy, Ratzinger's interpretation of monarchianism is interesting and illuminating. But it is when he turns to "the subsequent history of Monarchianism in modern thinking" that we begin to see what is really at stake in his analysis of the error. He identifies the theological drift of German idealism as a modern variety of monarchianism:

> Hegel and Schelling, in their efforts to interpret Christianity philosophically and to re-think philosophy from Christian premises, went back to this early attempt at a philosophy of Christianity and hoped by starting from here to make the doctrine of the Trinity rationally analyzable and useful, to elevate it in its allegedly pure philosophical sense into the true key to all understanding of Being.[29]

The thoroughly historicized ontology of Hegelian speculation treats the doctrine of the Trinity as "the expression of the historical side of God and therefore of the way in which God appears in history." The moderns, for various reasons, were able to develop the logic of monarchianism to its full extent.

---

27. Ratzinger, *Introduction to Christianity*, 119.
28. Ratzinger, *Introduction to Christianity*, 119.
29. Ratzinger, *Introduction to Christianity*, 119.

Inasmuch as Hegel and—in a different way—Schelling push this idea to its logical conclusion, they reach the point where they no longer distinguish this process of a historical self-revelation of God from a God quietly resting in himself behind it all; instead, they now understand the process of history as the process of God himself. The historical form of God then becomes the gradual self-realization of the divine; thus history certainly becomes the process of the *logos,* but even the *logos* is only real as the process of history.[30]

The contrast is stark: On the one side stands the classical Christian vision of "God quietly resting in himself behind it all," yet truly engaging with historical realities by "historical self-revelation" and by free, gracious divine action in the midst of that history. On the other side stands the modern possibility of history as "a process of God himself" and "the gradual self-realization of the divine." The submersion of the reality of God into the flux of historical process occurs with a pitiful splash; the fatal, final splash of Hans im Glück losing the last token of his inheritance in the stream below. "Thus the 'historicization' of the doctrine of the Trinity, as contained in Monarchianism, now becomes the 'historicization' of God."[31] We can define a historicized Trinity as a Trinity without its own ontology; a Trinity that requires history, our history, in order to be what it is.

In the folk tale with which Ratzinger began his *Introduction to Christianity,* Hans im Glück proceeded from one trade to another, accepting whatever came next and rationalizing an explanation of why each new exchange left him in a better position progressively. A thoroughly historicized modern trinitarianism likewise must accept whatever comes next, because whatever comes next is all there is. In this case, "meaning is no longer simply the creator of history; instead, history becomes the creator of meaning and the latter becomes its creation."[32]

---

30. Ratzinger, *Introduction to Christianity,* 120.
31. Ratzinger, *Introduction to Christianity,* 120.
32. Ratzinger, *Introduction to Christianity,* 120

This is why neither Hans im Glück nor modern revisionist trinitarianism can discern whether it is improving or degenerating: its standards of judgment, rather than being transcendent, must emerge in the course of history itself.

Ratzinger extends his analysis of modern monarchianism along lines that foreshadow the critical position he would later take with regard to the Marxist elements within liberation theology. For Ratzinger, consistent Marxism was itself the final result of the modern version of the monarchian error. "Karl Marx," he warned, "is the only one who continued to think resolutely along these lines, by asserting that if meaning does not precede man then it lies in the future, which man must himself bring about by his own struggles."[33] In the genealogy of Marxism that Ratzinger presupposes, the denial of a transcendent God "quietly resting in himself behind it all" is fundamental, and the struggle for meaning through praxis is the necessary consequence. Further, this loss of transcendence is what makes modern monarchianism so stridently political. By cutting the link to eternity, monarchianism has always tended toward not just historicization of Christian doctrine but also politicization of its core message:

> In its revival by Hegel and Marx it has a decidedly political tinge; it is "political theology." In the ancient Church it served the attempt to give the imperial monarchy a theological foundation; in Hegel it becomes the apotheosis of the Prussian state; and in Marx a programme of action to secure a sound future for humanity.[34]

Ratzinger's interventions in the controversy over liberation theology are among his most conspicuous and controversial public actions as head of the Congregation for the Doctrine of the Faith. In the deep background of his position on these issues lay his particular commitment to a classical Trinitarianism that confessed the Trinity's ontology as transcendent over history.

---

33. Ratzinger, *Introduction to Christianity*, 120.
34. Ratzinger, *Introduction to Christianity*, 121.

CONCLUSION

I began by admitting that Ratzinger is not a theologian whose work we would primarily characterize as Trinitarian, because that would not be as descriptive or distinctive as calling his work Christocentric, ecclesiological, or liturgical. But having attended to the foundational role played by his Trinitarian commitments, we can conclude by noting that his most characteristic theological interests all function in service of his background Trinitarian project. They all serve to guarantee and safeguard a recognition of God's transcendence over the flux of history. Ratzinger's constant return to pre-Christian philosophy served as a support, necessary but not sufficient, for his view of God's metaphysical exaltation and absoluteness. His pronounced philosophical personalism is explicitly connected to his interpretation of the doctrine of the Trinity. His insistence on the liturgical setting of theology served to anchor theological discourse in a reality that could be experienced precisely as an experience pointing comprehensively beyond experience, and in his liturgical reflections there is constant reference to the creedal and devotional language about the Father, Son, and Holy Spirit. And finally there is in Ratzinger's later work, especially the multivolume *Jesus of Nazareth*, a Christocentrism that digs deep into the history of Jesus Christ in all its detail, but without ever suggesting that to focus on Jesus is to turn attention away from his eternal, greater-than-historical relation to the Father and the Holy Spirit.[35] In fact it is precisely this set of relationships, among the Father, Son, and Holy Spirit, that transcend history and give to it, as a free gift of divine grace, its only possible meaning.

---

35. In addition to *Jesus of Nazareth*, the deepening Christocentrism of Ratzinger's thought can be seen in *Behold the Pierced One: An Approach to a Spiritual Christology*, trans. Graham Harrison (San Francisco: Ignatius, 1986). For excellent commentary on the relation between Ratzinger's Christocentrism and trinitarianism, see Peter John McGregor's *Heart to Heart: The Spiritual Christology of Joseph Ratzinger* (Eugene, OR: Pickwick, 2016).

9

Is the Pope (Roman) Catholic?

Joseph Ratzinger on Ecumenism

CARL R. TRUEMAN

O ne of the most fascinating aspects of the papacy of Benedict XVI was the enthusiasm for him among conservative Protestants. From his traditional stand on sexual ethics and identity to his critiques of relativism and his commitment to the idea of truth, Benedict resonated with conservative Protestants as none of his predecessors had ever done.

This Protestant enthusiasm for the pope stood somewhat at odds with the pope's own approach to ecumenism in general and Protestants in particular. From the moment of his election, Protestant delight at his stand on key moral issues contrasted dramatically with widespread concern about an approach to non-Catholic Christians that even the most infatuated of his Protestant supporters could only credibly describe as highly cautious.[1] Others have not been even that generous, expressing horror at his statements and actions. Thus, in 2007 Britain's *Guardian* ran an article by John Hooper and Stephen Bates with the headline "Dismay and Anger as Pope Declares

---

1. I am very grateful to my friend Professor Matthew Levering of Mundelein Theological Seminary for commenting on the section of this essay relative to tradition and also for drawing my attention to Joseph Ratzinger's 1968 essay on *Dei Verbum*. Thus, an article published in the *Baptist Standard* in the immediate aftermath of Benedict's election quotes Southern Baptist leader Richard Land enthusing about his appointment because he is likely to hold the traditional line on matters of sexuality. In the same article, Baptist ethicist David Gushee draws attention to the 2000 encyclical *Dominus Iesus* (which originated with then Cardinal Ratzinger) as sharply delimiting possibilities for ecumenical dialogue. Greg Warner, "Conservative Evangelicals Hope for New Ally in Pope Benedict XVI," *Baptist Standard*, April 22, 2005, https://www.baptiststandard.com/archives/2005-archives/conservative-evangelicals-hope-for-ally-in-new-pope-benedict-xvi50205/. It is also worth noting that Protestant enthusiasm for Benedict's moral stands depends on a somewhat eclectic, or perhaps better "selective," approach to Roman Catholicism. Roman Catholic opposition to homosexuality, for example, rests on a view of marriage that also sees artificial contraception as sinful, a point with which many conservative Protestants would disagree.

Protestants Cannot Have Churches." In fact, while the headline was designed to shock, the statement of Benedict's that had drawn such ire was really nothing more than a reaffirmation the teaching of Vatican II. Apparently, the idea that the pope might be, well, Catholic was extremely distressing to many of the newspaper's more liberal-minded readership.[2]

In fact, at the heart of Protestant confusion and shock at Benedict's approach to ecumenism lies a failure to understand the nature and depth of what separates Protestantism and Roman Catholicism. While Protestants can tend to think of Roman Catholicism as primarily different in terms of key doctrinal commitments, in fact the major issue is somewhat more complicated than that. Roman Catholicism is not simply Protestantism with a different set of doctrines. It is a different way of thinking about Christianity, a way that draws a very tight connection between Scripture, tradition, and the doctrine of the church in a manner alien to Protestantism.

THE FOUNDATION:
VATICAN II AND ECUMENISM

To understand this point, and to understand why Protestants found Benedict to be, on their own terms, a contradictory figure, it is necessary first to set his ecumenical thinking against the background of the work of the Second Vatican Council, at which he was a *peritus* (theological advisor) to Cardinal Frings of Cologne. In his own account of the council in his memoirs, Benedict mentions only the discussions of liturgical reform and of the nature of revelation.[3]

Nevertheless, Vatican II is clearly the framework for Benedict's own approach to ecumenism. Two documents are of particular importance

---

2. John Hooper and Stephen Bates, "Dismay and Anger as Pope Declares Protestants Cannot Have Churches," *The Guardian*, July 11, 2007, https://www.theguardian.com/world/2007/jul/11/catholicism.religion.

3. Ratzinger provides his own account of his role at the council in *Milestones: Memoirs 1927–1977*, trans. Erasmo Leiva-Merikakis (San Francisco: Ignatius, 1998), 120–31. In his published interviews with Peter Seewald, Benedict discusses his role at the council further but again gives no indication of having had any constructive role in the documents relating to ecumenism. See Joseph Ratzinger, *Salt of the Earth: The Church at the End of the Millennium; An Interview with Peter Seewald*, trans. Adrian Walker (San Francisco: Ignatius, 1997); see also Benedict XVI with Peter Seewald, *Last Testament: In His Own Words*, trans. Jacob Phillips (London: Bloomsbury, 2016).

here: *Lumen Gentium* and *Unitatis Redintegratio,* both dated November 21, 1964. The former, a dogmatic statement on the nature of the church, is the foundation of the latter, the decree on ecumenism.

The key passage in *Lumen Gentium,* and one to which Benedict would later refer when, as Cardinal Ratzinger, he was the guiding hand behind *Dominus Iesus* (2000), occurs in paragraph 8:

> This Church, constituted and organized as a society in the present world, subsists in the Catholic Church, which is governed by the successor of Peter and by the bishops in communion with him. Nevertheless, many elements of sanctification and of truth are found outside its visible confines. Since these are gifts belonging to the Church of Christ, they are forces impelling towards Catholic unity.[4]

There are a number of important elements in this passage. First, the subject is the true church or, to use the phrase from earlier in the same paragraph, "the sole Church of Christ which in the Creed we profess to be one, holy, catholic, and apostolic." Second—and crucially—this church is described as *subsisting* in the Catholic Church governed by the bishop of Rome. The choice of word is highly significant. To have declared that this church *is* that governed by the pope would have asserted an exclusivity that denied the existence of Christians outside of the Roman communion. The language of subsistence is somewhat more moderate, allowing that the primary and proper church is that of Rome, but that Christians can be found outside of its institutional boundaries. This is confirmed in the statement regarding the "many elements of sanctification and truth" found outside of its institutional boundaries.

Nevertheless, the council does not relativize the Roman communion in any absolute way. It is not claiming that Rome is the true church merely as a husband, for example, might claim that his wife is the most beautiful woman in the world. Whatever the strict logic of the latter statement, its personal nature means that the husband is not actually

---

4. Austin Flannery, ed., *Vatican Council II: The Conciliar and Post Conciliar Documents* (Collegeville, MN: Liturgical Press, 1975), 357.

making an absolute truth claim about the aesthetic inferiority of every other woman on the planet. By contrast, the council is here asserting the superiority of the Roman communion even if denying its strict monopoly of the title of church. The point is underscored by the observation that what signs of true Christianity do exist outside of the Roman church are forces pushing those groups or individuals toward unity with Rome.

Lumen Gentium makes explicit the assumptions that should guide Roman Catholic approaches to ecumenism. First, Rome is the true church in the deepest sense. Second, true churches, Christian communities, and individual believers can be found outside its institutional boundaries. And third, the aim of ecumenism (whether this can ever be achieved this side of the eschaton) is to bring such churches, communities, and individuals into formal, visible communion with Rome.

These points are clearly reflected in *Unitatis Redintegratio*, the council's statement on ecumenism. The decree begins by stating that the restoration of unity among Christians is one of the primary concerns of the council.[5] It proceeds to state that all who have been baptized have a right to be called Christians and then expands on the comment in *Lumen Gentium* concerning the existence of many aspects of true Christianity outside of the Roman communion:

> Some, even very many, of the most significant elements and endowments which together go to build up and give life to the Church itself, can exist outside the visible boundaries of the Catholic Church: the written Word of God; the life of grace; faith, hope and charity, with the other interior gifts of the Holy Spirit, as well as visible elements. All of these, which come from Christ and lead back to him, belong by right to the one Church of Christ.[6]

When reading this, it is important to remember that *Lumen Gentium* defines the "one Church of Christ" as subsisting in the Roman communion. Thus, this acknowledgment of Christianity elsewhere is not to be

---

5. *Lumen Gentium,* §1 (Flannery, *Vatican Council II,* 452).
6. *Unitatis Redintegratio,* §3 (Flannery, *Vatican Council II,* 455).

understood as relativizing Rome's claims to superiority, universal juris-diction, or to be the ultimate context for Christian unity.

Unitatis Redintegratio does elaborate on the status of the various churches and Christian communities that exist outside of the Roman Catholic Church. And here it makes an important distinction that is sig-nificant for understanding the ecumenical policies of Benedict: Rome sees a qualitative difference between the various churches we might bracket together as Eastern Orthodox, and the Western churches we might characterize as Protestant. As a result, there can be no strict sym-metry between ecumenism aimed at the East and ecumenism aimed at the West. To put the matter concisely, *Unitatis Redintegratio* grants that Eastern churches are true churches but only considers Protestant churches to be churches in an equivocal sense, preferring to refer to them as "ecclesial communities."

The reasons for making this distinction between East and West, Orthodox and Protestant, are important. In discussing the Orthodox churches, *Unitatis Redintegratio* acknowledges both their adherence to the doctrines of the Trinity and incarnation, and also the fact that these were defined at councils held in the East. If this was the major point of connection between Rome and the Orthodox, of course, orthodox Protestants would have grounds to ask why they too, as believers in Nicene and Chalcedonian theology, should not be placed in the same category. But the shared doctrinal commitments are not the decisive factor on this point. Rather, it is that the East is an ancient liturgical tradition, has a high view of Mary, which is reflected in its worship, and, most important of all, has a sacramental theology connected to a priesthood rooted in apostolic succession:

> These Churches although separated from us, yet possess true sacraments, above all—by apostolic succession—the priesthood and the Eucharist, whereby they are still joined to us in closest intimacy.[7]

---

7. *Unitatis Redintegratio*, §15 (Flannery, *Vatican Council II*, 465).

This should be a clear reminder to Protestants that, for Roman Catholics, the question of the true church cannot be separated from very specific questions of ecclesiology and that not in some vague, abstract sense but rather in very concrete, historical, and institutional forms—a point that Cardinal Ratzinger raises in an acute form relative to the Anglican– Roman Catholic discussions of the early 1980s. Indeed, in Ratzinger's mind the very question of truth itself cannot be separated from such ecclesiological considerations, a matter to which we shall return later.

Thus, when *Unitatis Redintegratio* addresses the issue of the Protestant churches, the approach is strikingly different. While acknowledging that baptism means that Protestants can be regarded as Christians, it notes that Protestant churches exhibit such diversity that it is very hard to describe them in any meaningfully coherent way, again an attitude that is reflected in later comments by Benedict.[8] The decree acknowledges Protestant love of Scripture (though it goes so far as to describe this as almost cultic).[9] Yet here again the decree makes a comment the significance of which needs to be grasped by Protestants:

> But when Christians separated from us affirm the divine author-
> ity of the sacred books, they think differently from us—differ-
> ent ones in different ways—about the relationship between the
> scriptures and the Church. For in the Church, according to
> Catholic belief, its authentic teaching office has a special place
> in expounding and preaching the written Word of God.[10]

Again, what is clear is that for Roman Catholics, questions of Christian truth cannot be isolated from questions of authority and therefore from questions of ecclesiology. Protestant churches lack apostolic succession and thus the sacramental ministry that rests on such. From Rome's

---

8. *Unitatis Redintegratio*, §19 (Flannery, *Vatican Council II*, 467). Cf. the comment of Benedict on the problems faced by him as pope in ecumenical engagement with Protestants: "With the Protestants, I would say the internal disagreements are the really big problem. One is always speaking only to a partial reality, which then excludes another partial reality. They themselves are in a major crisis, as we know." *Last Testament*, 203.
9. *Unitatis Redintegratio*, §21 (Flannery, *Vatican Council II*, 468).
10. *Unitatis Redintegratio*, §21 (Flannery, *Vatican Council II*, 468–69).

perspective, they are simply not legitimate churches in the sense that the Eastern Orthodox are.

That is a hard point for Protestants to understand, especially those from, say, evangelical traditions where ecclesiology is typically thin to nonexistent. But even more robust ecclesiological forms of Protestantism—say, Anglicanism or confessional Lutheranism and Presbyterianism—still operate with a Scripture principle that allows for the separation of questions of doctrinal truth and authority from a specific institutional ecclesiology—something that Rome excludes as a possibility. And that is vital to understanding why Benedict is for many Protestants a somewhat enigmatic figure in matters ecumenical.

Finally, *Unitatis Redintegratio* does offer a vision of what ecumenism might look like in practice. Again, this is worth noting because it is reflected in later comments by Benedict. Given the closeness of Rome and Eastern churches in terms of liturgy, sacraments, and priesthood, the decree specifically encourages some common worship, if circumstances allow for it and the church authorities grant their permission.[11] Roman Catholics are also to pray with other Christians for unity, sometimes in the context of formal gatherings with those from other churches and communities. Also, it is deemed appropriate for Roman Catholics to engage in social causes with other Christians as a means of demonstrating the servanthood of Christ to the wider world.[12]

This, then, is the ecumenical framework established by Vatican II, which is foundational to the ecumenism pursued by Benedict both as cardinal and as pope.

BENEDICT AND ECUMENISM

Benedict's own attitude to ecumenism is intended to be a careful application of the teaching of Vatican II, maintaining the essential superiority and therefore necessity of the papacy and the magisterium, and offering a modest and cautious vision of what is possible.

---

11. *Unitatis Redintegratio,* §15 (Flannery, *Vatican Council II,* 465).
12. *Unitatis Redintegratio,* §§5–12 (Flannery, *Vatican Council II,* 459–63).

Perhaps the most well-known act of Benedict's papacy in terms of Protestant ecumenism was the promulgation on November 9, 2009, of the Apostolic Constitution *Anglicanorum Coetibus*. This paved the way for the establishment of ordinariates—equivalents of dioceses—into which priests and members of the Anglican Church could enter in order to come into formal communion with Rome.[13] At the time it was widely interpreted as a somewhat aggressive gesture that undermined Roman Catholic and Anglican dialogue. Yet it was entirely consistent with both the direction set by Vatican II and with Benedict's own stated position on ecumenism and dialogue.

Nearly forty years before the *Anglicanorum Coetibus*, the Roman Catholic and Anglican churches had engaged in formal dialogue under the auspices of the Anglican Roman Catholic International Commission (ARCIC), which had been established in 1970 by Pope Paul VI and the then Archbishop of Canterbury Michael Ramsey. The first phase of ARCIC's work ended in 1981 with the production of a final report dealing with the Eucharist, ministry, and authority.[14]

The ARCIC discussions provided the then Cardinal Ratzinger, as prefect of the Congregation for the Doctrine of the Faith, with an opportunity to reflect critically on both the theory and practice of ecumenism in a 1983 essay, "Problems and Prospects of the Anglican-Catholic Dialogue."[15]

At the heart of Ratzinger's criticism lie the closely related issues of authority and tradition, both of which have to be addressed in terms of ecclesiology in order to stay faithful to the Roman Catholic Church's teaching. This is where Ratzinger correctly sees a conceptual problem or confusion lying at the heart at least of some Anglican convictions regarding the results of ARCIC.

---

13. See Benedict XVI, *Anglicanorum Coetibus*, Apostolic Constitution, November 4, 2009, http://w2.vatican.va/content/benedict-xvi/en/apost_constitutions/documents/hf_ben-xvi_apc_20091104_anglicanorum-coetibus.html.
14. The text of the final report is available at http://www.prounione.urbe.it/dia-int/arcic/doc/e_arcic_final.html.
15. Reprinted, along with a subsequent response to his critics, in Joseph Ratzinger, *Church, Ecumenism, and Politics: New Endeavors in Ecclesiology*, trans. Michael J. Miller et al. (San Francisco: Ignatius, 2008), 69–99.

In the essay, Ratzinger focuses on two specific but connected problems. First, there is the tendency of the ARCIC to speak about authority in the abstract without addressing what this looks like in practice.[16] Second, there is the slippery use of the term "tradition" as a means of relativizing the difference between communions. The two problems are clearly related as the concept of *tradition* is, for Ratzinger, a function of ecclesiology and thus a matter of particular, concrete, actual authority. As he expresses it,

> [The question of authority] is identical with the question of tradition and cannot be separated from that of the relation between universal Church and particular Church.[17]

The reason why the question of *tradition* is also a question of authority and of ecclesiology lies in the distinctive dogmatic sense of the term for Roman Catholicism. It is a truism that all Christian churches, from Roman Catholic to radical Anabaptist, have *tradition* in the sense that their beliefs and practices have historical roots, but that observation on its own achieves nothing of ecumenical value. While *tradition* might mean for a Protestant the received wisdom of the past, or simply the acknowledgment that contemporary dogmatic formulations have a specific history, for Roman Catholicism the term is loaded with theological and ecclesiological weight. It is inextricably bound to an understanding of the relationship between Scripture, the institutional church, and its dogmatic pronouncements. In a concise but precise manner Ratzinger defines the concept:

> "Tradition" means above all that the Church, living in the form of apostolic succession with the Petrine office at its center, is the place in which the Bible is lived and interpreted in a binding

---

16. "Any presentation of the theme 'Authority in the Church' that was really intended to lead to unity would have to take into account in a much more concrete way the actual form of authority in order to do justice to the question. ... It is of the essence of authority to be concrete; consequently, one can do justice to the theme only by naming the actual authorities and clarifying the position of each with regard to the other, instead of just theorizing about authority." Ratzinger, *Church, Ecumenism, and Politics*, 70–71.

17. Ratzinger, *Church, Ecumenism, and Politics*, 73.

way. This interpretation forms a historical continuity, setting fixed standards but never itself reaching a definitive point of completion after which it is a thing of the past.[18]

On this point, Ratzinger is simply reiterating once again the teaching of Vatican II, this time as contained in chapter 2 of *Dei Verbum*.[19]

This is a very important point for Protestants to understand. In recent years there has been a most welcome recognition among some confessional Reformed Protestants of the importance of tradition in doctrinal formulation. This is consistent with the position of the Reformers, who never questioned the importance of tradition in and of itself but rather rejected the idea of a stream of tradition that could stand as an authority independent of the Bible.[20] Yet it would be a mistake to see this appropriate awareness of the historical and ecclesiastical roots of contemporary doctrinal reflection as the Protestant analogue to the Roman understanding of tradition.[21]

For both Roman Catholics and Protestants, Scripture is in theory the norming norm of all theological statements, the material principle of theological formulation. The Westminster Confession of Faith chapter 1.6 is representative of Protestantism on this point.[22] Rome's view too is set forth in similar terms. Here is how Vatican II stated the matter in *Dei Verbum*:

18. Ratzinger, *Church, Ecumenism, and Politics*, 82.
19. Flannery, *Vatican Council II*, 753–56.
20. For a good manifesto of the Reformed retrieval project, see Michael Allen and Scott R. Swain, *Reformed Catholicity: The Promise of Retrieval for Theology and Biblical Interpretation* (Grand Rapids: Baker Academic, 2015). Reformation scholar Heiko A. Oberman made a distinction between different types of tradition and their relationship to Scripture, which is helpful here: Tradition I, which is church tradition that finds its source and its norm in Scripture; and Tradition II, which stands to some degree independent of Scripture as source and norm: see his *Forerunners of the Reformation: The Shape of Late Medieval Thought* (New York: Holt, Rinehart & Winston, 1966), 53–66.
21. Reflecting on ARCIC, Ratzinger himself clearly feared that a loose use of the term *tradition* was a surreptitious means of smuggling relativism into the discussion: "I had maintained that lurking behind the new concept of tradition was the elimination of the question of truth." *Church, Ecumenism, and Politics*, 93.
22. "The whole counsel of God concerning all things necessary for his own glory, man's salvation, faith and life, is either expressly set down in Scripture, or by good and necessary consequence may be deduced from Scripture: unto which nothing at any time is to be added, whether by new revelations of the Spirit, or traditions of men."

162

Since [the Scriptures] are inspired by God and committed to writing once and for all time, they present God's own Word in an unalterable form, and they make the voice of the Holy Spirit sound again and again in the words of the prophets and apostles. It follows that all the preaching of the Church, as indeed the entire Christian religion, should be nourished and ruled by sacred Scripture.[23]

There is a key difference, however, and that is on the matter of who is able to offer the authoritative interpretation and application of Scripture. The answer for Protestants rests heavily upon notions of Scripture's perspicuity and the internal testimony of the Holy Spirit in the individual believer, although forms of Protestantism with higher and more self-conscious ecclesiologies (e.g., Anglican, Lutheran, and Presbyterian) may well place more ministerial authority in the historic testimony of their particular communions. The answer for Roman Catholics is the Magisterium of the Church. *Dei verbum* again:

The task of giving an authentic interpretation of the Word of God, whether in its written form or in the form of Tradition, has been entrusted to the living teaching office of the Church alone. Its authority in this matter is exercised in the name of Jesus Christ. Yet this Magisterium is not superior to the Word of God, but is its servant. It teaches only what has been handed on to it. At the divine command and with the help of the Holy Spirit, it listens to this devotedly, guards it with dedication and expounds it faithfully. All that it proposes for belief as being divinely revealed is drawn from this single deposit of faith.[24]

The precise relationship of tradition, Scripture, and the church's teaching is a point of some discussion even among Roman Catholic theologians, but the essential difference with Protestantism is clear: for the Roman

---

23. *Dei Verbum*, §21 (Flannery, *Vatican Council II*, 762).
24. *Dei Verbum*, §10 (Flannery, *Vatican Council II*, 755–56).

Catholic, dogmatic truth claims cannot be separated from ecclesiology.[25] This is why Ratzinger was concerned that the ARCIC tended toward reducing the difference between Rome and Canterbury to matters of Marian dogma and Roman primacy. These are certainly differences between Roman Catholicism and Protestantism, but they cannot be relativized or treated in isolation. These two matters are inseparable and central to the issue of authority; and it is the issue of authority that lies at the fundamental breach between Rome and Protestantism.[26]

Again, this is important for Protestants to understand. When a confessional Protestant looks at the work of a theologian like Benedict and finds a shared commitment to supernaturalism, to Nicene Trinitarianism, to Chalcedonian Christology, and to a biblical sexual ethic, it is tempting to see these shared convictions as a sign that the differences between orthodox Protestants and Roman Catholics are peripheral or of little importance. But that misses a very significant point: the bases on which the two groups know that these elements of Christianity are true are very different.

For the Protestant, an appeal to Scripture alone, or to tradition normed by Scripture without any reference to a specific ecclesiology, is deemed a sufficient foundation for their truth. For the Roman Catholic it is because the living voice of the apostolic church under the Roman pontiff has witnessed to their truth. That is not, of course, to be reduced to a simplistic "The church says it, so it must be infallibly true." The Roman Catholic Church has a finely parsed notion of its own authority

---

25. The relationship of Scripture, tradition, and church was hotly debated at Vatican II; see the brief account in John W. O'Malley, *What Happened at Vatican II* (Cambridge: Harvard University Press, 2008), 146–47, 227–28. The relationship between Scripture and tradition remains a point of contention even within Roman Catholic circles. Vatican II seems to allow for both the two-modes approach, whereby doctrine is rooted in Scripture and conveyed in the teaching tradition of the magisterium of the church. This is a form of Oberman's Tradition I but connected to the authoritative teaching office of the institutional church. The other is the two-source approach, which is Oberman's Tradition II.
26. Ratzinger, *Church, Ecumenism, and Politics*, 72. Ratzinger there makes the pointed observation about Marian dogma and the papal primacy that "in point of fact, both the aforesaid dogmas are only the most tangible symptoms of the overall problem of authority in the Church. The way one views the structure of Christianity will necessarily affect in some measure, great or small, one's attitude to various particular matters contained within the whole."

in such matters, acknowledging that not everything it says is infallible, as is made clear in *Lumen Gentium* 25 and the Code of Canon Law 749–54.[27]

Ratzinger himself offered significant commentary on key chapters of *Dei Verbum* in a collection of essays originally published in English in 1968.[28] Ratzinger here expresses disappointment in this essay that the council had not addressed the issue of the fallibility of the church and the need for criticism of tradition.[29] But most importantly, he identifies the issue of sola Scriptura in Protestantism as ultimately raising ecclesiological questions:

> The firm emphasis on the unity of Scripture and tradition [in *Dei Verbum*] has aroused the strongest opposition and shown that the Protestant idea of *sola scriptura* is less concerned with the material origin of the individual statements of faith as with the problem of the judging function of Scripture in relation to the Church.[30]

Ratzinger then proceeds to engage with the critique of *Verbum Dei* offered by the Protestant theologian Oscar Cullman. Acknowledging Cullman's criticism of the council, that it offered no substantial discussion of how the church might critique tradition, he nonetheless argues that Cullman's own position essentially sets Scripture against church in a manner that hands the definition of the faith over to whatever happens to be the latest scholarly consensus and thereby reduces faith itself to an acceptance of mere probabilities. This constitutes what he characterizes as "the inner difficulties of the Protestant position."[31]

It is beyond the scope of this essay to address the specific issue of the relationship of Scripture, tradition, and church in Protestantism. What is important to note here is simply the point of fact: Doctrine and the issue of authority cannot be separated; and given the teaching

---

27. Flannery, *Vatican Council II*, 379–81. For the canon law, see the Code of Canon Law, book 3, http://www.vatican.va/archive/ENG1104/__P2H.HTM.
28. Joseph Ratzinger, "Commentary on *Dei Verbum*," in *Commentary on the Documents of Vatican II*, ed. Herbert Vorgrimler (New York: Crossroad, 1989), 3:184–98.
29. Ratzinger, "Commentary," 185.
30. Ratzinger, "Commentary," 191.
31. Ratzinger, "Commentary," 193.

of the Roman Catholic Church—that it is the Spirit-filled and Spirit-led body that has responsibility for the transmission of the faith from generation to generation—this has profound implications for the nature of ecumenism, a point that Joseph Ratzinger has clearly stated throughout his career, first as theologian and then as pope.[32]

Given all this, we are now in a position to comment on both the establishment of the ordinariate and *Dominus Iesus*, the earlier controversial document produced by Ratzinger when prefect, both of which Protestants found to be offensive.

As to *Dominus Iesus*, the theology contained therein draws explicitly on the earlier teaching of *Lumen Gentium* and even offers commentary on it. Specifically, *Dominus Iesus* seeks to clarify the position between Rome and other churches and other ecclesial communions. *Dominus Iesus* 16 speaks as follows:

> With the expression *subsistit in*, the Second Vatican Council sought to harmonize two doctrinal statements: on the one hand, that the Church of Christ, despite the divisions which exist among Christians, continues to exist fully only in the Catholic Church, and on the other hand, that "outside of her structure, many elements can be found of sanctification and truth," that is, in those Churches and ecclesial communities which are not yet in full communion with the Catholic Church. But with respect to these, it needs to be stated that "they derive their efficacy from the very fullness of grace and truth entrusted to the Catholic Church.[33]

Dominus Iesus 17 then continues: Rome is the communion in which the true church subsists; other churches and communions may have

---

32. It is also worth noting that the International Theological Commission's 2014 document *Sensus Fidei* articulates a positive role for the laity in the Roman Catholic Church in the task of recognizing whether particular doctrines belong to the apostolic faith. The document is available at http://www.vatican.va/roman_curia/congregations/cfaith/cti_documents/rc_cti_20140610_sensus-fidei_en.html.

33. *Dominus Iesus*, §16. Congregation for the Doctrine of the Faith, *Dominus Iesus*, August 6, 2000, http://www.vatican.va/roman_curia/congregations/cfaith/documents/rc_con_cfaith_doc_20000806_dominus-iesus_en.html.

aspects of the truth, but those that lack the valid episcopate (one rooted in apostolic succession) and a valid Eucharist are not churches in the proper sense, though Rome recognizes individuals in such groups as Christians because of their baptism.[34] It is clear why Protestants and perhaps progressive Roman Catholics would find this offensive; but it is also clear that it says nothing that is not consistent with the ecumenical teaching of Vatican II.

And it is this teaching that lies theologically behind the establishment of the ordinariate. Again, as offensive as it might be to Anglicans, the Church of England does not stand in the same relation to Rome as the Eastern Orthodox churches because it lacks the proper episcopate and the eucharistic mystery. Further, if the purpose of ecumenism according to Vatican II is to bring separated churches and communions into formal fellowship with Rome, under the authority of the bishop of Rome and the magisterium, then the ordinariate makes perfect sense. Of course, the politics of its timing are a different matter; but theologically the move is again consistent with Vatican II and does not represent a hardening of Rome's theological and ecclesiological position. Pope Benedict XVI was simply acting in a manner consistent with the theology of Cardinal Ratzinger.

CONCLUSION

Orthodox Protestants have found much to admire in the writings and policies of Benedict XVI, not only the commitments noted above to Nicene and Chalcedonian doctrine and to traditional sexual ethics but also in the model of gracious learning and clear thinking that he embodies. Indeed, his thoughtful and appreciative engagement with the figure and thought of Martin Luther is a case in point. Given this, his approach

---

34. "Apostolic succession" is the teaching that authoritative continuity in the leadership of the church (the bishops) is rooted in the unbroken historical succession of the same going back to the time of the apostles. A valdid Eucharist preserves the "eucharistic mystery," that is, the belief that the whole Christ is really present in the elements of the Eucharist. See Heinrich Ott, *Fundamentals of Catholic Dogma*, ed. James Canon Bastible (Charlotte: TAN, 1974), 308–9, 381.

to ecumenism might seem surprisingly cautious and even chauvinistic to Protestants who see in him a kindred spirit in our postmodern moment.[35]

Yet Protestants need to understand that ecumenism is always an ecclesiastical activity and thus presupposes an ecclesiology. And for Benedict that ecclesiology is carefully defined by the tradition of thinking that was formally elaborated and codified at Vatican II. His appreciation for the learning, insights, and faith of a Luther or a Melanchthon is one thing; acknowledging that Lutheranism is an equally legitimate form of the Christian church to that of Rome is quite another.

Benedict's ecumenism, in theory and in practice, has been consistent with the teaching of Vatican II. That it has been the subject of Protestant disappointment and criticism is perhaps predictable, but it is ultimately a testimony to the fidelity of Benedict to his church and its teaching. As has proved increasingly the case over recent decades, the pope is often considered to be most offensive when he speaks or acts in ways that are most faithfully Roman Catholic. And that is surely a matter of some considerable irony. Perhaps, in fact, he poses the greatest challenge to Protestants by giving us an example of what it means to be faithful to our convictions even—perhaps especially—when they are in conflict with a broader Christian culture that has, in its own subtle ways, absorbed more of the surrounding relativism than it cares to admit.

---

35. For Ratzinger on Luther, specifically in the context of ecumenical questions, see "Luther and the Unity of the Churches," in *Church, Ecumenism, and Politics*, 100–31.

10

Recentering Ministry on Christ

Joseph Ratzinger on the Priesthood

DAVID NEY

As Cardinal Fring's official theological advisor at the Second Vatican Council, Joseph Ratzinger, later Pope Benedict XVI, had an important role in crafting its documents, including *Lumen Gentium*. *Lumen Gentium* affirms the priesthood of all believers and even claims that the baptized all join in the priestly act of offering the Eucharist to God by virtue of their royal priesthood.[1] The document equally affirms that the ministerial priesthood, the priesthood into which men are initiated through holy orders, differs from this baptismal priesthood in kind and not only in degree. The ministerial priest "teaches and rules the priestly people; acting in the person of Christ, he makes present the Eucharistic sacrifice, and offers it to God in the name of all the people."[2]

As priest, archbishop, and pope, Ratzinger continued to affirm *Lumen Gentium's* understanding of the priesthood of all believers, which in the *Catechism of the Catholic Church* is called the "common priesthood." Yet throughout his ministry, he has taken a particular interest in the ministerial priesthood, which comprises the order of bishops and the order of priests. While he holds, with Roman Catholic tradition, that the fullness of the priesthood is embodied in bishops as icons of Catholic unity, he consistently has focused on priests that are not bishops because he believes that the renewal

---

1. *Lumen Gentium*, Dogmatic Constitution on the Church, November 21, 1964, §9, http://www.vatican.va/archive/hist_councils/ii_vatican_council/documents/vat-ii_const_19641121_lumen-gentium-en.html.
2. *Lumen Gentium*, §10.

of the Roman Catholic Church must come through the christological recentering of parochial ministry. For Ratzinger, Christ is the source of the ministerial priesthood and the one who is manifest through it.

THE PRIESTHOOD'S CHRISTOLOGICAL CENTER

Ratzinger believes that there are two doctrines pertaining to the priesthood that must be reengaged in order to guide the process of christological renewal. The first is the doctrine of apostolic succession, and the second is the sacerdotal understanding of holy orders and therefore Eucharist. For Ratzinger the pastoral function of the doctrine of apostolic succession is to remind priests that the source of their priestly ministry is not themselves but Christ. This source determines the nature of priestly ministry: priests are set apart by holy orders so that Christ's presence might be manifest to the world.

Ratzinger believes that the New Testament basis of the doctrine of apostolic succession is crystal clear. He insists that the Gospels manifestly confirm that while Christ had many followers, he chose twelve men and gave them apostolic authority as the guardians and conduits of his ministry.[3] Yet in a 2011 homily Benedict is careful to maintain that the basis of apostolic succession is not the ministry of these twelve men, but Christ's own ministry. Christ is "the new and eternal priest who made of himself a perfect offering."[4] "Apostolic succession" therefore denotes Christ's continued exercise of his own priesthood through his apostles and their ecclesial descendants. There are priests today—priests are consecrated today—because Christ himself is the great High Priest.

For Benedict, apostolic succession defines priestly ordination as prayer. The role that the church plays in "making" priests is simply to ask the Lord to bestow the exercise of his own priestly ministry on particular members of his body:

---

3. *Lumen Gentium*, §19.
4. Benedict XVI, homily at the Cathedral of Santa Maria la real de la Almudena, Madrid, World Youth Day, August 20, 2011, https://w2.vatican.va/content/benedict-xvi/en/homilies/2011/documents/hf_ben-xvi_hom_20110820_seminaristi-madrid.html.

No man can make another man a priest or a Bishop. It is the Lord himself, through the words of prayer and the act of the imposition of hands, who takes that man totally into his service, draws him into his own Priesthood. It is he himself who consecrates those chosen. He himself the one High Priest who offered the one sacrifice for us all confers on him participation in his own Priesthood so that his word and his work may be present in all the ages.[5]

Priests do not exercise their own authority. Christ is not merely the historic source of the ministerial priesthood; he *continues* to be the source of priestly ministry within the Roman Catholic Church.

Priests are Christ's representatives on earth. The priestly vocation demands that priests remain in the background so that Christ might minister through them.[6] The godly priest does not exercise priestly authority in a way that puts him in competition with Christ and with Christ's exercise of his own priestly authority. To borrow from Aquinas, the priest is the efficient cause of Christ's priestly ministry today. We might even appeal to the classic Reformed distinction between sufficiency and efficiency, and say that while Christ's sacrifice is sufficient, in every respect, there is always the question of efficiency, the human appropriation of this sacrifice, and this is where holy orders come into play.

We thus come to Ratzinger's second theological emphasis, the sacerdotal nature of the ministerial priesthood, which centers on the Eucharist. Ratzinger affirms the traditional Roman Catholic belief that ordination confers the special ability to confect the Eucharist. As the *Catechism* (which shows clear marks of Ratzinger's editorial hand) puts it, the grace conferred by the sacrament of holy orders is the grace of being configured to Christ, and therefore "ordered" to Christ, in a new

5. Benedict XVI, homily, Vatican Basilica, September 12, 2009, https://w2.vatican.va/content/benedict-xvi/en/homilies/2009/documents/hf_ben-xvi_hom_20090912_ord-episcopale.html.
6. Joseph Ratzinger with Vittorio Messori, *The Ratzinger Report: An Exclusive Interview on the State of the Church,* trans. Salvator Attanasio and Graham Harrison (San Francisco: Ignatius, 1985), 56–57.

way. It is thus that ordination newly "orders" the priest to the Eucharist, making him the conduit through which Christ's presence is made known. Historically, Protestants have worried that the Roman Catholic understanding of holy orders puts priests at the center of the church, but Ratzinger celebrates holy orders as a gift that God gives to the church as his appointed means of centering the church not on the priest but on Christ. And what is true with respect to holy orders, for Ratzinger, is true of the Eucharist itself. The celebration of the Eucharist gathers all of God's people, priests and lay people alike and both in their own way, in adoration, around Christ.

Ratzinger reaffirms the traditional Roman Catholic understanding of the ministerial priest as one who bears the yoke of apostolic ministry within the Roman Catholic Church.[7] His particular contribution is to emphasize the christological center of this definition: the priest is one who enters Christ's priesthood in order to exercise Christ's apostolic ministry. It is thus that holy oil becomes, for Ratzinger, an icon of the priesthood. The oil that is brought to the altar and consecrated at the chrism Mass on the eve of Holy Thursday is perfectly good oil, suitable for many mundane purposes, but it has not yet been set apart as sacramental. Once consecrated, however, it acquires elevated functions for the anointing of the sick and baptismal chrism. This oil, though, is not merely blessed in some generic sense; it is brought to the cathedral and to the altar and thus to the center, and this is the key element of its consecration. It *must* be brought to the center before it can be sent out into the world. "This one altar," says Ratzinger,

> which expresses our local Church of Munich and Freising, our diocese in its unity, is in turn, a reference to Jesus Christ himself, who is simultaneously the living altar and the priest. We receive from and in this one cathedral the holy oils, which now go out so that the same sacraments throughout the diocese come

---

7. *Catechism of the Catholic Church*, §427, http://www.vatican.va/archive/ENG0015/__P1D.HTM.

from this one center and thus appear visibly as the fruit of the one sacrament of the death and Resurrection of Jesus Christ.[8]

So too the priest, says Ratzinger. His being consecrated is his coming to the center, who is Christ, so that he might go out and thereby bring Christ to the world. It is thus that the chrism Mass is also what evangelicals might call a time of rededication, the opportunity for priests to reaffirm their vows. As we come to the cathedral and the altar bearing oil for chrism, Ratzinger says to his fellow priests, "it is as though we enter again into the center from which all our strength and mission come. We start again with the Lord, so that once more the life-giving oil might overcome the dryness of everyday routine and bring to life in us the joy of Christ's victory" so that "[in every place] we are the aroma of Christ."[9]

The meaning of priestly ministry is thus, for Ratzinger, found in the two central gestures of priestly ordination: laying on of hands and anointing with oil. First, the bishop, and then other priests, lay hands on the head of the ordinand and the bishop asks Christ, the anointed one, to fill and anoint the ordinand. Second, the bishop anoints the ordinand's hands: having been anointed by Christ, the newly ordained priest is thus consecrated for the purpose of passing on Christ to the world. A priest is someone who is blessed so that he might bless others.[10] Christ has given to him so that he might go out into the world and give Christ to others.

The responsibility of ministering Christ to the world does not elevate the priest but rather brings him to his knees. The priest is one who elevates the host. As priest, bishop, and pope, Ratzinger thus consistently distinguished his office from his person. The supreme statement of this distinction was his decision to step down from his role as pope because of his inability to perform the functions the office requires. Only the Lord knows how heavy bearing the office of the papacy was for

---

8. Benedict XVI, *Teaching and Learning the Love of God: Being a Priest Today*, trans. Michael J. Miller (San Francisco: Ignatius, 2017), 37.
9. Benedict XVI, *Teaching and Learning*, 28.
10. Benedict XVI, *Teaching and Learning*, 189–96.

Benedict. Indeed, the weight of this office would seem unbearable given his humble valuation of himself. In his interview with Peter Seewald, for example, he was asked if he experienced the "dark nights" of the saints of old: "Not as intensely," the Pope Emeritus confesses. "Maybe because I am not holy enough to get so deep into the darkness."[11] Yet Benedict transforms this modest self-assessment into an impetus for prayer: "I need more help from him," he confesses, "but if he lays the yoke on my shoulders, he must also help me bear it."[12]

RECENTERING THE PRIESTHOOD

Joseph Ratzinger is convinced that priestly renewal is never simply a matter of strategically addressing particular clerical problems, because these problems are always symptomatic of a deeper, more troubling, reality: as Christians, priests have lost their connection with Christ, the head "from whom the whole body, supported and held together by its ligaments and sinews, grows as God causes it to grow" (Col 2:19 NIV). Thus, for Ratzinger, the way to protect the church and the world from clerical abuse is to call priests to deeper devotion to Christ. As priests recenter their lives on Christ their ministries will be renewed with the gift of fruitfulness.

Ratzinger's was one of the early voices that drew attention to the new and unprecedented challenges facing the Roman Catholic Church in Europe after the Second World War. In his 1958 lecture "The New Pagans and the Church," Ratzinger enraged church leaders by claiming that the Catholic Church was full of unformed Christians who deserve rather to be called "pagans."[13] Ratzinger has consistently played the role of prophet through his candid analysis of ecclesial predicaments and sins: in particular, the temptation to adapt to modern culture, the

---

11. Benedict XVI with Peter Seewald, *Last Testament: In His Own Words,* trans. Jacob Phillips (London: Bloomsbury, 2017), 9.

12. Benedict XVI with Seewald, *Last Testament,* 184.

13. Joseph Ratzinger, "The New Pagans and the Church: A 1958 Lecture by Joseph Ratzinger (Pope Benedict XVI)," trans. Kenneth Baker, SJ, *Homiletic and Pastoral Review,* January 30, 2017, https://www.hprweb.com/2017/01/the-new-pagans-and-the-church/. This lecture was the fruit of his work among the young people of his parish as a transitional deacon.

continuing appeal of Protestant theological sensibilities, the challenge of clerical celibacy, the problem of clerical abuse, and the problem of declining numbers of priests.

Ratzinger does not regard all church problems as clerical problems. Yet he consistently zeroes in on the clerical dimension of the problems he addresses. In his 1984 interview with Vittorio Messori, Ratzinger went so far as to claim that "the crisis of the Church today is before all else a crisis of priests and religious orders," and of these two groups, it is certainly priests who receive the lion's share of his attention.[14] Ratzinger was never one to stand up on his soapbox and preach clerical reform, but he has steadfastly dedicated himself to the renewal of the ministerial priesthood as the key to church-wide reform. In this, his entire career addresses what critics of the Second Vatican Council regarded as a lack of attention given to the parochial ministry.

Again in his interview with Messori, Ratzinger the prophet complained that the "lostness" of modern culture is its loss of confidence in the certitude that once anchored it, namely, the belief that the bishop and his priests are the "successor of the apostles and hold the fullness of the sacrament of orders."[15] The primary challenge for parish priests today is that the people they are sent to minister to have succumbed to what Ratzinger calls "Protestant arguments."[16] They no longer believe that priests carry the authority of Christ as his representatives on earth.[17]

As he searches for words of encouragement for young ordinands, Ratzinger turns to the prophet Ezekiel. Reflecting on the destruction of Solomon's temple, he concludes that the modern West has analogously experienced a "spiritual destruction of the temple, a crumbling of what had been our spiritual home." "There are no temples in this new world," he says. Young men that "celebrate the Holy Sacrifice for the first time have had an experience like Ezekiel's."[18] Ratzinger's heart goes out to

---

14. Ratzinger with Messori, *Ratzinger Report*, 55.
15. Ratzinger with Messori, *Ratzinger Report*, 58.
16. Joseph Ratzinger, "Biblical Foundations of Priesthood," *Communio* 17, no. 4 (1990): 617–27.
17. Ratzinger with Messori, *Ratzinger Report*, 56.
18. Benedict XVI, *Teaching and Learning*, 218.

these young ordinands, for he believes that they suffer on account of the truth. They share with Ezekiel the conviction that: "God is necessary right now if men are to survive," and they believe that their ministry is necessary only because of this fact.[19] Yet they are told that the world no longer needs them since they are members of an outdated institution.

The renewal of the ministerial priesthood, for Ratzinger, is clearly not a matter of making it compatible with modern sensibilities. Specifically, Ratzinger insists that the institution of priestly celibacy must not be called into question. The distinction between priests and their congregations must remain despite the mounting pressure to redefine the priest as merely a representative of the congregation. The established order of the Roman Catholic priesthood is not in question. Indeed, the world that rejects this priesthood needs it more than ever.

Benedict's high estimation of the ministerial priesthood is, of course, something he has inherited from Roman Catholic tradition. But it is also grounded in personal experience. Benedict speaks of his own ordination as "the high point of his life." He remembers with deep affection the way that his Catholic community gathered around him and his fellow ordinands with fervency and joy in order to see them through the process as an act of devotion to Christ.[20] He also remembers, with special fondness, a mentor whom he upholds as the model priest, a man who died while administering the sacrament to a dying parishioner.[21] Benedict has such high aspirations for the priesthood because he has experienced just how effective it can be.

Benedict believes both that Christ is the source of the priesthood, and that Christ is the one who is made manifest through it irrespective of what the church on earth experiences, whether growth or decline, victory or defeat. As we would expect, Benedict sides with Augustine against the Donatists. Yet the assumption that undergirds his platform of renewal is that greater priestly effectiveness accompanies greater priestly holiness. "The holiness of the Church," said Benedict in a homily

---

19. Benedict XVI, *Teaching and Learning*, 218.
20. Benedict XVI with Seewald, *Last Testament*, 99–100.
21. Benedict XVI with Seewald, *Last Testament*, 100.

in 2011, "is above all the objective holiness of the very person of Christ, of his Gospel and his sacraments, the holiness of that power from on high which enlivens and impels it." But this does not mean that the personal holiness of Christ's ministers is incidental. "We have to be saints," he continues, as he addresses his fellow priests, "so as not to create a contradiction between the sign that we are and the reality that we wish to signify."[22] Christ's holiness must be visible in his ministers if the church on earth is to thrive.

At root, to speak of Ratzinger and the priesthood is to speak of his calling priests to return to the Lord. The renewal of the priesthood that Ratzinger envisions is priests returning, one by one, in faith, to Christ, the source and strength of their ministry. That's the solution—to the problem of clerical abuse, worldwide clerical numerical decline—and any other potential problem that might befall priesthood. "Without a connection to God," Ratzinger says, "we become like satellites that have left their orbits and then hurtle randomly into the void and not only destroy themselves but also threaten others."[23]

Parochial renewal will only take place when priests are "re-collected" to Christ, for priests cannot hope to "collect" others to Christ if they are "unre-collected."[24] The priest, says Ratzinger, "must first and foremost be a *man who believes*," for "the people are waiting for someone to believe before they do," and they rightly expect "above all a priest with deep faith, a priest who prays, a priest who lives according to the program of the Beatitudes."[25] Christ must be more than just the historic foundation of the priest's sacerdotal ministry. He must daily be its source, its inner strength and sustenance. "How should you behave during these years of preparation?" Pope Benedict asks a group of seminarians on their way to priestly ordination. "First of all," he says, "they should be years of interior silence, of unceasing prayer, of constant study and of gradual

22. Benedict XVI, homily, World Youth Day, August 20, 2011.
23. Benedict XVI, *Teaching and Learning*, 70.
24. Benedict XVI, *Teaching and Learning*, 49. See also Romano Guardini, *The Art of Praying: The Principles and Methods of Christian Prayer* (Manchester, NH: Sophia Institute, 1985), 11–17.
25. Benedict XVI, *Teaching and Learning*, 42.

insertion into the pastoral activity and structures of the Church."[26] In other words, inwardness must be the foundation of outward ministry, which should only be pursued modestly and incrementally as the inward life that directs it grows.

Benedict's christological vision for the priesthood emanates from his own devotion to Christ. The very fact that Benedict took the time during his busy pontificate to write his three-volume work on Jesus of Nazareth speaks volumes about his ambition for his church, and his heart. Those who have read even a single volume know something of the depth of his devotion.[27] As he speaks to veterans of the priesthood in a sermon titled "Bringing Christ to the People and the People to Christ," he reminds them, "He sent you, not only to hand on his words, but also to make him known personally, just as you had the privilege of becoming acquainted with him."[28] In his pontifical letter proclaiming a year for priests, he says quite explicitly that the year was inaugurated "to deepen the commitment of all priests to interior renewal for the sake of a stronger and more incisive witness to the Gospel in today's world."[29] Benedict believes that the primary mark of the ministerial priesthood must be friendship with God.

THE CRISIS OF PRIEST SHORTAGE

For Ratzinger, the christological renewal of the priesthood is not an abstract concept. It is his answer, or rather Christ's answer, to even the most troubling realities of history. Embedded in Ratzinger's claim that the renewal of the priesthood must come through its christological recentering is the conviction that whatever the crisis, however great the crisis, Christ is able to overcome it, because he is able to do more than

---

26. Benedict XVI, homily, August 20, 2011.
27. Evangelical readers find in this devotion language they often use for themselves. For example, as Ratzinger reflects on the Lord's Prayer he says, "Each of us, along with our totally personal relationship with God, is received into, and sheltered within this prayer." In 2011, Ratzinger, as Pope Benedict XVI, told the young people at World Youth Day that "Christian faith is not only a matter of believing that certain things are true, but above all a personal relationship with Jesus Christ." Benedict XVI, homily, World Youth Day, August 20, 2011.
28. Benedict XVI, *Teaching and Learning*, 346; see also 103, 106–7, 299.
29. Benedict XVI, *Teaching and Learning*, 355.

we can ask or imagine (Eph 3:20). Of all the enormous challenges facing the ministerial priesthood today, the challenge Ratzinger has given the most attention to, at least publicly, is the crisis of priest shortage.[30] As he engages this crisis we find him palpably wrestling with the idea of christological renewal. Yet it is through these wrestlings that Ratzinger manages to transform ministerial deprivation into an impetus to return to the Lord.

For Ratzinger, the current crisis of the priesthood is just this: fewer and fewer men are entering the priesthood each year.[31] The ordination of new priests thus became, for Ratzinger, a time not merely of celebration, but of apprehension about the future of the church he loves. This apprehension was palpable in 1973 as Ratzinger addressed four ordinands at their first mass in Traunstein (his childhood home), in the Diocese of Munich-Freising.

> I am often overcome by a depressing vision: today in Freising
> four priests are being ordained for a diocese of more than two
> million Catholics. Last year there were five. And the trend will
> continue this way. You can calculate statistically the day on
> which there will be no more priests for the magnificent churches
> of our homeland. And then more will have disappeared than
> a bit of folklore, the way other customs die out. This will be a

---

30. It is impossible to speak either of the crisis of the priesthood, or indeed of Ratzinger's experience of the priesthood, without addressing the problem of clerical abuse. It continues to be appropriate to ask whether the response of the Roman Catholic Church to the revelations of widespread abuse has been adequate. This being said, a thorough investigation of this question falls beyond the scope of this essay. Here it suffices to say that while Ratzinger did not handle things perfectly, we must not forget that he publicly chastised perpetrators and complicit bishops on several occasions, most notably in his pastoral visits to the United States, Malta, Australia, and the United Kingdom, and in his 2010 letter to the Church in Ireland. He also worked hard to ensure that perpetrators were brought to justice in a timely manner, and what is unprecedented, took time out of his busy schedule to meet with victims. The new policy which the Vatican ratified in order to deal with clerical abuse, called *The Sexual Abuse of Minors*, was mandated at Ratzinger's initiative in order to increase the efficiency of investigation and to make sure that guilty priests were stripped of their license to serve. Ratzinger publicly bemoans that "the church suffers as a consequence of infidelity on the part of some of her ministers," and he even claims that "the greatest persecution of the Church comes not from her enemies without, but arises from sin within the Church." Benedict XVI, interview, May 11, 2010, http://w2.vatican.va content/benedict-xvi/en/speeches/2010/may/documents/hf_ben-xvi_spe_20100511_portogallo-interview.html.

31. Ratzinger with Messori, *Ratzinger Report*, 55.

landslide of a completely different sort. A desertification of the spiritual landscape that can horrify even someone who has little use for faith and religion.[32]

Ratzinger cannot imagine a future for a priestless church, because the priesthood, which comprises bishops and the priests that assist him, is a "permanent basic structure of the Church's life, which gives continuity to the organization of the Church throughout history."[33]

Yet for Ratzinger, the problem of priest shortage is not just an administrative or institutional problem within the Roman Catholic Church. It is a problem for the human family at large. The priesthood is a primary conduit, perhaps *the* primary conduit, not merely of God's grace, but of God's very presence within the world. Thus, in his pastoral letter inaugurating the Year of the Priest, Pope Benedict quotes with approval Saint John Mary Vianney, the patron saint of parish priests: "Without the sacrament of Holy Orders, we would not have the Lord."[34]

Ratzinger has always cherished great hopes for spiritual renewal among Catholic youth. One of the most consistent features of his pontificate was his presence at the World Youth Days. Benedict personally addressed Catholic youth at these gatherings in every year of his pontificate, with the exception of the first, and in these addresses, he consistently appealed to young men to consider pursuing priestly ordination. Thus in 2010, for example, he urged "young men and boys to consider if the Lord is inviting them to a greater gift, along the path of priestly ministry." "I ask them," he continued, "to be willing to embrace with generosity and enthusiasm this sign of a special love and to embark on the necessary path of discernment with the help of a priest or a spiritual director."[35]

---

32. Benedict XVI, *Teaching and Learning*, 223.
33. Joseph Ratzinger, "The Theological Locus of Ecclesial Movements," *Communio* 25, no. 3 (1998): 482.
34. Benedict XVI, *Teaching and Learning*, 357.
35. Benedict XVI, message on World Youth Day, March 28, 2010, https://w2.vatican.va/content/benedict-xvi/en/messages/youth/documents/hf_ben-xvi_mes_20100222_youth.html.

Young men must receive the call from the Lord himself. This can only mean one thing. The solution to the problem of numerical decline rests in God's hands. God himself, in his providence, must call more young men to the priesthood for the office of the priesthood, and perhaps for the Roman Catholic Church itself, to survive. Ratzinger stares the mystery of providence square in the face: God himself has given his church over to its current shortage. The primary response of the faithful church to the crisis, therefore, is not improved marketing but rather prayer. Ratzinger made this point explicitly in a farewell address to his priests and deacons when he left his post as archbishop of Munich and Freising to serve under Pope John Paul II as prefect of the Congregation for the Doctrine of the Faith: "The harvest is great, but the laborers are few," Ratzinger reminds them. "Therefore pray the Lord of the harvest to send laborers into the harvest" (Matt 9:38; Luke 10:2).[36]

The experience and mystery of priest shortage is, for Ratzinger, an opportunity to humbly return to the Lord. John Paul II's story of faithful Roman Catholics under Soviet rule became paradigmatic for Ratzinger. John Paul tells of "a custom that developed in many localities behind the Iron Curtain where persecution left no priests."[37] The faithful would gather in an abandoned church or around the tombstone of a deceased priest. They would place a priestly stole on the altar or tombstone and recite the liturgy. Then, at the moment where the consecration of the elements occurs, they would stop, and enter a time of penetrating silence that was often interrupted only by weeping. Ratzinger invites the Catholic faithful of the world to enter into this silence, for it is a silence that providentially calls them back to Christ, the great High Priest.

CONCLUSION

Joseph Ratzinger fully admits that the structures of the Roman Catholic Church often lose their way. But he insists they are not to be jettisoned. They are to be retained because they are redeemable, and their redemption will only come when they are recentered on Christ and are thus

---

36. Benedict XVI, *Teaching and Learning*, 63.
37. Benedict XVI, *Teaching and Learning*, 39.

reoriented toward making Christ known in the world. Ratzinger takes for granted that all Roman Catholic faithful should assist in this process of recentering, but he advocates prayerfulness rather than activism, since Christ is the only hope for the redemption of both the priesthood and the church.

In the face of the revelation of widespread clerical abuse and rapidly falling numbers of ordinations, Roman Catholics can be heartened by Ratzinger's steadfast conviction that the Roman Catholic priesthood is yet redeemable through Christ. As someone who lives in a nation in which 15 of 145 dioceses have declared bankruptcy in the face of lawsuits over clerical abuse, and a diocese in which some priests have been given charge of four parishes as a response to the crisis of priestly shortage, I might be tempted to challenge Ratzinger as overly optimistic. But Ratzinger audaciously faces the bleak circumstances head on: it is this priesthood, and not some other one, that God wishes to redeem, because it is this priesthood, and not some other one, that God has given to his people. To give up on this priesthood would be to give up on Christ. Now as ever, the Roman Catholic priesthood is redeemable not because of its righteousness but because of Christ's righteousness. There is thus no calculus of redeemability.

It is relatively easy to give intellectual assent to the idea of providence, the idea that history is subject to God's benevolent government. But it is easier still to doubt that our personal and ecclesial histories are subject to this government, even as we celebrate the subjection of others. It is one thing to give intellectual assent to the idea that God has redeemed other fallen people and their fallen institutions, but it is quite something else to believe that the fallen people and fallen institutions God has given to us are yet redeemable, often because we have been so deeply wounded by them. Yet Ratzinger insists that to speak of the realm of redemption is to speak of the things that now surround us, the specific, given realities that constitute our individual lives.

Ratzinger's emphasis on the singular redeemability of the Roman Catholic priesthood presupposes the entrenched polemics of Christian division. Yet his steadfast and prayerful hope is laden with ecumenical potential, because of his willingness to engage the troubling circumstances of Christians suffering ministerial deprivation. We might take his reflections on the experience of priest shortage behind the Iron Curtain as paradigmatic. For some Protestants and evangelicals, the way to respond to these reflections is to engage Ratzinger in an argument about the validity of Roman Catholic orders. But to do so is to miss what is most important, and most sacred, about the experience in question: it is not just the experience of a particular group of Roman Catholics waiting for someone with the right kind of collar. It is the experience of Christians waiting for their great High Priest to return. Waiting and praying was their faithful response, as Roman Catholics, to the experience of ministerial deprivation. They were drinking this earthly cup "to its very dregs" as an act of Christian hope.[38]

Ratzinger's christological recentering of the priesthood demands an alternative understanding of what it means to be in a state of ministerial deprivation. Priest or no priest, Christians all find themselves ministerially deprived as they await the parousia, because, ultimately, they are not waiting for someone with a collar. They are groaning inwardly for the perfect ministrations of Christ, the great High Priest (Rom 8:23). Protestants disheartened by the failure of synodal and episcopal accountability structures and evangelicals worried that congregational authority has been hopelessly corrupted by a syncretistic embrace of the corporate leadership model easily lose heart. But it is these failings that bring Protestants and evangelicals into fraternal kinship with Roman Catholics. These failings force Protestants and evangelicals to acknowledge that they are likewise, under God, members of the first Adam, subject to original sin, and therefore directed to live their lives outside of the garden. Having thus acknowledged this status, God invites Protestants and evangelicals to get down on their knees as an act of solidarity with other members of the second Adam who call out, "Come, Lord Jesus" in the face of ministerial deprivation. So perhaps Protestants and evangelicals that refuse to apply a calculus of

---

38. Dietrich Bonhoeffer, *Letters and Papers from Prison*, ed. Eberhard Bethge (New York: Touchstone, 1997), 337.

redeemability to their own church structures honor Ratzinger's legacy. And more importantly, perhaps they honor Christ, for this refusal is their articulated Christian hope.

> It is good for a man to bear the yoke
>> while he is young.
> Let him sit alone in silence,
>> for the Lord has laid it on him. (Lam 3:27–28 NIV)

PART II

LITURGICAL THEOLOGY

11

One Book, One Body

Joseph Ratzinger on the Bible and the Liturgy

PETER J. LEITHART

In a discussion of Sabbath and Sunday, Joseph Ratzinger[1] observes, "As with all the major themes of theology, the issue of correctly determining the relationship between the Old and the New Testament proves to be fundamental here."[2] It is a characteristic and penetrating comment. It is characteristic in that it highlights Ratzinger's commitment to working out theological conclusions, and liturgical theology in particular, from Scripture. It is penetrating in the way it isolates a key problem of all Christian theology, especially in liturgical theology.

Ratzinger's treatment of Sabbath and Sunday illustrates the complexities of adjudicating the relation of Old and New. What Ignatius identified as a move from being a "follower of the Sabbath" to life "according to the Day of the Lord"[3] is, Ratzinger discerns, far more than a change of schedule. It was bound up with the eventual divergence of the church and synagogue. Sabbath and Lord's Day "confront each other as two fundamentally different life-styles," the first embedded within a set of ordinances and the latter a "life from what is to come, from hope."[4]

---

1. In this paper, I identify the subject primarily as "Joseph Ratzinger," sometimes as "Benedict XVI." My usage does not distinguish between pre- and postpapal writings. Many of his writings on liturgy were published in some form prior to his accession to the papacy.

2. Joseph Ratzinger, *Collected Works*, vol. 2, *Theology of the Liturgy: The Sacramental Foundation of Christian Existence*, ed. Michael J. Miller, trans. John Saward et al. (San Francisco: Ignatius, 2014), 201. Hereafter, this volume will be cited as *Theology of the Liturgy*. The discussion of Sabbath and Sunday is from the essay "The Resurrection as the Foundation of Christian Liturgy—On the Meaning of Sunday for Christian Prayer and Christian Life," originally published as part of Ratzinger's book *A New Song for the Lord: Faith in Christ and Liturgy Today*, trans. Martha M. Matesich, 2nd ed. (New York: Crossroad, 2005).

3. Quoted in Ratzinger, *Theology of the Liturgy*, 194.

4. Ratzinger, *Theology of the Liturgy*, 194.

Yet the day of the Lord is not a complete *novum,* but rises from and completes the biblical theology of the Sabbath. The seventh day of creation is God's definitive judgment that creation is good, and links creation to covenant. The Sabbath establishes that redemption cannot become a "worldless piety" or ignore metaphysics, and the Christian Sunday affirms the same: "Wherever the Sabbath or Sunday is cherished, creation is cherished as well."[5] Sabbath is a sign of Israel's liberation from Egyptian slavery, a promise of continuing release "of all the children of God and creation's release from anxiety." Masters and slaves share the rest of the Sabbath, and thus "the Sabbath is the heart of social legislation."[6] Insofar as the Sabbath anticipates the "messianic hour," Israel's entry into rest imitates God and engages in "a preliminary exercise in the world to come." The cult of Sabbath runs contrary to pagan cult, where "the gods create men in order to be fed by them" and "men need the gods to keep the course of the world in order." For a Sabbath-keeping people, "cult means the liberation of man through their participation in the freedom of God" and therefore the "liberation of creation itself." In the Sabbath, in short, cultic, social, and eschatological dimensions are inseparable.[7] In this profound sense, Sabbath is made for man, not man for the Sabbath.

Jesus' apparent Sabbath-breaking was in fact a defense of "the essential meaning of the Sabbath as a feast of freedom." It is a radical error to think that "the meaning of the Sabbath is completely opposed to that of Sunday."[8] In his resurrection on the first day, the day after the Sabbath, Jesus "brings the approval of the seventh day of creation, his saying that all is good, to completion." In the incarnation, God the Son takes the creation to himself; in his resurrection he transforms it "into a permanence beyond all transience."[9] With Sabbath as with all Torah, Jesus comes to fulfill and not to destroy.

---

5. Ratzinger, *Theology of the Liturgy,* 197–98.
6. Ratzinger, *Theology of the Liturgy,* 198. Here as elsewhere, Ratzinger understands liturgical theology as a mode of public theology.
7. Ratzinger, *Theology of the Liturgy,* 199.
8. Ratzinger, *Theology of the Liturgy,* 200–201.
9. Ratzinger, *Theology of the Liturgy,* 192.

Maintaining a strong link between Old and New enables Ratzinger to link Christian liturgy with "natural sacramentality," with cultural practices, and with metaphysics. Sacraments, material things that are transparent to God, point to the general truth that "things are more than things." Things "are not known exhaustively when one has understood their chemical and physical properties, because then another whole dimension of their reality still eludes one: their transparency toward the creative power of God." Since things are not merely things, human beings are not mere functionaries who manipulate things; "rather, only by examining the world with respect to its eternal first cause does man learn who he himself is: someone called by God and to God."[10]

For instance, even outside of explicitly liturgical settings, meals are sacramental occasions:

> Human eating is something different from the food intake of an animal: eating attains its human dimension by becoming a meal. Having a meal, however, means experiencing the delightfulness of those things whereby men are supplied with the gift of the earth's fertility, and having a meal means to experience also ... the company of other men: a meal creates community, eating is complete only when it happens in company. ... In this way the meal becomes a very penetrating interpretation of what it means to be a man, of human existence. ... In a meal man discovers that he is not the founder of his own being but lives his existence in receptivity.[11]

Liturgy does not occupy a zone of narrowly religious devotion, but intersects with, sometimes criticizes and judges, the practices of human culture more broadly. As with pagan sacramentality, the Christian concept of sacrament implies "an interpretation of the world, of man, and of God."[12]

---

10. Ratzinger, *Theology of the Liturgy*, 161–62.
11. Ratzinger, *Theology of the Liturgy*, 156–57.
12. Ratzinger, *Theology of the Liturgy*, 161.

Because Ratzinger strives to be a biblical theologian, the problem of relating the Old to the New is fundamental to his thought.[13] He insists that Christianity is a historical religion, and that the Bible is a record of that salvation history. It is a single history, unified by the purpose of God to unite humanity in one family, to give all nations a share in the history of Abraham and Israel. This, he insists, is the mission of Jesus.[14] That purpose was originally announced in the covenant with Abraham, which begins "God's great plan to make humanity one family through the covenant with a new people." Initiated with Abraham, implemented throughout Israel's history, the purpose comes to a climax in Christ.[15] Ratzinger's understanding of the unity of salvation history grounds a typological reading in which the shadows of the Old Testament anticipate the fulfillment of the new. Yet, for all his stress on the unity of this sacred history, Benedict is also aware of the discontinuities; fulfillment is not simply a repetition of the promise, but transcends the promise. Fulfillment transposes the Old into a New key, as the concealed is revealed in Jesus.

This framework leaves the biblical theologian with a delicate task. If one ignores the transforming discontinuity of the incarnation and resurrection, we are stuck in the Old, in the flesh with a Torah that cannot give life. Yet if we uproot Christian time-keeping from Israel's Sabbath, Christianity "becomes a clublike pastime and liturgy turns into entertainment."[16] Different Christian traditions have veered in one direction or another. Some, overwhelmed by the radical newness of the New, fail to see that it fulfills the Old; others replicate patterns of liturgy and life from the Old and run the risk of a form of Judaizing. For Ratzinger, getting the relation of Old and New right is essential to maintaining

---

13. For a superb summary of Ratzinger's thought on this issue, see Scott W. Hahn, *Covenant and Communion: The Biblical Theology of Pope Benedict XVI* (Grand Rapids: Brazos, 2009), especially chaps. 5–6.

14. Joseph Ratzinger, *Many Religions, One Covenant: Israel, the Church and the World*, trans. Graham Harrison (San Francisco: Ignatius, 1999), 26–28, quoted in Hahn, *Covenant and Communion*, 132.

15. Benedict XVI, Homily, Solemnity of the Epiphany of the Lord, January 6, 2018, quoted in Hahn, *Covenant and Communion*, 123.

16. Ratzinger, *Theology of the Liturgy*, 200–201.

orthodoxy and catholicity. If there is to be one church, she has to theologize and live in accord with the revelation of a unified Bible.

This demands a restoration of the typological interpretation of the Bible, which is the basis for the "Catholic concept of *sacramentum*." When the Old Testament is not read typologically, the church loses track of the New as well as the Old. The New Testament is not a new Scripture but offers "directions on how to understand the Christic content of the Old Testament." It is possible to gain a historical and literal understanding of the Old Testament without typology, but in rejecting typology the modern reader "radically rejects the New Testament and its understanding of the Old."[17]

In the following, I explore two issues of liturgical theology in some detail, both of which illustrate Ratzinger's interest in (obsession with?) the Old-New relationship: Church music and the essential nature of Eucharist.[18] Though both issues illustrate Ratzinger's profoundly biblical liturgical theology, they also highlight a tension between Ratzinger's commitment to the Catholic tradition and his interest in rapprochement with Protestants. Ratzinger demonstrates the ecumenical potency of a biblically grounded liturgical theology; but at a crucial point he fails to find common ground, and he does so, I argue, precisely because he fails to follow through consistently with his approach to the Old-New relation.[19]

---

17. Ratzinger, *Theology of the Liturgy*, 177–78. For Ratzinger, scriptural words are themselves *sacramenta futuri*, and the events of Israel's history are *"sacramenta* of what is to come." Israel's liturgical forms are also *sacramenta*, while the sacraments of the new are old promises fulfilled (179). This, he argues, provides a proper basis for understanding the Catholic affirmation of *ex opera operato Christi*, which means "the sacraments now no longer work by foreshadowing and asking; rather, they are effective as a result of what has already happened, and therein is manifest the act of liberation accomplished by Christ" (180).

18. Ratzinger applies this pattern of biblical reasoning to church architecture in "'Built from Living Stones': The House of God and the Christian Way of Worshipping God," in *Theology of the Liturgy*, 371–89. This essay is also found in *A New Song for the Lord*, 78–93.

19. See Michael Horton's criticisms of Ratzinger's covenant theology in *Covenant and Salvation: Union with Christ* (Louisville: Westminster John Knox, 2007), 25–29. Horton charges that Ratzinger is inconsistent, but that in the final analysis the pope absorbs law into gospel. Horton's criticisms depend on an understanding of covenant and the law-gospel distinction that I do not share.

THEOLOGY OF CHURCH MUSIC

Music is dear to Ratzinger's heart.[20] His brother, Georg, served for many years as the choirmaster of the Regensburg Cathedral. In an address delivered on the occasion of his brother's retirement,[21] Ratzinger suggests that "one cannot speak of liturgy without also talking about the music of worship."[22] Elsewhere he makes the point more strongly: "Wherever people praise God, words alone do not suffice. ... Everywhere it has called on music for help." Worship "is singing in unison with that which all things bespeak."[23]

Music is not, as some theologians suggest, merely a utilitarian matter, nor a matter of popular taste and style, nor a merely aesthetic adornment of an essentially nonmusical liturgy. Liturgy *is* musical, and the kind of music that the church uses is a question for theological analysis.

In Ratzinger's view, the church is ill-equipped to grapple with issues surrounding liturgical music because of the "somewhat cool" relation between theology and church music. When Thomas Aquinas turns to music in *Summa theologiae* II–II, he has to reckon with three authorities critical of church music. Jerome urges Christian to "sing to God with their hearts, not with their voices"; Gregory the Great warns that a beautiful voice might be a cover for an evil life; Thomas picks up another patristic theme when he rejects the use of musical instruments in the church "lest she appear to be falling back into Jewish ways."[24]

Ratzinger is not dismissive of these critiques, but probes to discover their "positive significance." While the church aims to transform "creation into the mode of being of the Holy Spirit," this transformation necessarily involves both death and renewal. For that reason, "the

---

20. The same material has been published in both Ratzinger, *Theology of the Liturgy*, 421–79, and Ratzinger, *The Feast of Faith: Approaches to a Theology of the Liturgy*, trans. Graham Harrison (San Francisco: Ignatius, 1986), 97–126. See also Ratzinger, *The Spirit of the Liturgy*, trans. John Saward (San Francisco: Ignatius, 2000), 136–56.

21. Joseph Ratzinger, "'In the Presence of the Angels I will Sing Your Praise': The Regensburg Tradition and the Reform of the Liturgy," in *Theology of the Liturgy*, 461–79.

22. Ratzinger, *Theology of the Liturgy*, 470.

23. Ratzinger, *Theology of the Liturgy*, 443. This is from an essay titled "The Image of the World and of Man in the Liturgy and Its Expression in Church Music," originally published in *A New Song for the Lord*.

24. Ratzinger, *Theology of the Liturgy*, 425–27.

Church has had to be critical of all ethnic music; it could not be allowed untransformed into the sanctuary." Pagan music is often *a-logikos*, and therefore unfit for worship in and of the *Logos*. The music of the pagan theater is often the target of the early church's attacks, and Ratzinger believes that such music *needed* to be critiqued and set aside.

Ratzinger is not afraid to make applications to contemporary music, which, he argues, fails to express a biblical anthropology. Ratzinger finds a key to liturgical music in Romans 12, where Paul exhorts the Romans to offer "reasonable service," *logikē latreia*. *Logos* here does not merely mean reason or language. Logos is "self-interpreting, self-communicating spirit," and ultimately refers to the living reality of the incarnate Word.[25] Worship and its music must engage the whole person. Music offers sensuous and emotional experiences, but it must also be *intelligible*. Dionysian music has no place in Christian liturgy, and by Dionysian Ratzinger means pop and rock music. He does not mince words:

> Music has become today the decisive vehicle of a counterreli-
> gion and thus the showplace for the discerning of spirits. On
> the one hand, since rock music seeks redemption by way of
> liberation from the personality and its responsibility, it fits very
> precisely into the anarchistic ideas of freedom that are manifest-
> ing themselves more openly all over the world. But that is also
> exactly why such music is diametrically opposed to the Christian
> notions of redemption and freedom, indeed their true contra-
> diction. Music of this type must be excluded from the Church,
> not for aesthetic reasons, not out of reactionary stubbornness,
> not because of historical rigidity, but because of its very nature.[26]

This may seem no more than a rant from a grumpy nonagenarian. In fact, Ratzinger's assessment of rock music is consistent with his approach to modernity. Tracey Rowland has suggestively observed that John Paul

---

25. Ratzinger, *Theology of the Liturgy*, 453.
26. Ratzinger, *Theology of the Liturgy*, 456. One can hardly contemplate what would happen if Benedict were to step into an evangelical megachurch worship service. Nonagenarian though he is, I suspect the result would be somewhat analogous to overturning tables of money changers.

battled obvious expressions of what he called the "culture of death"—abortion, dehumanizing sexuality, war, economic degradation. In terms of the transcendentals, John Paul was an advocate for the true and the good. Benedict has focused more on the modern corrosion of the third transcendental, beauty. He zeroes in on "practices which diminish the possibilities of the soul or the self, for its own transcendence. The marketing of vulgar art, music, and literature and the generation of a very low, even barbaric, mass culture is seen by Ratzinger to be one of the serious pathologies of contemporary western culture."[27]

While acknowledging the force of the patristic and medieval critiques of music, Ratzinger is remarkably blunt in criticizing the tradition, especially its handling of the relation of Old and New. The fundamental problem with the patristic critique of music is "a one-sidedly 'spiritual' understanding of the relationship between the Old and New Testaments, between law and gospel." The musical worship and instruments of temple worship were spiritualized into human voices or, in some extreme cases, into purely interior song. Ratzinger sniffs something Greek here. He admits that the church and Platonism "pursue parallel courses for quite a distance," but the church must follow a different course when Platonism opposes allegorizing to the world of sense. With regard to music, the church fathers were too Platonist. With its early and resolute opposition to Gnosticism, the church certainly did not follow Platonism fully down this path, but it did follow it too far.[28]

Another factor behind the critique of music was the church's fraught connection with the synagogue. Ratzinger argues that the earliest liturgies "linked up as a matter of historical necessity with the synagogue, not the Temple," and this lent a "more or less puritan form" to Christian worship. Though Christians did not imitate temple worship in their liturgical forms, they struggled to express the church's continuity with temple liturgy. Ratzinger highlights the question of priesthood: Did the church make "a definitive and fundamental break with the idea of

27. Tracey Rowland, Ratzinger's *Faith: The Theology of Pope Benedict XVI* (Oxford: Oxford University Press, 2008), 9.
28. Ratzinger, *Theology of the Liturgy*, 428–29.

priesthood, or must the Temple's authentic inheritance be continued, once it has undergone a christological transformation?"[29]

Platonic allegory and attachment to the synagogue produced an ambiguity about music in worship. On the one hand, God should be praised in the heart not by the body, and so "no status can be accorded to music, to the audible form of this praise." But then there was the obvious fact that Christians actually did sing in worship. To get around this impasse, music was "relegated to a secondary level," pedagogically useful but not essential to the worship of God. Thomas concluded that music was necessary "not for God's sake, but for the sake of the worshipper," a sign, Ratzinger thinks, of how deeply "the ancient world's concept of God's absolute immutability and impassibility had entered into Christian thought through Greek philosophy."[30]

A more deeply Christian understanding of church music requires a more Christian approach to the Old-New problem. Even the apostles read the Old Testament "spiritually" and "allegorically," yet a genuinely Christian reading is not merely a spiritualization; "it also implies incarnation,"[31] or, we might say, a "humanization" of the temple and its worship. In this framework, the church can affirm the Psalms' "utterly unpuritanical delight in music," share joy "through celebratory music-making," and so manifest that joy as "the presence of the glory that is God." In liturgical song, the Creator's glory is manifested "in the music of creation" and "in its creative transformation by the mind of the believing and beholding man." With a proper "incarnational" grasp of the relation of Old and New, the church's liturgical music is not longer simply utilitarian, an aid to piety, or a dangerous distraction. Liturgical music instead takes on "cosmic" dimension, as it orchestrates "the mystery of Christ with all the voices of creation" and ascends to God in praise.[32]

---

29. Ratzinger, *Theology of the Liturgy*, 429–30. Priesthood, Ratzinger observes, illustrates "how intractable, so far, the problem of the relationship of the Testaments to one another has proved" (430).

30. Ratzinger, *Theology of the Liturgy*, 431–32; cf. 165.

31. Ratzinger, *Theology of the Liturgy*, 428.

32. Ratzinger, *Theology of the Liturgy*, 433–34.

Ratzinger's explication of the church's theology of liturgical music is thrilling, but the path toward his final celebration needs to be carefully noted: Everything depends on getting the Old-New relation right, and, importantly, depends on recognizing where the church has *failed* to get it right. Unfortunately, Ratzinger is not always as skeptical about the tradition as he is in regard to music.

MEAL OR EUCHARIST?

One of the central debates among Catholic theologians following Vatican II had to do with the essential character of the Mass: Is the Mass a sacrifice or a meal? Behind this is the liturgical movement, which focused not on the traditional dogmatic questions about real presence but on ritual and its structures. From an analysis of the Last Supper, liturgical theologians concluded that "the Eucharist's basic structure was unequivocally that of a meal."[33] This raised a problem for Roman Catholics: "Was this not the same as Luther's position, which was condemned by Trent?" This approach also seemed to sideline the sacrificial character of the Mass, defended and elaborated by dogmatic theologians in the Catholic tradition.[34] Ratzinger also spies here a central problem of modern theology: If Jesus instituted a ritual *meal* and the church celebrates something else, then a gap is opened between Jesus and the church that might become a chasm.

Ratzinger worries that, post–Vatican II, the church will be reduced to a purely human community. A meal concept of the Eucharist can treat the church as a self-enclosed community, sitting in a circle looking at and to one another. The church, however, is the body of *Christ*, and lives only by looking away from herself, upward to the source of

---

33. Ratzinger, *Theology of the Liturgy*, 300. Much of what follows is from Ratzinger, "Form and Content of the Eucharistic Celebration," also published in *Feast of Faith*, 33–60.
34. Ratzinger, *Theology of the Liturgy*, 300–301.

her life. Insisting on the sacrificial dimension of the Mass protects the church from collapsing into clubbishness.[35]

Ratzinger offers several lines of argument in defense of a dogmatic approach to the Eucharist. Arguments in favor of a "meal structure" often appeal directly to the founding texts that describe Jesus' Last Supper with his disciples. It seems a decisive argument. After all, "Can there ever be any other standard than that given by Jesus himself?"[36] But there are complications. Jesus ate a full Passover meal with his disciples, yet no one proposes that the church perpetuate the entire Passover feast.[37] Passover was a "household meal," but from the first the church celebrated the Eucharist as the "household of Jesus Christ." What was instituted at the Last Supper was not so much the meal as the eucharistic action: "Jesus' command to repeat the action does not refer to the Last Supper as a whole at all, but to the specifically Eucharistic action,"[38] the giving of thanks, understood as a sacrifice.

Ratzinger argues that the development of the Mass bears out his point. He cites Joseph Pascher's argument that the Eucharist inserts sacrificial themes—the separation of body and blood especially—into the meal pattern, thus fundamentally affecting the nature of the event. He acknowledges that in apostolic times the Eucharist was linked with community meals, but, following Josef Jungmann, Ratzinger claims that by the end of the first century, meal and eucharist were decoupled, leaving a fundamental *eucharistic* structure in place. Prior to Luther's use in the sixteenth century, only Paul had described the event as a "Supper"

---

35. Ratzinger, *Theology of the Liturgy*, 361. This point also comes out in Ratzinger's discussions of eucharistic orientation. He expresses concern about the postconciliar tendency to "make the congregation into a closed circle that is no longer aware of the explosive trinitarian dynamisms that gives the Eucharist its greatness." The church, he insists, "does not carry on a dialogue with itself; it is engaged on a common journey toward the returning Lord" (*Theology of the Liturgy*, 390). This is overstated. Insofar as those who receive the Spirit become "rivers of living water," a church is never merely "a dialogue with itself." Ratzinger's argument assumes a one-directional flow of grace from God through the priest to the people, rather than the more complex pattern of Paul's description of the body of Christ, in which the Spirit equips *every* member to contribute to the body's self-edification (Rom 12; 1 Cor 12; Eph 4).

36. Ratzinger, Theology of the Liturgy, 303.

37. Ratzinger, Theology of the Liturgy, 357 (from an essay titled "Eucharist—Communio—Solidarity").

38. Ratzinger, *Theology of the Liturgy*, 305–6.

(1 Cor 11:20).[39] Calling the event a "Eucharist," the church tapped into the late antique notion of a "verbal sacrifice and gave it a deeper religious and theological significance":

> The Eucharistic Prayer is an entering into the prayer of Jesus Christ himself; hence it is the Church's entering into the Logos, the Father's Word, into the Logos' self-surrender to the Father, which, in the Cross, has also become the surrender of mankind to him. So, on the one hand, *eucharistia* made a bridge to Jesus' words of blessing at the Last Supper, in which he actually underwent, in an inward and anticipatory manner, his death on the cross; and, on the other hand, it built a bridge to the theology of the Logos and hence to a Trinitarian deepening of the theology of Eucharist and of the Cross.[40]

In the experience of Christians, this means that death has been "transformed into a word of acceptance and self-surrender."[41] By his death, the *Logos* makes *the* absurd—death—*logikos*. For Ratzinger, recognizing that the Mass is fundamentally Eucharist heals the apparent breach between liturgy and dogma, Jesus and the church. It shows the continuity between the performed liturgy and the development of sacramental theology, and between the institution of Jesus and the practice of the church.

This analysis supports the traditional Roman Catholic practice of the Mass, in which the meal is radically subordinated to the eucharistic prayer and sacrificial action of the priest. Ratzinger provides a biblically grounded way of justifying celebrations of the Eucharist performed in the absence of a congregation, or performed without the host and cup being offered to a present congregation.

---

39. For Protestants, of course, this hardly counts as decisive. It only means that the church mislaid an essential dimension of the Eucharist very early. Pascher and Jungmann were both pioneers of Catholic liturgical reform in the decades prior to the Second Vatican Council. Recent liturgical theologians have questioned central details of Jungmann's historical account and his vision of liturgical reform. See Alcuin Reid, *The Organic Development of the Liturgy*, 2nd ed. (San Francisco: Ignatius, 2005), 164–72.
40. Ratzinger, *Theology of the Liturgy*, 302.
41. Ratzinger, *Theology of the Liturgy*, 302–3.

Yet Ratzinger's argument takes a number of odd twists. For starters, Ratzinger is unwilling to consider the possibility that the church deviated in any way from the apostolic trajectory.[42] It is hardly surprising that Ratzinger refrains from criticizing the Catholic tradition at this point, given the historical, dogmatic, and practical stakes. Yet his unwillingness to concede the possibility of error is striking given his sharp critique of patristic thought about music. It seems *possible*, at least, that a church that misconstrues the Old-New relation with regard to music might do something similar with regard to food.

Besides, the substance of his arguments does not always fully support his conclusions. He concludes that "*eucharistia* is the gift of *communio* in which the Lord becomes our food," as well as signifying "the self-offering of Jesus Christ, perfecting his Trinitarian Yes to the Father by his consent to the Cross and reconciling us all to the Father in this 'sacrifice.'"[43] First Corinthians 11:16–17 is in the background, since there Paul links the *koinōnia* in the body and blood with *breaking* the bread and *blessing* the cup, not with eating and drinking. Even if we grant the point, though, on Ratzinger's formulation the eucharistic action is directed toward the Lord-made-food. That is, *eucharistia* is ordered to the end of eating and drinking.[44] To prioritize the Eucharist over the meal, to treat the Eucharist as if it is a separable action, is as odd as offering table prayer for a meal that is not eaten. Biblically put, if Ratzinger can find some Pauline support, he ignores the Johannine theme: Unless you *eat* my flesh and *drink* my blood, you have no life in yourselves (John 6:53).

Ratzinger's treatment of this question is wrapped up in his understanding of the Old-New relation. In a postscript to his essay on the form and content of the eucharistic celebration, Ratzinger summarizes

42. He states this claim explicitly: Though "what is fine, sublime, about the Church is that she is growing, maturing, understanding the mystery more profoundly," still "we have to say that the Church could not possibly have been celebrating the Eucharist unworthily for nine hundred years" (*Theology of the Liturgy*, 281). Putting it so strongly prejudices the case, however. Even if the church celebrated Eucharist "worthily," she could have celebrated immaturely or even with some taints of error.

43. Ratzinger, *Theology of the Liturgy*, 311.

44. I assume here that Ratzinger is actually speaking about food and not about a communion that partakes of Christ in some food-like fashion, yet without physical food.

the work of Hartmut Gese on the origin of the Lord's Supper.[45] Though Gese acknowledges that Jesus' death fulfilled the Passover, he denies that the Eucharist originated in the Passover meal.[46] Instead, Gese argues, the Lord's Supper took its origin from a form of the peace offering, the tôdâ, "thank offering."

The *tôdâ* was a type of "peace offering" or "sacrifice" (*zebah*; Lev 7:11–18), offered in gratitude for rescue from death, illness, or persecution. A *tôdâ* celebrates a state of shalom following deliverance from danger. The worshiper confesses God's deliverance, often in a song of thanks, and invites members of his community to share a feast. Psalms 22, 40, and 69 are *tôdâ*, celebrating Yahweh's saving acts in the context of a feast, and Gese argues that lament psalms that conclude with thanksgiving for deliverance also reflect the *Sitz im Leben* of the *tôdâ* meal. *Tôdâ* offerings are not gifts to God but offer homage to God as deliverer. They are a fitting celebratory response to deliverance. The feast embodies the reality of deliverance, "God's gift that the one rescued can begin his life anew in the sacred meal."[47]

Though the *tôdâ* was originally confined to a few friends of the thankful worshiper, over time it took on eschatological coloration and came to represent the hope of Israel and the nations: "the basic experience of death and deliverance in the *todah* spirituality could be made into an absolute, and deliverance from death led to the conversion of the world, to enabling the dead to participate in life, and to eternal proclamation of salvation."[48]

---

45. The postscript is found in *Theology of the Liturgy*, 312–18. Gese's article was originally published as "Die Herkunft des Herrenmahls," in *Zur biblischen Theologie* (Munich: Kaiser, 1977), 107–27. An English translation is found in Hartmut Gese, "The Origin of the Lord's Supper," in *Essays on Biblical Theology*, trans. Keith Crim (Minneapolis: Augsburg, 1981), 117–40. Tim Gray has developed Gese's argument in *From Jewish Passover to Christian Eucharist: The Todah Sacrifice as Background for the Last Supper* (Steubenville, OH: Emmaeus Road, 2006).

46. Gese may be correct that the *form* of the Eucharist is not indebted to these earlier meal events (though cf. the use of "take, give thanks" in Matt 15:36 and John 6:11). Still, Gese, in my judgment, minimizes the connections between these various meals and the Eucharist. The fact that Jesus ate and drank regularly with his disciples, and performed food miracles, provides some of the background to the church's continuing memorialization of Jesus in a meal.

47. Gese, "Origin," 128–29.

48. Gese, "Origin," 133.

Gese points to several details that link the *tôdâ* ritual with the eucha-ristic rite. In Psalm 116, the psalmist raises the "cup of salvation," a ges-ture connected with the proclamation of Yahweh's salvation. Further, in contrast to the grain offering (*minhâ*, "tribute"; Lev 2), the *tôdâ* is cele-brated with everyday leavened bread rather than the unleavened bread of the Passover.[49] The *tôdâ*, in short, combines several elements that later appear in eucharistic liturgies: Thanksgiving; a recital of Yahweh's mighty acts; bread and wine, loaf, and cup.[50] Against this background, Gese criticizes penitential performances of the Supper and silent litur-gies that do not proclaim Jesus' victory and deliverance.[51]

The *tôdâ* also fills out the *theology* of the Eucharist. The Last Supper, which institutes a continuous sacramental meal, is the "dedication of Jesus as the sacrifice, prior to his death." Jesus sets His own death in motion, but he does so in confidence that he will be raised. The contin-uation of the Supper in the church is the "thank offering ... of the One who is risen," the form of "the new beginning of Jesus' life from death," a celebration of the "Easter event of deliverance." By drinking from the cup of Jesus' thanksgiving, a worshiper "becomes a party to this cove-nant of blood," participates in the rescue of Jesus.[52]

For Ratzinger, this perspective on the Eucharist can help to heal the historical breach between Catholic and Protestant, since "it gives us a genuinely New Testament concept of sacrifice that both preserves the complete Catholic inheritance ... and ... is receptive to Luther's central intentions." This ecumenical synthesis is possible because Gese's thesis brings the "inner unity of both Testaments to light."[53]

But Ratzinger is able to so fully endorse Gese's argument only because he distorts Gese's conclusions. Ratzinger rightly notes that the *tôdâ* includes a notion of verbal sacrifice that takes the form of a *eucharis-tia*. Yet Gese nowhere suggests that the *tôdâ* aims at a "total interiorizing

---

49. Gese, "Origin," 130. Though leavened bread is prescribed for the todah (Lev 7:13), it is not clear that it constitutes an exception to offering leaven on the altar (cf. Lev 2:11).
50. The use of wine is not as unique to the *tôdâ* as Gese suggests. Num 15:1–16 prescribes offerings of bread and wine for every "burnt offering" ('ôlâ) and sacrifice (zebaḥ).
51. Gese, "Origin," 138–39.
52. Gese, "Origin," 135–38.
53. Ratzinger, *Theology of the Liturgy*, 317.

of the *torah*."[54] Nor, it would seem, does Ratzinger want any such thing from the Eucharist. His conclusion that Gese proves that "*eucharistia*, or *eulogia*, is the determining 'form' in the Eucharist" is misleading.[55] Gese does not set Eucharist over against a sacred meal, or raise the thankful confession to a place of primacy over the secondary meal; rather, the meal is the setting for *eucharistia*, and eating and drinking is both the form of thanksgiving and a participation in the salvation of Jesus. Ratzinger can only find support in Gese's article by changing the meaning of *eucharistia*.[56]

Ratzinger, in short, does not carry through his stated method in dealing with the *tôdâ*. By subordinating the meal dimension of the Eucharist, his treatment verges toward the "over-spiritualization" reflected in patristic treatments of music. He is not, at this point, fully incarnational; instead, he places a caesura between the festive food event of the *tôdâ* and the verbal event of the Eucharist. And precisely for this reason, he does not take full advantage of the ecumenical import of Gese's work on the thank offering, but instead defends the features of the Roman Catholic Eucharist that Protestants find most offensive.

CONCLUSION

Ratzinger has no liturgical theology that he would wish to identify as "his." He instead seeks to illuminate, explain, and at times correct the inherited liturgical life and theology of the church. But he is a creative thinker just the same, not least in his use of Scripture and his focus on the crucial problem of relating the Old and New. He is completely compelling when he stresses the ecumenical potential of a whole-Bible

---

54. Ratzinger, *Theology of the Liturgy*, 316.

55. Ratzinger, *Theology of the Liturgy*, 318.

56. More generally, Ratzinger fails to define "sacrifice" in biblical terms. His contrast of "sacrifice" and "meal" makes no sense in a Levitical framework. Self-offering and death are moments in the liturgical sequence of Levitical sacrifice, but not the whole. Every Levitical offering is a food rite; sometimes Yahweh alone "consumes" the meal in fire, and sometimes human beings eat from Yahweh's altar-table. But every time an Israelite sacrificed, he was part of a meal event. When he asks "Is the Eucharist a Sacrifice?" (*Theology of the Liturgy*, 207–17) he unfortunately assumes that we already know the content of the "idea of sacrifice," and attempts only to decide whether it is present in the New Testament account of the Eucharist.

approach to liturgy; he is least compelling when his treatment of the Old-New relation is unsatisfactory, when he uncharacteristically tends toward spiritualization rather than incarnation. In this way, Ratzinger points both to the possibilities and current limits of ecumenical liturgical theology. He is a great exemplar and guide, also for Protestants. But the church will be more deeply and fully one only when she wholeheartedly and accurately embraces the one Bible. A fully incarnational one-Bible theology alone gives hope for reuniting the church into one body.

12

"This Intimate Explosion of Good"

Joseph Ratzinger on the Eucharist

JOEY ROYAL

The Eucharist is *the* central Christian rite. Even if we call it "the Lord's Supper" or simply "Communion" it remains—with very few exceptions—something that all Christians in all places do as an act of devotion to and remembrance of Jesus Christ. For St. Paul the Eucharist was both a picture and the source of Christian unity: "Because there is one bread, we who are many are one body, for we all partake of the one bread" (1 Cor 10:17). What a sad irony it is, then, that this rite of Christian unity has become a barrier to unity; Roman Catholics and Protestants have cursed one another over rival interpretations, while Protestants have divided one from another over the same.

Fortunately, the fiery polemics of the Reformation have begun to cool, and many Christians are realizing the only way forward is to talk and, more importantly, to listen. What follows is an attempt to learn from Joseph Ratzinger and, in this spirit of ecumenical listening, to pay attention to aspects of his eucharistic thought where he can clarify and challenge Protestants. A close reading of Ratzinger's work can reveal surprising points of agreement on matters that have long divided Christians. Even where disagreements remain, they must be held in a spirit of love, with the awareness that "now we see in a mirror, dimly, but then we will see face to face" (1 Cor 13:12 NRSV).

THE LITURGY AS GOD'S MYSTERIOUS WORK

Born in early twentieth-century Germany, Joseph Ratzinger grew up in a now vanished Catholic culture, an experience he looks on with no small amount of nostalgia: "I can still smell those carpets of flowers and the freshness of the birch trees: I can see all the houses decorated, the banners, the singing; I can still hear the village band. ... I remember the *joie de vivre* of the local lads, firing their gun salutes."[1] Our past cannot help but shape us, and in Ratzinger's case it seems to have formed a person with a deep appreciation of tradition who has used his keen intellect to articulate the beautiful strangeness of Catholic Christianity. That said, his formative years were far from insular; some of his earliest theological work on the Eucharist was written in dialogue with Protestant theologians.[2]

We cannot fully appreciate Ratzinger's contribution to eucharistic theology, however, without briefly discussing the Second Vatican Council (1962–1965). Then a young professor, Ratzinger attended the council as a theological consultant. Despite the complexity of the council's deliberations and decisions, it is commonly accepted that it led to a "revisionist, progressivist spirit"[3] in the Roman Catholic Church. This ethos is perhaps most visible in the subsequent revisions made to the church's liturgy. Although the actual decisions of the council were fairly conservative, the responsibility to implement the councils mandates was handed to liturgical commissions who made far-reaching liturgical changes.[4] The most visible result was the almost complete displacement of Latin as the main liturgical language in favor of vernacular languages. In the process, most liturgical texts were revised, leading to increased pluralism in how the Mass was conducted. This is most obvious at the parish level, where participating in the Mass today is a vastly different

---

1. Joseph Ratzinger, *The Feast of Faith: Approaches to a Theology of the Liturgy,* trans. Graham Harrison (San Francisco: Ignatius, 1986), 127.
2. Eamon Duffy, "Benedict XVI and the Eucharist," *New Blackfriars* 88, no. 1014 (2007): 196.
3. Paul D. Murray, "Roman Catholic Theology after Vatican II," in *The Modern Theologians*, ed. David F. Ford with Rachel Muers, 3rd ed. (Malden, MA: Blackwell, 2005), 265.
4. See Tracey Rowland, *Ratzinger's Faith: The Theology of Pope Benedict XVI* (Oxford: Oxford University Press, 2008), 123–43, for a survey of liturgical changes since Vatican II.

experience than it was several generations ago. In Ratzinger's judgment these innovations went well beyond the intent of the council.[5] He has often expressed caution about revising the liturgy, urging that we receive the liturgy as a divine gift and not as something that can be molded and manipulated to suit our needs. Fr. Emery de Gaál glosses Ratzinger's position here: "The liturgy is essentially God's mysterious work, mutable on the outside but never fabricated."[6]

In order to properly understand the centrality of the Eucharist for Ratzinger, we must understand the place of the church in God's providential ordering of history. The *Catechism of the Catholic Church* puts it this way: "The gift of the Spirit ushers in a new era ... during which Christ manifests, makes present, and communicates his work of salvation through the liturgy of the Church. ... He acts through the sacraments in what the common Tradition of East and West calls 'the sacramental economy.'"[7] In other words, the worship of the church, exhibited most clearly in the Eucharist, shows us the very purpose and fulfillment of God's plan of salvation, which is a renewed creation in right relationship with God. Scott Hahn says this well: "The liturgy of the Church is the work of Jesus continuing in time, transforming history and divinizing men and women by transforming them into 'new creations,' children of God, and partakers of divine nature."[8] The Eucharist is not simply something the church does; rather "the Church is the Eucharist,"[9] which is to say that the Eucharist is the means whereby Christ's saving presence is perpetuated in time as he draws all creation to himself. It is difficult to overstate the centrality of the Eucharist for Ratzinger's theology; it is "the animating centre of the Church, the very centre of Christian life."[10]

---

5. Joseph Ratzinger, *Milestones: Memoirs 1927–1977*, trans. Erasmo Leiva-Merikakis (San Francisco: Ignatius, 1998), 182.

6. Emery de Gaál, *The Theology of Pope Benedict XVI: The Christocentric Shift* (New York: Palgrave Macmillan, 2010), 240.

7. *The Catechism of the Catholic Church* (Toronto: Random House Canada, 1995), 304.

8. Scott W. Hahn, *Covenant and Communion: The Biblical Theology of Pope Benedict XVI* (Grand Rapids: Brazos, 2009), 166–67.

9. Joseph Ratzinger, *Pilgrim Fellowship of Faith: The Church as Communion*, ed. Stephan Otto Horn and Vinzenz Pfnür, trans. Henry Taylor (San Francisco: Ignatius, 2005), 103.

10. Duffy, "Benedict XVI and the Eucharist," 198.

THE NEW PASSOVER

To understand why this is so we will turn to the scriptural basis for the Eucharist. In *Jesus of Nazareth* Ratzinger, now Pope Benedict XVI, devotes considerable attention to Jesus' Last Supper with his disciples.[11] The earliest account is from St. Paul's First Letter to the Corinthians:

> For I received from the Lord what I also handed on to you, that the Lord Jesus on the night when he was betrayed took a loaf of bread, and when he had given thanks, he broke it and said, "This is my body that is for you. Do this in remembrance of me." In the same way he took the cup also, after supper, saying, "This cup is the new covenant in my blood. Do this, as often as you drink it, in remembrance of me." For as often as you eat this bread and drink the cup, you proclaim the Lord's death until he comes. (1 Cor 11:23–26 NRSV)

The Synoptic Gospels recount this event, with some variance in detail (Matt 26:26–30; Mark 14:22–25; Luke 22:14–23). Although the Gospel of John does recount Jesus' Last Supper with his disciples (John 13:1–30), the words of institution are not included. There is a further discrepancy between the Synoptic Gospels and John's Gospel on the timing of Jesus' death. The discrepancy concerns whether Jesus died on Passover (as the Synoptics allege) or whether he died the day before Passover (as John alleges). Many have sought to reconcile these accounts,[12] but Benedict sees them as irreconcilable. He believes John's account is historically most likely and thus believes that Jesus ate the Last Supper and died on the day before Passover when the paschal lambs would have been slaughtered in the temple.[13] This latter point he sees as significant: "Jesus died at the hour when the Passover lambs were being slaughtered in the Temple. That Christians later saw this as no coincidence, that they

---

11. Benedict XVI, *Jesus of Nazareth*, vol. 2, *Holy Week: From the Entrance Into Jerusalem to the Resurrection*, trans. Philip J. Whitmore (San Francisco: Ignatius, 2011), 103–44.

12. *Ignatius Catholic Study Bible* (San Francisco: Ignatius, 2010), 188.

13. Benedict XVI, *Holy Week*, 107–9.

recognized Jesus as the true Lamb, that in this way they came to see the true meaning of the ritual of the lambs."[14]

Why then do the Synoptics—and presumably a tradition that predates their writing—identify Jesus' death with Passover itself? According to Benedict,

> Jesus knew that he was about to die. He knew that he would not be able to eat the Passover again. Fully aware of this, he invited his disciples to a Last Supper of a very special kind, one that followed no specific Jewish ritual but, rather, constituted his farewell; during the meal he gave them something new: he gave them himself as the true Lamb and thereby instituted his Passover.[15]

He cites a mysterious line in Luke, in which Jesus says, "I have eagerly desired to eat this Passover with you before I suffer; for I tell you, I will not eat it until it is fulfilled in the kingdom of God" (Luke 22:15–16 NRSV). From this Benedict infers,

> This farewell meal was not the old Passover, but the new one, which Jesus accomplished in this context. Even though the meal that Jesus shared with the Twelve was not a Passover meal according to the ritual prescriptions of Judaism, nevertheless, in retrospect, the inner connection of the whole event with Jesus' death and Resurrection stood out clearly. It was Jesus' Passover. And in this sense, he both did and did not celebrate the Passover: the old rituals could not be carried out—when their time came, Jesus had already died. But he had given himself, and thus he had truly celebrated the Passover with them. The old was not abolished; it was simply brought to its full meaning.[16]

Jesus' Last Supper echoed the Old Testament tradition of commemorating God's rescuing the Israelites from Egypt, and yet it was not simply a repetition of that tradition. What Jesus did instead is offer something

14. Benedict XVI, *Holy Week*, 112.
15. Benedict XVI, *Holy Week*, 113.
16. Benedict XVI, *Holy Week*, 114.

new that brought the old ritual to its fulfilment; it was a new Passover, in which the paschal lamb is Jesus himself. At the center of this new rite is Jesus' words of thanksgiving: "The early Christians recognized that the essential thing that took place at the Last Supper was ... the great prayer of praise that now contained Jesus' words of institution as its centerpiece. With these words he had transformed his death into the gift of himself, so that we can now give thanks for this death."[17] The Last Supper was anticipatory; without the cross it was incomplete. Now with the reality of Christ's work on the cross finished, believers are invited to participate in an ongoing way in Christ's self-offering. In a moving passage Benedict articulates this:

> At the celebration of the Eucharist, we find ourselves in the "hour" of Jesus. ... Through the Eucharist this "hour" of Jesus becomes our own hour, his presence in our midst. Together with the disciples he celebrated the Passover of Israel. ... He recites over the bread the prayer of praise and blessing. But then something new happens. He thanks God not only for the great works of the past; he thanks him for his own exaltation, soon to be accomplished through the Cross and Resurrection, and he speaks to the disciples in words that sum up the whole of the Law and the Prophets: "This is my Body, given in sacrifice for you. This cup is the New Covenant in my Blood." He then distributes the bread and the cup, and instructs them to repeat his words and actions of that moment over and over again in his memory. What is happening? How can Jesus distribute his Body and his Blood? By making the bread into his Body and the wine into his Blood, he anticipates his death, he accepts it in his heart, and he transforms it into an action of love. What on the outside is simply brutal violence—the Crucifixion—from within becomes an act of total self-giving love. ... Since this act transmutes death into love, death as such is already conquered from within, the Resurrection is already present in it. Death is,

17. Joseph Ratzinger, *On the Way to Jesus Christ*, trans. Michael J. Miller (San Francisco: Ignatius, 2005), 173.

so to speak, mortally wounded, so that it can no longer have the last word.

To use an image well known to us today, this is like inducing nuclear fission in the very heart of being—the victory of love over hatred, the victory of love over death. Only this intimate explosion of good conquering evil can then trigger off the series of transformations that little by little will change the world.[18]

Jesus not only died for us and rose from the dead, but he also gave us a means to participate in his victory over death. To use Benedict's memorable phrase: the Eucharist is like a "nuclear fission in the very heart of being"—it brings us into regular contact with his presence. Every time the church gathers as the body of Christ and celebrates the Eucharist, we are brought into intimate contact with Christ in his life-giving sacrifice.

AN UNBLOODY SACRIFICE

This brings us to an idea that has been contentious since the Reformation, the idea of the Eucharist as a sacrifice. The *Catechism of the Catholic Church* unambiguously describes the Eucharist as a "Holy Sacrifice," which "makes present the one sacrifice of Christ the Savior and includes the Church's offering."[19] Benedict, too, makes the same claim: "In instituting the sacrifice of the Eucharist, Jesus anticipates and makes present the sacrifice of the Cross and the victory of the resurrection."[20] We should note the phrase "makes present," which is vital if we are to properly understand the sacrificial nature of the Eucharist.

To Martin Luther (1483–1546) belief in the eucharistic sacrifice sounded like a denial of the sufficiency of Christ's death on the cross and seemed to call for a continual "resacrifice" of Christ.[21] Ratzinger sees

18. Benedict XVI, *Heart of the Christian Life: Thoughts on Holy Mass* (San Francisco: Ignatius, 2010), 31.

19. *Catechism of the Catholic Church*, 370.

20. Benedict XVI, *Sacramentum Caritatis*, Post-Synodal Apostolic Exhortation, February 22, 2007, §10, http://w2.vatican.va/content/benedict-xvi/en/apost_exhortations/documents/hf_ben-xvi_exh_20070222_sacramentum-caritatis.html.

21. Denis R. Janz, *The Westminster Handbook to Martin Luther* (Louisville: Westminster John Knox, 2010), 86–87.

many contemporary Roman Catholics siding with Luther on this issue: "A sizable party of Catholic liturgists seems to have practically arrived at the conclusion that Luther, rather than Trent, was substantially right."[22]

Protestants would do well to recognize that, since at least the second century, it was commonplace to speak of the Eucharist as a sacrifice.[23] For example, in an ancient eucharistic prayer, *The Liturgy of St. James*, the priest prays the following over the bread and wine:

> Making remembrance of his life-giving sufferings, his saving cross and death, his burial and resurrection on the third day from the dead, and his session at the right hand of You his God and Father, and his second glorious and fearful coming when he will judge the living and the dead. ... we offer to You O Lord, this *awesome and unbloody sacrifice*, beseeching You to deal with us not according to our sins ... but according to Your great mercy and love.[24]

This part of the eucharistic prayer is often referred to as the "anaphora" or the "canon," which is the point at which the bread and wine become the body and blood of Christ. Note that the Eucharist here is called a sacrifice, although an "unbloody" one, as contrasted with the "bloody" sacrifice of the cross. That distinction is meant to clarify that the Eucharist is not a "resacrifice" of Christ, as if his death on the cross were insufficient. It is rather a "re-presentation" of that one sacrifice, which is now made present in the Eucharist. In a sermon on Hebrews 9, John Chrysostom (ca. 347–407) emphasizes this crucial distinction:

> Do we not offer the sacrifice daily? Indeed we do offer it daily, re-presenting his death. How then is it one sacrifice and not many? ... We offer the same person, not one sheep one day and

---

22. Benedict XVI, "Theology of the Liturgy," in *The Essential Pope Benedict XVI*, ed. John F. Thornton and Susan B. Varenne (San Francisco: HarperOne, 2007), 143.

23. C. P. M. Jones and C. J. A. Hickling, "The New Testament," in *The Study of Liturgy*, ed. Cheslyn Jones, Geoffrey Wainwright, Edward Yarnold, SJ, and Paul Bradshaw (Oxford: Oxford University Press, 1992), 205.

24. Quoted in Robert Louis Wilken, *The Spirit of Early Christian Thought* (New Haven: Yale University Press, 2003), 25 (emphasis added).

tomorrow a different one, but always the same offering. ... There is one sacrifice and one high priest who offered the sacrifice that cleanses us. Today we offer that which was once offered, a sacrifice that is inexhaustible. This is done as a remembrance [*anamnesis*] of that which was done then, for he said, "Do this in remembrance of me." We do not offer another sacrifice as the priest offered of old, but we always offer the same sacrifice. Or rather we re-present the sacrifice.[25]

The key word here is "remembrance," which is an English rendering of the Greek word *anamnesis* (a form of which St. Luke and St. Paul use when recounting the Last Supper). The church historian Robert Louis Wilken argues that the word, used in this liturgical context, means "recall by making present."[26] To remember, in this sense, is more than simply bringing something to mind; it is rather to fully participate in a rite which blurs past, present, and future together: "In the Eucharist the life-giving events of Christ's death and Resurrection escape the restrictions of time and become what the early church called mysteries, ritual actions by which Christ's saving work is re-presented under the veil of the consecrated bread and wine."[27] Understood thus, the sacrifice of the Eucharist is not a *different* sacrifice than the sacrifice of Christ's life on the cross. It is rather a making present of that same sacrifice, an instance of our being brought into contact with an event that is no longer simply past, but also present and future.

Let us reflect, for a moment, on the idea of sacrifice more generally. It is a concept found widely in the Old Testament and refers to the offering of something (usually an animal) to God. Although there were sacrifices that did not include animals (for example, grain and wine), the animal sacrifices were nonetheless the most common and the most important. The New Testament, in particular the book of Hebrews, links Christ's death with sacrifice, claiming that Christ is both high

"This Intimate Explosion of Good"

priest and sacrificial lamb (Heb 7:26–27). This concept can become so familiar that we often fail to ask the most obvious question: What exactly is a sacrifice?

In his book *The Spirit of the Liturgy*, Ratzinger distinguishes two rival definitions of sacrifice. The first, which he claims is the common view, sees sacrifice as the destruction of something good in order to please God. Ratzinger rejects that view, arguing that God takes no pleasure in destruction.[28] Ratzinger instead draws from St. Augustine of Hippo (354–430) to argue that the essence of sacrifice is self-offering rooted in love, with the goal of union between Creator and creature. After all, we cannot offer God any "thing" that is not already his. What we can offer, and what he ultimately desires, is our love. Augustine cites Psalm 51:16–17, in which the psalmist prays: "For you have no delight in sacrifice; if I were to give a burnt offering, you would not be pleased. The sacrifice acceptable to God is a broken spirit; a broken and contrite heart, O God, you will not despise."[29] For Augustine, the entire Old Testament sacrificial system points to this. Ratzinger distinguishes these rival definitions of sacrifice this way:

> People commonly consider sacrifice as the destruction of something precious in the eyes of man; in destroying it, man wants to consecrate this reality to God, to recognize his sovereignty. In fact, however, a destruction does not honor God. The slaughtering of animals or whatever else can't honor God. ... What, then, does sacrifice consist of? Not in destruction, not in this or that thing, but in the transformation of man. In the fact that he becomes himself conformed to God. He becomes conformed to God when he becomes love.[30]

For Ratzinger (and Augustine) to sacrifice oneself is to give oneself wholly to God in thanksgiving. It is an act of total surrender, but rather than destroying the self it leads to freedom for the self. The Eucharist

---

28. Joseph Ratzinger, *The Spirit of the Liturgy*, trans. John Saward (San Francisco: Ignatius, 2000), 28.

29. Augustine, *City of God*, trans. Henry Bettenson (New York: Penguin, 1972), 10.5.

30. Benedict XVI, "Theology of the Liturgy," 148.

is this act of thanksgiving, where we again and again re-present the once-and-for-all sacrifice of Christ. We also offer ourselves as a "living sacrifice" to God (Rom 12:1). The irony of course is that we are only offering back to God what properly belongs to him, including our very bodies. Nonetheless God desires our love, and the path to union with God—what is often called "divinization"—is sacrifice, re-presented in the Eucharist and constantly renewed in our lives. According to Ratzinger, "The Eucharist draws us into Jesus' act of self-oblation. More than just statically receiving the incarnate Logos, we enter into the very dynamic of his self-giving."[31] We are transformed in the process and empowered to live in charity with God and with our neighbor.

TRANSFORMED BY LOVE

It may surprise some readers to have come this far having barely mentioned transubstantiation. After all, the *Catechism of the Catholic Church* unambiguously describes the change that occurs to the consecrated bread and wine as "fittingly and properly called transubstantiation."[32] Ratzinger, however, is reluctant to rely exclusively on this language: "There are plenty of reasons not to put too much emphasis on the word 'transubstantiation' in contemporary theology; … it is right to push it aside from the central position that it wrongly acquired in a theology excessively oriented to philosophy."[33] Nevertheless, Ratzinger does believe the doctrine must be clarified and defended, if only for the reason that it is so often misunderstood.

Transubstantiation is a doctrine that attempts to provide a rational account of Christ's substantial presence in the Eucharist. The most famous exponent of the doctrine, Thomas Aquinas (1225–1274), used the conceptual language of Aristotle (384–322 BC) to show how consecrated bread and wine can truly be the body and blood of Christ while keeping the appearances of bread and wine. To make this argument,

31. Benedict XVI, *Heart of the Christian Life*, 56.
32. *Catechism of the Catholic Church*, 1376.
33. Joseph Ratzinger, *Collected Works*, vol. 2, *Theology of the Liturgy: The Sacramental Foundation of Christian Existence*, ed. Michael J. Miller, trans. John Saward et al. (San Francisco: Ignatius, 2014), 567.

he used the categories of "substance" (what a thing is) and "accidents" (what characteristics a thing *has*). Thomas taught that at the celebration of the Eucharist "the substance of bread was changed (transubstantiated) into the body of Christ, even though the accidental features of the bread remained."[34] When an ordained priest—acting *in persona Christi*—consecrates the bread and wine a permanent change is affected at the deepest level of reality.

Ratzinger clarifies what Thomas means by an accident: "Not only the 'when' but also the 'where' is an accident; that is to say, not only the process unfolding over the course of time but also the structure existing in space is an accident. In still other words: not just the quality but also the quantity is considered an accident."[35] For Thomas, all spatial and temporal characteristics of a thing are accidents; the substance is what lies beneath, and what remains imperceptible to our senses. How then can we speak of the substance of a thing if it exists independently of any characteristics? This question is especially difficult for modern people, who are accustomed to thinking of the world in scientific terms, and for whom metaphysical concepts are strange and foreign. Ratzinger again provides clarity:

> For the High Middle Ages, "matter" as *materia prima* is a pre-physical, precisely meta-physical entity; it is pure potentiality, and as such it does not become intelligible anywhere; it can only be grasped speculatively, metaphysically as the one root of physically observable material being. The same is true of "substance," which refers to the metaphysical reality of the subsistence of an existing thing, but not to the appearing thing as phenomenon.[36]

---

34. James R. Ginther, *The Westminster Handbook to Medieval Theology* (Louisville: Westminster John Knox, 2009), 177. Interestingly he used Aristotle's language to develop a position that Aristotle himself could not accept, namely, that the substance of a thing could be entirely separated from its accidents.

35. Ratzinger, *Theology of the Liturgy*, 599.

36. Ratzinger, *Theology of the Liturgy*, 601.

For Thomas, matter is a formless primeval material from which the universe is made. Likewise, substance refers to a stable, permanent reality that underlies all perceptible things.[37] To apply this to Thomas's eucharistic theology, then, is to identify substance with the underlying reality of the consecrated bread and wine, which is the body and blood of Christ. The accidents then refer to any and all characteristics of the bread and wine, including their location in space and time. Our natural faculties can only grasp the accidents of the Eucharist; the substance of the consecrated bread and wine lies entirely outside the realm of appearances, impressions, and physical phenomena.[38]

It may help to clarify what this doctrine is *not* claiming. It is emphatically not saying that the bread and wine undergo a physical or chemical change. Ratzinger makes this point with startling clarity:

> Viewed from the perspective of physics and chemistry, absolutely nothing takes place in the gifts—not even somewhere in a microscopic realm; considered physically and chemically, after the transformation, they are exactly the same as they were before it. Only great speculative naïveté and a complete misunderstanding of what faithful Catholic thinking means by transubstantiation could contest this statement. ... Physically and chemically nothing happens in the Eucharist. That is not its level of reality. But a faith-filled approach to reality includes at the same time the conviction that physics and chemistry do not exhaust the totality of being; therefore it cannot be said that where nothing happens in the physical order nothing at all has happened. On the contrary: the reality lies behind the physical.[39]

What is being affirmed rather is that a metaphysical change has occurred, transforming the bread and wine at the deepest levels of reality into something altogether new. That transformation is only perceptible through the eyes of faith, not through scientific analysis. In other words,

37. F. L. Cross and E. A. Livingstone, eds., *The Oxford Dictionary of the Christian Church*, 3rd ed. (Oxford: Oxford University Press, 2005), 1553.
38. Ratzinger, *Theology of the Liturgy*, 606.
39. Ratzinger, *Theology of the Liturgy*, 606–7.

the appearances of the consecrated bread and wine no longer tell us what they fundamentally are; Christ has taken hold of them, and now they are entirely "signs that have lost their creaturely peculiarity and exist no longer for themselves but only for him, through him, in him."[40]

This can all sound very abstract and technical, so it is important to be reminded that transubstantiation is not intended to be an explanation for a mechanical process. It is, rather, intended as an invitation to share in the mystery of Christ's presence. It is meant to lead us to worship the risen Christ, who comes near to us and touches us. Here is Ratzinger at his most pastoral:

What we eat in Holy Communion is not a piece of matter; this food is an entirely different food: it is the Son of God who became man. Eating this new food therefore does not mean eating something; it is an encounter of my I with the I of the Son of God, it is a heart-to-heart communion. Eucharistic Communion is not something external: Communion with the Son of God, who gives himself in the Host, is an encounter with the Son of God and, therefore, a form of communication and adoration. We can receive it only by adoring, by opening up our whole existence to his presence, by opening ourselves so that he becomes the strength of our life.[41]

In other words, to receive the Eucharist in faith is to commune with Jesus. It is a true meeting between two persons, as Jesus gives himself in love to his people through the means of the sacraments. Ratzinger is fond of citing Augustine's account of a vision he had in which he heard the Lord say to him, "This is a different food; you are not to assimilate me, but you are to be assimilated by me."[42] The Eucharist provides a different sort of nourishment. When we eat ordinary food we take something into our bodies by destroying it and extracting the nutrients.

40. Ratzinger, *Theology of the Liturgy*, 610.
41. Benedict XVI, *Teaching and Learning the Love of God: Being a Priest Today*, trans. Michael J. Miller (San Francisco: Ignatius, 2017), 121–22.
42. Benedict XVI, *Teaching and Learning*, 122.

With the Eucharist, however, we are drawn into Christ by eating his body and blood.

CONCLUSION

I began this chapter with an admonition to listen carefully to Ratzinger in the hope that he can clarify our understanding and challenge our assumptions. I will now briefly point to several areas where I think his work can challenge Protestant assumptions in some productive ways.

First, his understanding of the Eucharist is grounded in an impressively wide-ranging biblical theology. This allows him to evaluate innovations in liturgical practice by determining whether these changes are faithful to the gospel. In my experience, Protestants pay far less attention to what we do in worship; we are, more often than not, pragmatists. In many churches, music is chosen based solely on the preference of the worship leader, the order of service is purely functional, and the Eucharist is tacked on at the end of the service, if it is celebrated at all. What if we were to base our decisions about worship on a rich scriptural theology, and not on the latest fads? What if meeting Christ in the Eucharist became the focal point of our gatherings?

Second, Ratzinger's explanation of transubstantiation and eucharistic sacrifice clears away many Protestant misunderstandings (such as the claim that it's nonsense, or arises purely from pagan philosophy, or calls for the continual "resacrifice" of Christ). Can we acknowledge that *ideas* about the Eucharist need no longer be a barrier between Roman Catholics and Protestants who affirm the real presence of Christ in the Eucharist?[43] I do not mean to imply that there are no longer any

43. There still remains significant disagreement between those who affirm the real presence of Christ in the Eucharist (Roman Catholics, Anglicans, Calvinists, Lutherans, etc.) and those who argue against the real presence of Christ in the Eucharist, following Huldrych Zwingli (1484–1531). Granted, most North American evangelicals are Zwinglians by default, but it is my impression that this position is often simply assumed rather than argued. In addition, there is a sizeable population of young evangelicals who are drawn to certain kinds of Calvinist theology (as evidenced by the popularity of John Piper, Tim Keller, and The Gospel Coalition), as well as a move within certain Reformed quarters toward more deliberate reflection on the centrality of liturgical practices (e.g., see the recent work on cultural liturgies by James K. A. Smith). It remains to be seen whether these theological currents will lead to larger-scale evangelical rethinking of Zwinglian assumptions.

barriers to unity at all (there clearly still are, particularly in the area of ecclesiology) but only that we may be closer to one another in this particular area. It is noteworthy that Anglicans—who are perhaps the most liturgical of Protestants—joined with Roman Catholics several decades ago to produce a document called *Eucharistic Doctrine*, which affirms the following:

> We believe that we have reached substantial agreement on the doctrine of the eucharist. Although we are all conditioned by the traditional ways in which we have expressed and practised our eucharistic faith, we are convinced that if there are any remaining points of disagreement they can be resolved on the principles here established. We acknowledge a variety of theological approaches within both our communions. But we have seen it as our task to find a way of advancing together beyond the doctrinal disagreements of the past. It is our hope that, in view of the agreement which we have reached on eucharistic faith, this doctrine will no longer constitute an obstacle to the unity we seek.[44]

That is clearly a step in the right direction. If Protestants and Roman Catholics can move beyond needless quarrels, we can better focus our energy on resolving the substantial disputes that remain.

Third and last, there is a warm piety to Ratzinger's eucharistic theology, which communicates a profound love for Jesus Christ. This should be welcomed by evangelicals in particular, who have long emphasized the need for a Christian faith that moves the heart. Even at his most theologically complex, Ratzinger's writing is shot through with an intimacy and a tenderness; he speaks of touching Christ and of encountering him as one encounters a friend. Perhaps the "physicality" of this can be a challenge to evangelical piety, which can tend to be overly individualized and interiorized. Can evangelicals not affirm the real presence of Christ in the Eucharist, as well as his presence in our hearts?

---

44. First Anglican/Roman Catholic International Commission, *Eucharistic Doctrine*, 1971, http://www.vatican.va/roman_curia/pontifical_councils/chrstuni/angl-comm-docs/rc_pc_chrstuni_doc_1971_eucharistic-doctrine_en.html.

In a beautiful sermon on Jesus healing the leper (Mark 1:40–45), Ratzinger provides a wonderful summation of the awe-inspiring strangeness of the Eucharist, the ritual where Jesus, ever faithful to his promise, continues to touch us with healing and with hope:

> Jesus touches him. ... The Fathers viewed this touch of Jesus as the symbol for the whole sacramental dimension of the Church. In the sacraments he is still here and corporeally walks shoulder to shoulder with us, touches our body with his body in a bodily way and so causes us even now to sense that it is true: σπλαγχνισυείς—"his bowels were moved with pity" (Mk 1:41). With his body he rescues and delivers our body.[45]

---

45. Benedict XVI, *Teaching and Learning*, 183.

13

Servant of the
Clear, Wide Word

Joseph Ratzinger on Preaching

ANNETTE BROWNLEE

In his first apostolic exhortation to the church, *Sacramentum Caritatis* (Sacrament of charity), Pope Benedict XVI states that "the quality of homilies need to be improved."[1] Though perhaps not intended, with this authoritative observation the pope establishes common ground with Protestants in the parched soil of contemporary preaching: it all stands in need of improvement. It comes as no surprise that for Ratzinger preaching is a theological practice. It is as a theologian that he lays out both the reasons behind the current crisis in preaching and a faithful remedy or response. That response is given in the Word itself.[2]

Benedict offers three reasons behind the current crisis in preaching: the difficulty of preaching to and in an unbelieving world, the low regard for the church, and the loss of accepted norms for preaching in the Roman Catholic Church.[3] All three lead to a lack of clarity about the content of preaching and to a loss of hope on behalf of many in receiving any direction from Scripture.[4] Benedict is not one who has lost such hope. He believes, despite the "primeval forest" of hermeneutic problems, that there is a self-illuminating clarity to

---

1. Benedict XVI, *Sacramentum Caritatis*, Post-Synodal Apostolic Exhortation, February 22, 2007, §46, http://w2.vatican.va/content/benedict-xvi/en/apost_exhortations/documents/hf_ben-xvi_exh_20070222_sacramentum-caritatis.html.
2. Joseph Ratzinger, *Dogma and Preaching: Applying Christian Doctrine to Daily Life*, trans. Michael J. Miller and Matthew J. O'Connell, ed. Michael J. Miller (San Francisco: Ignatius Press, 2011).
3. Joseph Ratzinger, "Standards for Preaching the Gospel Today," in *Dogma and Preaching*, 26–39.
4. Ratzinger, "Standards for Preaching the Gospel Today," 27.

Scripture characterized by its univocal character.[5] He turns to Luther's understanding of Scripture's *perspicuitas* to describe its self-illuminating clarity within the church.[6] Working theologically from Scripture's center, which is the crucified Christ, Benedict lays out three key characteristics of the church's preaching that are given in the Word itself. All three provide a response to the difficulty of preaching today. First, the clarity of what to preach is given in the Word's center, Jesus Christ. Benedict stands firm in preaching the particularity of Jesus Christ. "The fact that Jesus is God is God's deed, his act, which is the foundation for the 'actuality' of what is preached. ... If preaching abandons this, it becomes irrelevant, even if it is decked out in a way that is subjectively interesting."[7] Second, the Word supplies the *direction* of the church's appropriation of Scripture in response to human questions about God. A close look at some of his sermons indicates the steps or approach he employs as he moves from human questions about God to the Word's response. Third, the Word supplies the ecclesial shape of the faith proclaimed. The shape of God's Word is ecclesial because it is always a gathering word.

Scripture's self-illuminating clarity provides the content of the church's proclamation, the direction of the church's appropriation of Scripture, and the shape of the faith proclaimed. This essay explores Benedict's understanding of the direction of the church's appropriation of Scripture for preaching and the shape of the faith proclaimed, coming out of Scripture's center, Jesus Christ, as a response to the difficulties of preaching today. At the end of the essay, I will briefly address some of the differences between Benedict's theology of preaching and those employed by Protestant theologians. But given the parched landscape of all Christian preaching, such differences are not reason enough to allow the common ground Benedict shares with Protestants in this area to lie fallow. Benedict's remedy for the impoverished state of preaching is found in his theological mining of the provisions the Word itself provides for the church's faithful proclamation. Thus, as described below,

5. Ratzinger, "Standards for Preaching the Gospel Today," 28
6. Ratzinger, "Standards for Preaching the Gospel Today," 27.
7. Joseph Ratzinger, "Christocentrism in Preaching?," in *Dogma and Preaching,* 43.

when preaching either to those who have faith or to those who have difficulty believing, Benedict does not translate Scripture into extrabiblical categories or stray from its ecclesial center, because both—the direction and shape of the faith proclaimed—are *themselves* a part of Scripture's clarity and are thus essential. Only by looking at the whole of Scripture, within the living context of faith and the church, can its single voice be grasped.[8] His is a remedy not only for the ailing homilies of the Roman Catholic Church. In *Verbum Domini*, the post-synodal apostolic exhortation he issued in 2010, which addresses how the Catholic Church should approach the Bible, Benedict writes, "The faithful should be able to perceive clearly that the preacher has a compelling desire to present Christ, who must stand at the center of every homily. For this reason preachers need to be in close and constant contact with the sacred text."[9]

PREACHING IN AN UNBELIEVING WORLD

In a homily on the occasion of a new priest's first celebration of the Eucharist, Benedict says in his straightforward style, "It is difficult to proclaim God's Word today in a world that is sated with every kind of sensation."[10] This is challenge enough for the preacher, but he continues, "It is difficult to proclaim God's Word today in a world in which the priest himself must grope his way with difficulty through the darkness and must choose between saying what no one will understand or, in a

8. Ratzinger, "Christocentricism in Preaching?," 43.

9. Benedict XVI, *Verbum Domini*, Post-Synodal Apostolic Exhortation, September 30, 2012, §59, http://w2.vatican.va/content/benedict-xvi/en/apost_exhortations/documents/hf_ben-xvi_exh_20100930_verbum-domini.html. Pope Benedict is reiterating the teaching of his church on the centrality of Scripture in the life of the church: "The Second Vatican Council states that, by necessity, all the clergy, primarily priests and deacons, ought to have continual contact with the Scriptures, though assiduous reading and attentive study of the sacred texts, so as not to become idle preachers of the Word of God, hearing the Word only with their ears while not hearing it with their hearts (cf. DV 25; PO 4)." General Assembly of the Synod of Bishops, *The Word of God in the Life and Mission of the Church: Instrumentum Laboris*, Synod of Bishops, Twelfth Ordinary General Assembly, 2008, http://www.vatican.va/roman_curia/synod/documents/rc_synod_doc_20080511_instrlabor-xii-assembly_en.html.

10. Joseph Ratzinger, "Meditations on the Day of a First Mass," In *Dogma and Preaching*, 372.

hesitant and inadequate way, translating for our world which is so far removed from our everyday experience."[11]

Benedict is a keen observer of the climate of positivism that has made the reality of God increasingly inaccessible for many. But he lays blame for the crisis of preaching in an unbelieving world squarely on the shoulders of the church.

> The crisis in Christian preaching, which we have experienced in growing proportions for a century is based in no small part on the fact that the Christian answers have ignored man's questions; they were and remain right, but because they were not developed from and within the question they remain ineffective. Hence to question along with man who seeks is an indispensable part of preaching itself, because only in this way can the Word [*Wort*] become an answer [*Ant-wort*].[12]

Benedict's openness to an unbelieving world is rooted in the understanding of Christ's openness to the world expressed in Vatican II. He lays out as the great task before the church preaching that takes seriously the difficulty of belief today, whether preaching to those whose faith must grow deeper and more vibrant or to the church that is yet to be created. For this task he turns to the character of Christ's embrace of reality to shape the pattern of the church's openness to the world and its questions about God. The crucified Christ's embrace supplies the direction of the church's faithful appropriation of Scripture for and in an unbelieving world. In *Eschatology: Death and Eternal Life* Ratzinger indicates the direction the Word itself supplies for the faithful appropriation of the Word in preaching.

> Faithful appropriation of that Word treads the narrow path between archaism and Modernism: Issuing as it does from the crucified and risen Christ, the Word indicates a given direction

11. Ratzinger, "Meditations on the Day of a First Mass," 372.

12. Joseph Ratzinger, "Contemporary Man Facing the Question of God," in *Dogma and Preaching*, 77. Throughout his writings Benedict uses "man" to indicate human beings. In this essay I maintain his usage and his usage of the male pronoun to refer to the preacher.

which is wide enough to receive all reality into itself, yet clear enough to confront it with a definite measuring-rod of its own.[13]

In his incarnation Christ does not leave the world as it is. Benedict states this with the utmost simplicity: "God does not just become the world's companion."[14] His Yes is mission, "and that means the penetration of the world by God's Word and its consequent transformation by a union of love with God himself."[15] Benedict speaks of openness in preaching in terms of translation. However, given the character of Christ's embrace of all reality, translation in preaching is not simply a two-way street. It is not dialogue between equal partners or companions, such as translating Mandarin into French and French into Mandarin. It involves entering into human uncertainty and questions about God and rediscovering and speaking about God from within them. This is the only way the Word can become an answer.

A close reading of some of his sermons and homiletic addresses reveals a process by which Benedict enters into human questions about God and speaks about God from within them. It is too much to claim this as his homiletic method. However, by identifying steps within his faithful appropriation of Scripture, Benedict provides an enormous aid to preachers who are trying to do likewise. In the essay "Contemporary Man Facing the Question of God," Benedict describes three steps by

---

13. Joseph Ratzinger, *Eschatology: Death and Eternal Life,* trans. Michael Waldstein and Aidan Nichols (Washington, DC: Catholic University of America Press, 1988), 18, as quoted in Aidan Nichols, *The Thought of Pope Benedict XVI: An Introduction to the Theology of Joseph Ratzinger* (London: Burns & Oates, 2007), 117–18.

14. "The Gospel of redemption cannot be made an object of dialogical treatment: it is kerygma, proclamation. Yet alongside mission there is a place for dialogue: for the Christian message can only be heard in its full integrity by way of response to human questioning." Nichols, *Thought of Pope Benedict XVI,* 106.

15. Nichols, *Thought of Pope Benedict XVI,* 106.

which he enters into human questions about God and then responds to them from within Scripture's self-illuminating clarity.[16]

Briefly, Benedict's three-step approach for a faithful appropriation of Scripture in preaching is as follows: (1) Enter into human questions about God and the underlying difficulty of how to know God as contemporary men and women experience it (even if they are unaware of this). (2) Move into Scripture and approach these questions from within the interior of the Christian image of God, trying to receive Scripture on its own terms. Pay attention to how God is known within the biblical witness (through his creation, through following him, through the witness of others, etc.). (3) Ask how the fundamental understanding of life and the world expressed in the Christian image of God can be brought to bear on the questions at hand in and for an unbelieving world. The goal of this process is to be able to enter into the uncertainty about God many experience so as to be able to rediscover and speak about God from within that experience. This direction for the faithful appropriation of Scripture, supplied by the Word, leads to an epistemology also supplied by the Word. He says in his homily for Pentecost 2011, "God shows himself in Jesus and by doing so gives us the truth about ourselves."[17] His Easter sermon "Resurrection as Mission" provides an example of his use of these steps.[18]

"Resurrection as Mission" is addressed to those who already have faith. His first step in the three-step process is to begin with a question that either believers or those who do not yet have faith might have: How can we know the resurrected Jesus? How can anyone? To draw out this

16. Ratzinger, "Contemporary Man Facing the Question of God," 77–87. Here Benedict employs an intratextual hermeneutic, though he does not use that term. The key characteristic of an intratextual hermeneutic is the direction of interpretation. It moves from text or story to reality. It does not translate Scripture into extrabiblical categories. It redescribes reality within a scriptural framework. This is the hallmark of George Lindbeck's approach to Scripture. "A Scriptural world is thus able to absorb the universe. It supplies the interpretative framework within which believers seek to live their lives and understand reality." George Lindbeck, *The Nature of Doctrine: Religion and Theology in a Postliberal Age* (Louisville: Westminster, 1984), 106.

17. Benedict XVI, homily delivered at the Vatican Basilica, June 12, 2011, §4, http://w2.vatican.va/content/benedict-xvi/en/homilies/2011/documents/hf_ben-xvi_hom_20110612_pentecoste.html.

18. Joseph Ratzinger, "On the Spirit of Brotherhood," in *Dogma and Preaching*, 207–9; Ratzinger, "Resurrection as Mission," in *Dogma and Preaching*, 301–4.

question he uses the contradictory statements in John's narrative that the resurrected Jesus makes about touching him.[19] On Easter morning Jesus tells Mary Magdalene not to hold onto him because he has not yet ascended (John 20:17). A week later he tells Thomas to touch his wounds (John 20:27).

In his second step, Benedict reads these two Gospel narratives on their own terms and in relation to one another. He looks to the narrative about Thomas to make "the earlier scene intelligible."[20] Mary wants to have her teacher back as he was before his death and resurrection. But that is not possible because "Jesus has now become the one who is exalted at the Father's side and accessible to everyone. He can be touched only as the One who is with the Father, as the One who has ascended."[21] Thomas may touch him because the wounds are meant to make the cross unforgettable (in contrast to Mary who wanted to forget about it). The touch becomes for Thomas an act of worship and a call to the mission of witnessing.

Finally, in the third step, Benedict directly addresses the Word's answer to the question, How do we know the risen Christ? We know the risen Christ not through private friendship, but only by entering his way, ascending with him and, in union with the Father and the Son, belonging to all. Our attempts to hold on to him are replaced by a mission: "To know the risen Christ then is to launch out on a journey that has him for its point of origin."[22]

In reading for Scripture's self-illuminating clarity, the Word becomes an answer to the question about how God can be known in an unbelieving world. Benedict's three-step approach does not abandon scriptural language in favor of worldly language. He recasts worldly discourse into discourse about God so as to classify "the whole of reality under the comprehensive dominion of God."[23] His approach, characterized by its starting place and direction, is given by Christ himself in Scripture.

19. Ratzinger, "Resurrection and Mission," 301–4.
20. Ratzinger, "Resurrection and Mission," 302.
21. Ratzinger, "Resurrection and Mission," 302.
22. Ratzinger, "Resurrection and Mission," 303.
23. Joseph Ratzinger, "Preaching God Today," in Dogma and Preaching, 101.

227

Jesus did not start from ground zero in his proclamation. Nor does
the church. The preacher brings forth from the old what is new, like a
learned scribe, renewing but holding on to a coherent language "that
has not just now been created by him."[24]

PREACHING IN A DIMINISHED CHURCH

Faith can only exist ecclesially, Benedict claims, and yet, as he says
bluntly, "the church does not have a good reputation today."[25] "Whereas
formerly no one doubted that Church was the standard and locus of
preaching, now she stands almost as an obstacle to it: preaching, it
seems, must become a critical corrective to Church instead of being
subordinate to her and allowing her to be normative."[26] With this observation Benedict points to a second source of the crisis in preaching:
the diminished state of the church. Here too the remedy he offers is
supplied by the Word itself. For just as Benedict believes there is a
self-illuminating clarity to Scripture, characterized by its unequivocal
character, so too he believes there is a coherent universal faith in the One
who stands at its center across ages and cultures. Despite the church's
diminished authority, Benedict does not stray from preaching's ecclesial
center because both the direction and shape of the faith proclaimed are
themselves a part of Scripture's clarity and thus essential. How can the
church receive, listen to, guard, proclaim, inhabit, and be reformed by
the full and universal expression of faith found in the self-illuminating
clarity of Scripture? How can she take this as "the standard of authenticity"?[27] Only by inhabiting, holding on to, and preaching the whole

---

24. Ratzinger, "Preaching God Today," 101.
25. Joseph Ratzinger, "Church as Locus of Service the Faith," in *Dogma and Preaching*, 222.
26. Joseph Ratzinger, "Church as the *Place of Preaching*," in Dogma and Preaching, 15.
"The standard of preaching lies in what the universal Church, the Church of all ages, testifies to communally. The judge of this testimony is the Magisterium, which can demand
unconditional respect when it speaks in the name of the whole Church and her Lord.
Scripture and dogma are to be read in the living faith of the universal Church and receive
from her their univocal character, just as, conversely, the Church takes her direction from
them." Ratzinger, "Standards for Preaching the Gospel Today," 39.
27. Ratzinger, "Church as the Place of Preaching Today," 25.

because "the standard of all preaching lies in what the universal Church, the Church of all ages testifies to communally."[28]

Benedict acknowledges that the growing suspicion of Scripture, creeds, and dogma, as well as the disregard of the magisterium, has led to a rediscovery of the faith and positive witness of living Christian communities.[29] But he is critical of this trend when it leads to redefining faith as whatever each community thinks, based on the religious experience of that community, rather than on the common objective faith of the universal church.[30] This trend leads to an abandonment of preaching in the strictest sense. Proclamation is replaced by "dialogue," which he describes as a "form of talking to itself amidst the echoes of old traditions."[31]

THE ACTING SUBJECT OF PREACHING

Benedict argues that the shape of faith received in the crucified and risen Christ is ecclesial because faith in the Trinitarian God disclosed in Scripture is a gathering faith. Benedict declares as fiction any notion that the Bible is not an ecclesial book or stands opposed to the church.[32] He describes the relationship of church and Word as both unity and opposition. The Word is in the church and the source of the church. The Word also is above the church and is its judge.[33] From this central claim that faith can only exist ecclesially, Benedict posits two claims about preaching, given in the Word itself. First, the church is the location of preaching. Second, the church is the subject that acts in preaching. Both claims provide a response to the ecclesial crisis of today.

First, the church is the location of preaching. In *Verbum Domini*, Ratzinger states that Christ himself "is present in his word, since it is he

28. Ratzinger, "Standards for Preaching the Gospel Today," 39.
29. Ratzinger, "Standards for Preaching the Gospel Today," 31.
30. Ratzinger, "Standards for Preaching the Gospel Today," 31.
31. Ratzinger, "Standards for Preaching the Gospel Today," 31–32.
32. Ratzinger, "Church as Place of Preaching," 22.
33. The Bible is the form and norm for preaching its center Jesus Christ because it is the "sole universal book of universal Christianity as a whole, just as the most central creed—the resurrection of the Lord, the rescue of the truly Just man from the pit of death—is at the same the most universal." Ratzinger, "Standards for Preaching the Gospel Today," 25.

who speaks when Scripture is read in Church."[34] Benedict then turns to the use of the word *ecclesia* in the New Testament to describe the fruit of Christ's Word. He notes that the church is not something preexisting and static. Christ speaks in Scripture to call people together in himself and thereby to make them into the *ecclesia*.[35] Thus the Word creates the church but not in a static sense. The church that the Word creates is commissioned to go outside of itself in order to draw all people "into the thanksgiving of Christ, and to make them thankful with him."[36] Thus the creating character of the Word is the source of the two forms of preaching. The church must preach to those who already have faith, who are already drawn into the *eucharistia* of Jesus and live it. The church must also preach to those who stand outside of the assembly, gathering them into the *ecclesia* of those who listen and are thankful.[37] In both cases, faith means emerging from the isolation of one's own existence and becoming "one body" with Christ, an existential unity with him.[38]

Because of the ecclesial shape of the Word, the liturgy is the home of the Word. And the homily is only one of the ways that the liturgy—in the unity of word and sacrament—is the complete and effective proclamation of Christ.[39] Even in preaching one must start from and return to the reality of the church and its liturgy, where the Word gathers those who listen into the *eucharistia* of Jesus and where the Christian

---

34. Benedict XVI, *Verbum Domini*, §52.

35. Ratzinger, "Church as the Place of Preaching," 19.

36. Ratzinger, "Church as the Place of Preaching," 19.

37. Ratzinger, "Church as the Place of Preaching," 20.

38. Ratzinger, "Church as the Place of Preaching," 22.

39. "The liturgical celebration becomes the continuing, complete and effective presentation of God's word. The word of God, constantly proclaimed in the liturgy, is always a living and effective word through the power of the Holy Spirit. It expresses the Father's love that never fails in its effectiveness towards us. The Church has always realized that in the liturgical action the word of God is accompanied by the interior working of the Holy Spirit who makes it effective in the hearts of the faithful." Benedict XVI, *Verbum Domini*, §52. In this post-synodal apostolic exhortation on the Word, only 1 of the 125 sections, paragraph 59, is explicitly devoted to preaching.

encounters the action of the present Christ: the divine worship of the church, which sits at table with the risen Lord.[40]

In a homily preached to university students in Rome on the first Sunday of Advent in 2012, Benedict describes this Eucharistic center.

> The liturgical year that we are beginning with these Vespers also represents for you the journey to live once again the mystery of this faithfulness of God, on which you are called to found your lives, as on a firm rock. In celebrating and living this itinerary of faith with the whole Church, you will experience that Jesus Christ is the one Lord of the cosmos and of history, without whom every human project risks coming to nothing. The liturgy, lived in its true spirit, is always the fundamental school for living the Christian faith, a "theological" faith which involves you in your whole being—spirit, soul and body—to make you living stones in the edifice of the Church and collaborators of the New Evangelization. Especially in the Eucharist the living God makes himself so close that he becomes food that supports us on the journey, a presence that transforms us with the fire of his love.[41]

Second, Benedict turns to the theological implications of the gathering Word on the role and identity of the preacher. The preacher preaches on behalf of the church. He does not preach on behalf of himself or personal faith, or on behalf of an individual congregation or situation. Nor does he preach on behalf of faith in Christ from above which has little to do with the church. Just as the preacher's faith can only exist ecclesially, the preacher's proclamation of the Word that awakens faith must also have an ecclesial character. Thus Benedict speaks of the church as "the human subject of the Bible."[42] The Bible is the witness to and

40. Ratzinger, "Christocentrism in Preaching?," 47 (emphasis original). For an excellent overview of the relationship of the sermon to the Eucharist in the Reformed tradition, see Paul Scott Wilson, "Preaching and the Sacrament of Holy Communion," in *Preaching in the Context of Worship*, ed. David M. Greenhaw and Ronald J. Allen (St. Louis: Chalice, 2000) 43–61.

41. Benedict XVI, homily at First Vespers, Vatican Basilica, December 1, 2012, http://w2.vatican.va/content/benedict-xvi/en/homilies/2012/documents/hf_ben-xvi_hom_20121201_vespri-avvento.html.

42. Ratzinger, "Church as the Place of Preaching," 23.

instrument of a shared faith, from Israel forward, through the long history of the establishment of the canon and its interpretation. His argument is based on locating inspiration within the church. Inspiration is not an individual charismatic process but essentially ecclesial and historic. "The 'Body' alone is the abode of the Spirit."[43] There cannot be any division in preaching between the body the Word creates and the Word that same body proclaims. "Those who have heard the Word about the exaltation [of Christ], the tidings that make us glad, and have been gathered in this Word are at the same time those who must carry it farther."[44] Because of this Benedict claims the church is the "acting subject of preaching."[45]

As a good Catholic, Benedict locates his approach to preaching in the doctrine of the church and its inspiration. Many Protestants acknowledge, following Martin Luther and John Calvin, that Word and church cannot be separated.[46] But they would locate their approach to preaching in their understanding of the inspiration of and authority of Scripture and not in the doctrine of the church. This difference has led to a range of commitments within Protestantism about the relationship of the human word and the divine word in preaching. Karl Barth digested and summarized this Reformation view well: speaking about God is a human impossibility and preaching is a unilateral act of God. He defines preaching as "the Word of God which he himself speaks, claiming for the purpose the exposition of a biblical text in free human

---

43. Ratzinger, "Church as the Place of Preaching," 22.

44. Ratzinger, "Church as the Place of Preaching," 24.

45. Ratzinger, "Church as the Place of Preaching," 21.

46. Calvin opposed those who thought they could know Christ outside of the church. See John Calvin, *Institutes of the Christian Religion*, ed. John T. McNeill, trans. Ford Lewis Battles (Philadelphia: Westminster, 1960.), 4.1.6, 4.1.9; see also Calvin, *Commentary on Galatians, Ephesians, Philippians, Colossians, I & II Timothy, Titus, and Philemon*, Calvin's Commentary Series 21 (Grand Rapids: Baker, 1979), 282. Luther likewise declares that the holy people of God, *the ecclesia santa catholica*, are recognized by their possession of the holy Word of God preached, believed, professed, and lived—and the holy sacraments of baptism and the altar, wherever they are, taught, believed, and administered according to Christ's ordinance. See Martin Luther, *On the Councils and the Church* (1539), trans. Charles M. Jacobs, in Luther's Works, vol. 41, *Church and Ministry III*, ed. Helmut T. Lehmann and Eric W. Gritsch (Philadelphia: Fortress, 1966), 146–68.

words."[47] In contrast to Barth and other neo-orthodox theologians, the Swiss theologian Emil Brunner argued, that there is some human capacity to receive the Word of God.[48] Most forms of Protestant preaching fall somewhere between these two poles. But in almost all cases, preaching is conceived of as an individual encounter with God through his preached Word. The Word and the sermon's location in liturgy among the gathered priesthood of all believers is rarely central.

Because of these differences, many Protestants locate the crisis in preaching in the decline in the authority of Scripture and the pervasiveness of a hermeneutic of suspicion. But as Protestants attempt to respond to the decline of their own churches and the growing number of people who identify as "spiritual but not religious," they too must address the crisis of ecclesial consciousnesses and its relationship to preaching. Some Protestant theologians are beginning to explore a more ecclesially based approach to preaching.[49] This welcome development is coming out of the larger movement of a theological interpretation of Scripture, which explores the implications of Scripture as the church's book.[50]

THE LIVING VOICE OF PREACHING

Benedict's own commitments can offer a guide to Protestants who are exploring ecclesiology as a possible starting place in preaching. Let me

47. Karl Barth, *Homiletics,* trans. Geoffrey William Bromiley and Donald E. Daniels (Louisville: Westminster John Knox, 1991), 53.

48. Emil Brunner and Karl Barth, *Natural Theology: Comprising "Nature and Grace" by Professor Dr. Emil Brunner and the Reply "No!" by Dr. Karl Barth,* trans. Peter Fraenkel (London: Bles; the Centenary Press, 1946). John W. Hart, *Karl Bart vs. Emil Bruner: The Formation and Dissolution of a Theological Alliance, 1916–1936* (New York: Peter Lang, 2001). For a discussion of the Brunner-Barth debate, see Alister McGrath, "Natural Theology? The Barth-Brunner Debate of 1934," in *Emil Brunner: A Reappraisal* (Chichester, UK: Wiley Blackwell, 2014), 90–132.

49. Charles Campbell, *Preaching Jesus: New Directions for Homiletics in Hans Frei's Postliberal Theology* (Grand Rapids: Eerdmans, 1997); David Lose, *Confessing Jesus Christ: Preaching Jesus Christ in a Postmodern World* (Grand Rapids: Eerdmans, 2003); P. W. T. Johnson, *The Mission of Preaching: Equipping the Community for Faithful Witness* (Downers Grove, IL: IVP Academic, 2015); Annette Brownlee, *Preaching Jesus Christ Today: Six Questions for Moving from Scripture to Sermon* (Grand Rapids: Baker Academic, 2018).

50. A. K. M. Adam, Stephen E. Fowl, Kevin J. Vanhoozer, and Francis Watson, *Reading Scripture with the Church: Toward a Hermeneutic for Theological Interpretation* (Grand Rapids: Baker Academic, 2006); Todd J. Billings, *The Word of God for the People of God: An Entryway to the Theological Interpretation of Scripture* (Grand Rapids: Eerdmans, 2010).

briefly make three observations. First, Benedict articulates the vocation
of the church regarding the Word and the responsibility and burden of
all Christian preaching. The Word of God makes the church possible,
yet it is also above it and its critical authority. Though the church is not
the Word, it is the place the Word dwells and lives. Thus, the vocation
of the church is to guard Scripture as a living and not a dying word.[51]
This involves proclaiming the Word in its unmistakable and cohesive
identity and making it new at the same time. This is the work of the Holy
Spirt, to be sure; and Benedict reminds the church that the vocation of
preaching includes the hard work of discerning between an authentic
word and the best thing humans can think of to say. It is a necessary
reminder. Often preachers quickly leave the text of Scripture for the
more accessible worlds of personal experience and stories, or the less
contested world of abstract principles such as love, justice, or justification. In doing so they avoid the burden and vocation of preaching as
Benedict lays out: "Somewhere between mummification and evaporation the church must find the way to serve the Word and to establish,
based on the Word, unity among past, present and future."[52]

Second, Benedict does not leave it up to the preacher or a congregation to discern the character of an authentic word. It is found in the
unity of past, present, and future in the crucified Jesus, who stands
in the center of Scripture as the Alpha and Omega. Only through the
peaching of an authentic word, located in the universal "I" of the church
across the ages, can the church fulfill its vocation to preach both to those
who already believe and to those who do not. Benedict's insistence on
discerning the character of an authentic word invites Protestants to do
likewise.

What are the criteria? What is the rule of faith? His insistence on
preaching an authentic word is a welcome response to the pressure for
relevant preaching, which too often uses Scripture to address listener's

---

51. "The Church is not the Word; she is the place where the Word dwells and in which
lives. That means, however, that she is obliged to be in reality the milieu or 'living
space' ... and not the 'dying space' ... of the Word." Ratzinger, "Church as the Place of
Preaching," 23.
52. Ratzinger, "Church as the Place of Preaching," 24.

felt needs—and nothing more. Benedict will have none of that. "The true ecclesial character of preaching, which is measured by what the Church authentically is ... is far from being a mere determination of what is generally accepted today. It is the most decided protest against the absolutizing of the present moment. It demands of the preacher and of the listener a readiness to go beyond themselves."[53] Benedict reminds all preachers that the stage of personal experience and felt need—the tyranny of the present moment—is a stage far too small on which to proclaim, inhabit, and witness to the gospel.

Third, by locating Scripture in the church across the ages, Benedict establishes the connection between the horizons of Scripture and the current day. Frequently in homiletic theory, the image used to describe this connection is a bridge.[54] But within Protestant homiletics there is no consensus about how to move from "then" to "now," or even if it is legitimate to make this move. Walter Brueggemann makes just this point: "The move very much depends on the interpreter's judgment about the needs and prospects of the present situation, a judgment inevitably personal."[55]

Benedict does not leave it to personal judgment, and in doing so challenges other preachers not to do so either.[56] For Benedict, God's Word in Scripture forms a single people across time, and what the church preaches across time is the actuality of Jesus Christ.[57] Scripture does not belong to the past because its subject is the single people of God, formed by the living Word. Thus those who listen today are not on the far side of a bridge from Scripture, though there is historical distance

---

53. Ratzinger, "Church as the Place of Preaching," 25.
54. Paul Scott Wilson, *Preaching and Homiletical Theory* (St. Louis: Chalice, 2004), 50.
55. As quoted in Wilson, Preaching and Homiletical Theory, 35.
56. The continuum of the church stands in contrast to application (the hallmark of expository preaching), where the preacher unearths Scripture's truths, often in propositions, and carries those across the bridge to parishioners or to liberal Protestant preaching, where the preacher unearths the universal and transcendent religious experiences embedded in the language of Scripture and likewise carries them across the bridge. This is an adaptation of Lindbeck's well-known threefold taxonomy of the function of doctrine in religious communities. Lindbeck's goal was to help religious communities understand one another for the sake of dialogue. Lindbeck, *Nature of Doctrine*, 1–34. For a more complete description of these models used in preaching, see Brownlee, *Preaching Jesus Christ Today*.
57. Ratzinger, "Christocentrism in Preaching?," 43.

to be crossed. They are a part of and a continuation of Scripture, which through the Holy Spirit addresses, builds, sustains, and judges the one church in each generation.[58] It is in this continuum that Ratzinger finds support for the preacher. "The preacher today is not alone; he does not stand before a two-thousand-year gulf between him and the Bible—the living interpretation in the experience of the saints is the inner connection which supports him, and without it intimate acquaintance with the Bible degenerates into mere historicism."[59]

Protestants will agree that preaching comes from and moves toward faith. But many will protest against Benedict's insistence on subordinating the Word and its proclamation to the church. They might challenge him to a further exploration of his own claim that the church must submit to Scripture's judgement in every era, what many Protestants would describes as its ongoing reformation.[60] But the rebuttal of *sola Scriptura* in response to Benedict's focus on ecclesial preaching is not the guarantee some might hope it is. The well-trod hermeneutical battlefields of our day have had their share of friendly fire. The declining practice of actually reading Scripture, in part, has led to the rise in arguments about various methods of reading and interpreting it. L. Gregory Jones notes, "Even evangelicals, who have a very high view of the Bible's authority, often have a rather low competence in reading and embodying Scripture."[61]

Pope Benedict does not have a low competence, and his sermons overflow with his love of, immersion in, and embodying of Scripture's self-illuminating clarity, revealing Jesus Christ, who stands and speaks at its center as he draws all creation to himself. Through Scripture Benedict interprets the world, history, the church, death, the state, humanity, and the future. Far more than in many Protestant sermons, Scripture

---

58. "We are in the story that Scripture tells." Robert W. Jenson, "Scripture's Authority in the Church," in *The Art of Reading Scripture*, ed. Ellen F. Davis and Richard B. Hays (Grand Rapids: Eerdmans, 2003), 27–37.

59. Ratzinger, "Preaching God Today," 101.

60. "The Church of this time and this place must always be measured against the Church of all times and all places, but especially against the exemplary self-expression of the faith that is found in the Bible." Ratzinger, "Church as the Place of Preaching," 24.

61. L. Gregory Jones, "Embodying Scripture in the Community of Faith," in Davis and Hays, *Art of Reading Scripture*, 145.

supplies the form and norm of his sermons, and their content is the crucified Christ, revealed there in word and deed. His sermons, whether lectionary based, centered on the church year, or marking specific ecclesial occasions, are deceptively straightforward. They contain little in the way of introductions, personal stories, or digressions. Their form is frequently narrative, leading to a one-point sermon; or he will take the three appointed Scripture lessons in order. His attentive reading of the texts and their interplay yields deep descriptions of the reality of God in the crucified Christ and the life of following in the church.

For example, in a sermon on the third Sunday of Advent, he moves from Zephaniah 3:14–18a to its fulfillment in Luke 1:28 to Philippians 4:5 and Romans 8, back to Zephaniah, all of it interpreted by the stories of John the Baptist in Luke 3. Such interplay of texts leads to a fulsome and sober description of the joy associated with that day.[62] The reality of the living God, who is the truth of all that is, who addresses us in Scripture, permeates his sermons. "People find that they are being addressed in the word of another and hear God's Word in the word of a man."[63]

The remedy Benedict offers the church for its impoverished preaching is given in the Word itself. The Word, issuing from the crucified and risen Christ, supplies the direction and shape of the church's listening and response. In this direction and shape the preacher is given his vocation. It is to develop practices of listening to Christ, who stands in the center of the self-illuminating Word, and responding in a coherent life in the church of charity, hope, suffering, and love. Benedict speaks of the preacher's vocation to personally be a hearer of the Word.[64] "'What are the Scriptures being proclaimed saying? What do they say to me personally? What should I say to the community in the light of its concrete situation?' The preacher 'should be the first to hear the Word of God which he proclaims,' since, as Saint Augustine says: 'He is undoubtedly

62. Benedict XVI, homily delivered at San Patrizio Al Colle Prenestino, Rome, December 16, 2012, http://w2.vatican.va/content/benedict-xvi/en/homilies/2012/documents/hf_ben-xvi_hom_20121216_parrocchia.html.
63. Ratzinger, "Christocentrism in Preaching?," 40.
64. Ratzinger, "Christocentrism in Preaching?," 57.

barren who preaches outwardly the Word of God without hearing it inwardly.'"[65]

PREACHING TO AN UNBELIEVING WORLD

The crisis in preaching to which Pope Benedict responds is not new. In his 1922 essay "The Need and Promise of Preaching," Karl Barth, like Benedict, speaks of the great need of preaching to speak from and within deep human questions about God.[66] People want to know, "Is it true, this talk of a loving and good God, who is more than one of the friendly idols whose rise is so easy to account for, and whose dominion is so brief? What the people want to find out and thoroughly understand is, Is it true?"[67] In his theology of preaching and his own homilies, Benedict offers the church a direction and shape for preaching the concrete reality of Jesus Christ in an age where both Scripture and the church are suspect. A truth that is both the hope and crisis of the world, and a way to follow.

Many Protestants will object to Benedict's locating of preaching in the church and its liturgy, subordinated on every side by its creeds, dogma, and magisterium. Many will insist on more open skies. But what cannot be denied—and perhaps could be received as a gift—is the sole purpose of this crowded landscape: to protect and serve the living Word, which, as Benedict says, "issuing as it does from the crucified and risen Christ, is wide enough to receive all reality into itself, yet clear enough to confront it with a definite measuring-rod of its own."[68] Preaching must address, as Barth says, the deep human questions about God. By rooting it in Scripture's single, self-illuminating voice and the objective reality of the church, Benedict's preaching does just this. "Man remains a being in which not only the stomach hungers but also the mind and the heart; a being which endures hunger not only for food but also for meaning, for love, for infinity and which cannot live with these truly

---

65. Benedict XVI, *Verbum Domini*, §59.
66. Karl Barth, "The Need and Promise of Christian Preaching," in *The Word of God and the Word of Man*, trans. Douglas Horton (New York: Harper, 1957), 97–135.
67. Barth, "Need and Promise of Christian Preaching," 108.
68. Ratzinger, *Eschatology*, 117–18.

human, no godly gifts."[69] Here, we end with what we agree on: the task, burden, privilege, and responsibility of the preaching of the church. The church across her many branches throughout time and space gives the world what "she alone can give: the Word of God, by which man lives no less than by the bread of this earth."[70]

---

69. Joseph Ratzinger, "The Christian and the Modern World," in *Dogma and Preaching*, 179.

70. Ratzinger, "Christian and the Modern World," 179.

14

Salvation, Will, and Agency

Joseph Ratzinger on Prayer

PRESTON D. S. PARSONS

B enedict famously spoke of his retirement from the papacy as an opportunity to spend time in prayer. This is perhaps no surprise; Benedict
has devoted himself to developing and articulating a theology of prayer in
volumes such as *The Spirit of the Liturgy* and *A New Song for the Lord*, and
his essays on liturgy appear in *The Feast of Faith* and his collected works. His
own prayers have been published in *The Wisdom and Prayers of the Pope*. In
addition to Benedict's discussion of prayer in the liturgy, Benedict has also
focused, in General Audiences given between May 4, 2011, and October 3,
2012, on prayer in Scripture; these are collected in *A School of Prayer*. They
give some insight especially into Benedict as a theological interpreter of
Scripture and as a biblical theologian. They are the focus of this essay.

A School of Prayer begins with two addresses on prayer as a universal
phenomena, and that is where this essay will begin as well, with a brief but
revealing section on the ways that humanity as whole yearns to reach out
to God. But most of the addresses arise directly from Benedict's reading of
Scripture, and I will follow suit, with sections on the prayer of the patriarchs,
the prayer of Jesus, and the prayer of the faithful, each referring to biblical
narratives of various sorts. This works well with the form of Benedict's
own homiletic commentaries on Scripture, and the shape of prayer revealed
through those scriptural figures and narratives.

While Benedict does not treat theological themes concerning prayer
systematically, his comments reveal some consistent systematic concerns
centered primarily on prayer's relation to doing God's will. This allows for
some compelling and generative conclusions about the relation between

humanity and God. For Benedict, human desires can be revelatory of God's own desires for others. As Christ prays for others, he invites them into an ongoing relationship with him and in him, in which we join our desires with God's desires, a desire for the well-being and salvation of others. This will raise some questions about the relationship between divine will, human will, and human agency.[1]

PRAYER AS A UNIVERSAL HUMAN PHENOMENON

Benedict describes prayer as "universally human." As he puts it, "practically always and everywhere [prayers] were addressed to God."[2] Benedict looks to an ancient Egyptian "petition by someone who is suffering"[3] and looking to God for relief. Benedict finds in ancient Mesopotamia hope for God's redemption and liberation in a prayer that seeks freedom, demonstrating "how the human being, in his search for God, had intuited, if vaguely, on the one hand, his own guilt and, on the other, aspects of divine mercy and goodness."[4] Socrates, too, is reported to have prayed that he might be a better person, asking God that he might have inner beauty and wisdom rather than wealth.[5] The unknown God of Greek tragedy is prayed to as "the one who guides the ways of the world."[6] Benedict finds "in the examples of prayer of the various cultures which we have considered ... a testimony of the religious dimension and of the desire for God engraved in the heart of every human being."[7]

---

1. An influential framework for understanding the noncompetitive relation between divine sovereignty and human agency comes from Kathryn Tanner's *God and Creation in Christian Theology* (Minneapolis: Fortress, 2005), 111–16; see also Rowan Williams, who similarly investigates the relation between divine and human will and agency in his Hulsean Lectures of 2016, revised for publication as *Christ: The Heart of Creation* (London: Bloomsbury, 2018).

2. Pope Benedict XVI, *A School of Prayer: The Saints Show Us How to Pray*, trans. L'Osservatore Romano (San Francisco: Ignatius, 2012), 10.

3. Benedict XVI, *School of Prayer*, 10.

4. Benedict XVI, *School of Prayer*, 10–11.

5. Benedict XVI, *School of Prayer*, 11. This petition is found in Plato's *Phaedrus*.

6. Benedict XVI, *School of Prayer*, 11.

7. Benedict XVI, *School of Prayer*, 13.

Even now, in an increasingly secular world, Benedict finds evidence of humans reaching out in their desire for God. Religious life persists; and following the *Catechism of the Catholic Church*, Benedict reports that "all religions bear witness to man's essential search for God."[8] This, for Benedict, is because God has made human beings in the image and likeness of God. The image persists, indelibly engraved on human beings, meaning that all human beings feel "the need to find light to give a response to the questions that concern the deep meaning of reality," a meaning that cannot be found in themselves "in progress, in empirical science."[9] Instead humans bear "the desire for God," an attraction given by God, which is "the soul of prayer."[10]

For Benedict, prayer is a cooperative venture, in both the ancient and contemporary world. Openness in prayer leads to a personal relationship with God, and "prayer appears as a reciprocal call, a covenant drama,"[11] a reciprocity found even among non-Christians. Marcus Aurelius, for example, "affirmed the need to pray in order to establish a fruitful cooperation between divine action and human action. ... The human creature who experiences weakness and impoverishment ... addresses his supplication to Heaven, and ... is endowed with an extraordinary dignity, so that in preparing to receive the divine revelation, finds himself able to enter into communion with God."[12]

Benedict's generosity here is not an absolute generosity. The ancient world did not experience the fullness of God's revelation; instead, they awaited "a word from heaven" that was eventually found in the "full expression in the Old and in the New Testament."[13] "Yet only in God who reveals himself does man's seeking find complete fulfillment."[14] So

---

8. Benedict XVI, *School of Prayer*, 16; *Catechism of the Catholic Church*, §2566.

9. Benedict XVI, *School of Prayer*, 16; Gen 1:26.

10. Benedict XVI, *School of Prayer*, 17.

11. Benedict XVI, *School of Prayer*, 19. Benedict is quoting the *Catechism* here (§2657): "In prayer, the faithful God's initiative of love always comes first; our own first step is always a response ... as God gradually reveals himself and reveals" humanity to itself, and "prayer appears as a reciprocal call, a covenant drama."

12. Benedict XVI, *School of Prayer*, 12–13.

13. Benedict XVI, *School of Prayer*, 13.

14. Benedict XVI, *School of Prayer*, 19.

for Benedict, human beings cannot rely only on themselves for prayer apart from God.

Nevertheless, humanity does experience a longing and a desire for God. And we see Benedict's concern about this longing and desire for God—even among non-Christians—continue as he turns to the prayer of Moses and Abraham, the prayer of Jesus, and the prayer of the faithful. For Benedict, prayer, justice, and salvation are deeply entwined; and further, the human will does not stand alone. Rather, prayer, as it depends on God's initiative, is nevertheless a cooperative venture where communion with God means that human will and divine will work together to accomplish God's own desires for the world.

THE PRAYER OF THE PATRIARCHS

Benedict understands the ultimate fulfillment of human will in adherence to the divine will. One of the ways this is accomplished is through prayer. But for Benedict, prayer is not simply listening to God in order to discern God's will. Rather, Benedict describes God's will as revealed through what Moses and Abraham ask of God. As Benedict looks to the prayers of Moses and Abraham, he sees intercession as a way that God's will is revealed, specifically in stories where intercessions are made for those who were at risk of suffering God's wrath. God's ultimate will is the salvation and well-being of others, which is revealed in and through those prayers of intercession for the mitigation of God's wrath and destruction of others.

Moses provides the primary example of intercession that reveals God's will for salvation. Benedict recounts the Sinai episode of Exodus 32, when Moses ascends the mountain, and where the people, under the direction of Aaron, make and pray to a golden calf. When God sends Moses down from Sinai in order to reveal the idolatry of Israel to him, he tells Moses that he will visit the people with his destructive wrath.[15] But for Benedict, God reveals his intentions to Moses "almost as though he did not want to act without Moses' consent."[16] Instead, God speaks

---

15. Benedict XVI, *School of Prayer*, 34–35.
16. Benedict XVI, *School of Prayer*, 35.

of his wrath so that "Moses might intervene and ask God not to do it, thereby revealing that what God always wants is salvation."[17] And Moses does ask God that he not bring disaster on his people.

For Benedict, there are two parallel things happening in Moses' intercession. First, there is God's anger, expressed as the "rejection of evil" through "punishment and destruction." And second, there is Moses' request, as intercessor, "intended to show the Lord's desire for forgiveness."[18] Moses' intercession reflects God's own will and desire for salvation of his people and his mercy toward them, but this begins as a denunciation of sin, "so that the sinner, having recognized and rejected his sin, may let God forgive and transform him."[19] So "prayers of intercession make active in the corrupt reality of sinful man divine mercy, which finds a voice in the entreaty of the person praying and is made present through him wherever there is a need for salvation."[20] In this way the guilt of an idolatrous people is not overlooked for Benedict. But the intercessor who desires the salvation of God's people does so for the sake of the people entrusted to him and because this outcome— the salvation of the people to whom Moses was entrusted—also brings about the "true reality of God."[21] As Benedict puts it, "Moses asked God to show himself more powerful than sin and death and, with his prayer, elicited this divine revelation of himself,"[22] making Moses' intercession revelatory of God and his will and desire for the salvation of others.

Similarly, Abraham, in his intercession for Sodom and Gomorrah, reveals God's will. In Benedict's reading of Genesis 18, Sodom and Gomorrah had reached such depravity that God's intervention had become necessary. But after God reveals to Abraham that Sodom and Gomorrah are to be destroyed on account of this depravity, Abraham chooses not simply to let that destruction happen, but to intercede for those who are about to be destroyed and to pray for their salvation.

---

17. Benedict XVI, *School of Prayer*, 35.
18. Benedict XVI, *School of Prayer*, 35.
19. Benedict XVI, *School of Prayer*, 35–36.
20. Benedict XVI, *School of Prayer*, 36.
21. Benedict XVI, *School of Prayer*, 36–37.
22. Benedict XVI, *School of Prayer*, 37.

Benedict says, "Abraham knows that God has other ways and means to stem the spread of evil."[23] So Abraham asks for Sodom and Gomorrah's salvation through calling on God's justice in two ways. First, he asks whether it is just for the righteous to be destroyed as though they were guilty. And second, he asks God to treat the guilty as innocent, thus offering the guilty the chance to confess their sin and as a result to become righteous themselves, and therefore no longer in need of punishment.[24]

There is at least one significant difference, however, in Benedict's recounting of Moses' and Abraham's intercession. In the story of Moses and the idolatry of the Israelites, the Israelites survive. But not one person in the Genesis account of Sodom and Gomorrah is saved from destruction.[25] Benedict takes this destruction of Sodom and Gomorrah into account by saying that God was willing and wanted to forgive the citizens of Sodom and Gomorrah, but "the cities were locked into a totalizing and paralyzing evil, without even a few innocents from whom to start in order to turn evil into good."[26] If a transformation from within is not possible, and there is no seed of goodness in Sodom and Gomorrah, then God and God's love have already been abandoned in sin, which already "bears the punishment in itself."[27]

Despite the destruction of the two cities, Abraham's intercession reveals God's own desire for the salvation of others. As Benedict puts it, it is not "punishment that must be eliminated but sin," and Sodom and Gomorrah's destruction is "the very path to salvation"[28] that Abraham was asking and hoping for. Abraham reveals God's will in his intercession as a "prayer to God for the salvation of others, the desire for salvation which God nourishes for sinful man."[29] Ultimately God's desire and God's will is "always to forgive, to save, to give life, to transform

---

23. Benedict XVI, *School of Prayer*, 23.

24. Benedict XVI, *School of Prayer*, 22.

25. Benedict neglects to mention the destruction of the three thousand by the sons of Levi and the plague visited on the survivors; cf. Exod 32:25–29, 35.

26. Benedict XVI, *School of Prayer*, 24; citing Gen 50:20; Rom 8:28.

27. Benedict XVI, *School of Prayer*, 24. Benedict is following Rom 1 here.

28. Benedict XVI, *School of Prayer*, 23.

29. Benedict XVI, *School of Prayer*, 23.

evil into good."[30] To this Abraham lends "his voice, and also his heart."[31] Because salvation is God's ultimate goal, God did not *necessarily* desire the destruction of Sodom; but "by voicing this prayer, Abraham was giving voice to what God wanted."[32] As such, Abraham reveals God's will and desire for the salvation of others.

So in Abraham and Moses, Benedict finds an intercessor who expresses God's will. Abraham's and Moses' desire that God's will be done leads them to ask that others be saved. In the end, in both Sodom and Gomorrah, and among the Israelites at the foot of Sinai, judgment nevertheless takes place. Abraham cannot find ten righteous people, and Sodom and Gomorrah are razed. Three thousand Israelites are killed by the sons of Levi, and others are visited by a plague. But Benedict does not confuse God's willingness to bring judgment and destruction on humanity with God's ultimate ends for humanity. Indeed, the intercession of Abraham and Moses reveals God's desire and will for the salvation of humanity.

Again, for Benedict, God initiates human desire for God and his salvation. God is, in this sense, sovereign. But God's will includes a human agency in which the human person, in prayer, can express God's own will for the salvation of others. So, according to Benedict, to do God's will is not to deny human agency. Instead, God works with human agency in order to make his ways known in the world, with Moses and Abraham acting as examples of intercessors that reveal God's will through their intercessions.

THE PRAYER OF JESUS

Benedict sees Jesus as the paragon of obedience to the Father's will. Abraham and Moses may take part in revealing God's own desire through their intercession, but, for Benedict, Jesus is the one who is most fully able to embody that will and to bring that will to bear on his own life through prayer.

---

30. Benedict XVI, *School of Prayer*, 23.
31. Benedict XVI, *School of Prayer*, 23.
32. Benedict XVI, *School of Prayer*, 23.

For Benedict, Jesus' own habit of prayer is derived from two sources: his life with his family and the traditions of Israel.[33] But Benedict draws a connection between family life and Jesus' own place in the traditions of Israel. As he puts it, the "deep, essential origins" of Jesus' prayer "are found in his being the Son of God and in his unique relationship with God the Father."[34] In this way, Jesus' relationship with the God of Israel is no less familial than his relationship with Mary and Joseph. This is revealed and summarized in Jesus' use of the term "Abba." Calling God "Father" in prayer expresses Jesus' own communion with the Father, what he calls "the central focus and source of every one of Jesus' prayers."[35]

But the familial relation only takes Benedict so far. As we saw in the previous section, on Moses and Abraham, prayer is also revelatory of God's will. Jesus is, after all, divine in the way that the Father is divine, and yet fully human. Thus, in "the unity of the Divine Person of the Son, the human will finds its complete fulfillment in the total abandonment of the I to the You of the Father."[36] So even though Jesus does ask, at Gethsemane, that the cup be removed from him—a human cry that he might not suffer the death he was facing—Jesus ends his cry with a prayer "in which the human will adheres to the divine will without reserve."[37] Benedict sees this communion of Father and Son as one of unity of will, revealed in Gethsemane through Jesus' saying that the will of the Father be done in him, according to that unity.

It is this unity of Jesus' will with the Father's, in prayer, that Benedict returns to most consistently. For example, Jesus in prayer is "completely faithful to the Father's will";[38] and prayer for Jesus "flows through the whole of his life like a secret channel that waters existence, relationships, and actions and guides them, with progressive firmness, to the total

---

33. Benedict XVI, *School of Prayer*, 119.
34. Benedict XVI, *School of Prayer*, 119.
35. Benedict XVI, *School of Prayer*, 124. On God as Father, see Joseph Ratzinger, *Dogma and Preaching: Applying Christian Doctrine to Daily Life*, trans. Michael J. Miller and Matthew J. O'Connell, ed. Michael J. Miller (San Francisco: Ignatius, 2011), 89–90.
36. Benedict XVI, *School of Prayer*, 156.
37. Benedict XVI, *School of Prayer*, 157.
38. Benedict XVI, *School of Prayer*, 120.

gift of self in accordance with the loving plan of God the Father."[39] This unity of will with the Father also extends to healing prayer. When he heals, Jesus seeks out his relation with the Father; Benedict points out that Jesus looks heavenward for the Father's direction when healing the deaf mute in Mark 7:32.[40] Benedict also points out that Jesus' offering of himself for others and for their salvation in the "Eucharistic memorial" shows "his identity and his determination to fulfill his mission of total love to the very end and of offering in obedience to the Father's will."[41] In the High Priestly prayer as well, Jesus is glorified by his "entry into full obedience to the Father."[42]

Benedict explores the relation between the Father's will and Jesus' prayer most fully in the address on the cry of exultation (Matt 11:25–30; Luke 10:21–22). Benedict calls this cry "the apex of a journey of prayer in which Jesus' profound and close communion with the life of the Father in the Holy Spirit clearly emerges and his divine sonship is revealed."[43] This is a personal connection. Jesus has true knowledge of the Father because of this "communion of being."[44] But most importantly for Benedict, the cry of exultation is a prayer that begins with a recognition of the Father's action—that the Father has hidden some things from the wise and revealed them to infants. Thus Jesus shows his own agreement with the way the Father acts and with the Father's will.[45] Jesus' perfect unity with the Father means perfect knowledge, a knowledge reserved for the Son and revealed in the Son. Jesus is joyful that the Father's will is to hide things from the wise, and to reveal them to the little ones. This is a manifestation of Jesus' communion with the Father.[46]

So for Benedict, Jesus at prayer offers evidence of the unity of the Father and Son, a unity that includes unity of will. This is not to the

---

39. Benedict XVI, *School of Prayer*, 116.
40. Benedict XVI, *School of Prayer*, 129.
41. Benedict XVI, *School of Prayer*, 145.
42. Benedict XVI, *School of Prayer*, 149.
43. Benedict XVI, *School of Prayer*, 123–24.
44. Benedict XVI, *School of Prayer*, 124.
45. Benedict XVI, *School of Prayer*, 123.
46. Benedict XVI, *School of Prayer*, 125.

exclusion of Jesus' involvement and care for others. Instead, the unity of will is bound up with the well-being of those for whom Jesus prays.

At two junctures, Benedict explores this connection between doing the will of the Father and concern for others: in Jesus' healing of the deaf mute in Mark 7 and in the raising of Lazarus in John 11. In Jesus' healing of the deaf mute, we see that even though Jesus looks first to the Father, he does so because of his human involvement with others and for the sake of others. It is this compassion toward others that prompts Jesus to pray to the Father. This is because prayer to the Father and Jesus' human involvement with others work together. As Jesus prays to the Father for others, "the human relationship of compassion with the man enters into the relationship with God and, thus, becomes healing."[47]

Benedict also sees this connection between compassion for others and the doing of God's will in Jesus' prayer for the healing of Lazarus. Benedict speaks specifically of Jesus' friendship with Lazarus, where the "bond of friendship and Jesus' participation and distress at the sorrow of Lazarus' relatives and acquaintances are connected throughout the narrative to a continuous, intense relationship with the Father."[48] Benedict points to the prayer at Lazarus' tomb as evidence of this dual dynamic: Jesus lifts up his eyes and thanks the Father for having heard him.[49] The friendship is strengthened even while Jesus remains "in communion with the Father's will, his plan of love, in which Lazarus' illness and death were to be considered as a place for the manifestation of God's glory."[50]

But it is the cross where Benedict sees Jesus' particular form of intercession. In this intercession Jesus identifies with humans; he is willing to be "blotted out" to ensure the salvation of others.[51] For Benedict, Moses' intercession prefigures Christ's intercession.[52] But unlike Moses' intercession, Christ's is an intercession that is contemporary to us, and

---

47. Benedict XVI, *School of Prayer*, 131.
48. Benedict XVI, *School of Prayer*, 131.
49. Benedict XVI, *School of Prayer*, 132; John 11:41.
50. Benedict XVI, *School of Prayer*, 132.
51. Benedict XVI, *School of Prayer*, 38.
52. Benedict XVI, *School of Prayer*, 38; Exod 32:32.

one in which humanity is welcomed into identity with him as one body and one spirit.[53] Benedict also sees Jesus' intercession as ongoing in the Eucharist. As we participate in the Eucharist, "we experience in an extraordinary manner the prayer that Jesus prayed and prays ceaselessly for every person."[54] And we see Jesus' ongoing intercession in the High Priestly prayer as well, in which Jesus prays for the church till the end of time.[55] But the fullness of the ongoing intercession, into which all of humanity is caught up, is seen on the cross, where the prayer of Jesus is about more than bringing his own will in harmony with that of the Father's: it also begins to graft all of humanity into his prayer.

So in Christ we find prayer that reveals the unity of will he shares with the Father. But this unity of will is shaped by Jesus' own human commitments and compassion for others: to his disciples, to those in need of healing, and to his friend Lazarus. This clearly shows us what God's desire for human salvation looks like: it looks like healing and the giving of life. And, like we saw in Moses and Abraham, this divine will, even in its sovereignty, works with created causes as they are found in Christ. Most importantly, by his intercession on the cross Jesus welcomes human beings and begins an ongoing relationship with them.

THE PRAYER OF THE FAITHFUL

Benedict's meditations on prayer, for the most part, begin by exploring prayer as it is described in Scripture. In the first section of *A School of Prayer* Benedict speaks of the prayers of Old Testament figures; in the central and most substantial section of the book, he explores Jesus' own habits of prayer. In most of his addresses, however, Benedict does not end with an exposition of the life of prayer of Abraham, Moses, or Jesus. Instead, he ends with an exhortation about how the life of prayer, as it is found in the lives of biblical figures—and preeminently in Jesus— teaches us how to pray. Benedict underlines this point by exhorting his hearers to pray *like* those figures, especially Jesus. More importantly,

---

53. Benedict XVI, *School of Prayer*, 38–39.
54. Benedict XVI, *School of Prayer*, 146.
55. Benedict XVI, *School of Prayer*, 151.

however, Benedict strives to point out that praying *like* those figures should be understood according to, and then lead to, an understanding of prayer *with* and *in* Christ. It is to the significance of prayer *like, with* and *in* Christ that we now turn.

For Benedict, praying the Psalms is one of the primary ways for the faithful to pray like Christ. Jesus, who looked to the traditions of Israel for his own formation in prayer, prayed the Psalms; so for us to pray the Psalms is to pray the same prayers Jesus himself knew and prayed. But the Psalms themselves foreshadow the messianic figure of Jesus. "Christians, therefore, in praying the Psalms pray to the Father in Christ and with Christ."[56] This adds depth to the correspondence between us at prayer and Christ at prayer. This depth of unity and correspondence leads Benedict to say that in other prayers—in the Eucharist, for example—we as the church are "drawn into this moment of prayer, of being united ever anew to Jesus' prayer."[57]

It should not be a surprise to see that Benedict connects this creaturely formation with the divine will. To return to the cry of exultation: Jesus' cry for the "little ones" "expresses his will to involve in his own filial knowledge of God all those whom the Father wishes to become sharers in it."[58] Through Jesus' relation to the Father in prayer, we learn to take our part in the will of the Father. Thus Benedict writes that "in our prayer, too, we must learn, increasingly, to enter this history of salvation of which Jesus is the summit, to renew before God our personal decision to open ourselves to his will, to ask him for the strength to conform our will to his will, throughout our life, in obedience to his design of love for us."[59] Benedict sees this unity of human and divine will, through prayer with Christ, especially in the Lord's Prayer. "Thy will be done on earth as it is in heaven." In this petition our own human will comes into harmony with Christ's, and thus with the will of the Father.

---

56. Benedict XVI, *School of Prayer*, 52.
57. Benedict XVI, *School of Prayer*, 147.
58. Benedict XVI, *School of Prayer*, 126.
59. Benedict XVI, *School of Prayer*, 120.

Again, this is not simply a matter of being like Christ as we pray; it is a matter of being "with Christ and in Christ."[60]

When praying with Christ and in Christ, the "horizon of the person praying thus opens to unexpected realities."[61] For example, in his address on Psalm 110 Benedict states that in praying we ask that we would be "ready to climb with him the mount of the Cross to attain glory with him" and be able "to contemplate him seated at the right hand of the Father, a victorious king and merciful priest who gives forgiveness and salvation to all men and women."[62] In this way, Benedict speaks to the dual identity of the person praying, being simultaneously formed christologically, while keeping a discrete creaturely identity.

So, when it comes to other prayers of Jesus, such as Jesus' High Priestly prayer, we see again that unity and creaturely vocation become entangled with one another, where the "unity of future disciples, in being united with Jesus—whom the Father sent into the world—is also the original source of the efficacy of the Christian mission in the world."[63] What Benedict sees, then, is a christological formation in prayer in which we become part of God's mission in the world.

Benedict describes this mission to the world as struggle and gift. Much like Jesus' prayer in Gethsemane, our prayers too can be a struggle. The struggle of prayer leads to the blessing God gives as "gratuitous gift."[64] But again, this gift is not simply for the person praying. As Benedict puts it, "whoever allows himself to be blessed by God, who abandons himself to God, who permits himself to be transformed by God, renders a blessing to the world."[65] In this sense, the gratuitous gift of prayer is not simply for the person praying; rather, this gift turns outward toward others, and as such renders prayer as part of God's mission of blessing.

Importantly, for Benedict, to be sent in mission is to exist for others. As he puts it in his address on the High Priestly prayer, "giving to God

60. Benedict XVI, *School of Prayer*, 126.
61. Benedict XVI, *School of Prayer*, 52.
62. Benedict XVI, *School of Prayer*, 115.
63. Benedict XVI, *School of Prayer*, 32.
64. Benedict XVI, *School of Prayer*, 151.
65. Benedict XVI, *School of Prayer*, 32.

means existing no longer for oneself, but for everyone. Whoever, like Jesus, is segregated from the world and set apart for God with a view to a task is, for this very reason, fully available to all."[66] This orientation toward others is partly revelatory: "Christians are called to be witnesses of prayer precisely because our world is often closed to the divine horizon and the hope that brings the encounter with God. ... Through our constant and faithful prayer we can open windows on God's Heaven."[67] Christ prays for the sake of the salvation of others and their well-being—that God's will be done—but now Christians themselves are entrusted with that mission of salvation. Just as Jesus prayed for the sick and suffering, so do we, and as such we become part of God's mission in and to the world; and just as Jesus loves both God and neighbor, he teaches us to do the same. Both the love of God and of others are to be part of our own prayers.[68] Benedict, in fact, puts it in no uncertain terms: "In prayer we must ... open ourselves to the needs and suffering of others."[69] And so just as Jesus gives attention to the needy and suffering, and acts compassionately toward friends and family,[70] this becomes the shape of our prayer as well. We not only to seek out the Father's will but also express the Father's will. We look to our relationship with God as a guide for the direction of that compassion.

While Benedict does not go into great detail on the Holy Spirit's part in prayer, he does not completely avoid the subject.[71] His pneumatology, as he speaks of prayer, is christologically centered. The Holy Spirit joins us into Jesus' sonship. "By involving us in his sonship, Jesus invites us, too, to open ourselves to the light of the Holy Spirit."[72] It is this Spirit that prays within us, revealing the Father's love. The gift of the Holy Spirit is what allows us to pray to God "with the confidence

---

66. Benedict XVI, *School of Prayer*, 150.
67. Benedict XVI, *School of Prayer*, 121.
68. Benedict XVI, *School of Prayer*, 133–34.
69. Benedict XVI, *School of Prayer*, 165.
70. Benedict XVI, *School of Prayer*, 134.
71. He spends much more time understanding prayer through Jesus' Sonship and our prayer as taking part in that "sonship."
72. Benedict XVI, *School of Prayer*, 127; following Rom 8:26–27.

of children, calling him by the name Father."[73] Thus the reception of
the Holy Spirit is what makes us "sons in Christ" and "places us in a
filial relationship with God ... like that of Jesus, even though its origin
and quality are different"; we become "sons in him ... through faith and
through the sacraments of Baptism and Confirmation."[74] Again, this is
related to prayer for Benedict, following Paul in Romans 8. Benedict
describes our prayers as "reciprocal" in the sense that it is not "one direction from us to God" because it is the Spirit that cries "Abba! Father!"[75]
In this sense, the relationship in prayer is one in which God acts first,
in the cry of the Holy Spirit within us, as an "act of the entire Church"
praying as a body and in Christ.[76]

So, for Benedict, Jesus sets an example of how to pray. Primarily he
suggests that we pray like Jesus by praying the Psalms he prayed. But to
pray like Christ is to pray with and in Christ. He invites us into God's
own horizon—even to become God's own creaturely agents in the world,
carrying out God's mission for the salvation and well-being of others.

CONCLUSION

Much more could be said about Benedict's understanding of prayer. In
School of Prayer Benedict speaks about silence and prayer,[77] Mary and
prayer,[78] contemplation,[79] saints such as Alphonsus Mary Liguori and
Dominic Guzmán,[80] and briefly of liturgical prayer.[81]

But the uniqueness of this volume is that Benedict's thoughts on
prayer are primarily guided by Scripture. In Abraham and Moses,
Benedict finds examples of people at prayer, who in prayer and in their
own hopes for the well-being of others bring God's own desire for the
well-being and salvation of others to light. Benedict sees a struggle in

73. Benedict XVI, *School of Prayer*, 128.
74. Benedict XVI, *School of Prayer*, 212.
75. Benedict XVI, *School of Prayer*, 214.
76. Benedict XVI, *School of Prayer*, 215.
77. Benedict XVI, *School of Prayer*, 172–76.
78. Benedict XVI, *School of Prayer*, 178–82, 250–53.
79. Benedict XVI, *School of Prayer*, 223–29.
80. Benedict XVI, *School of Prayer*, 243–45 and 246–49, respectively.
81. Benedict XVI, *School of Prayer*, 271–82.

Jesus between his humanity and his divinity, but a struggle in which Jesus' will is ultimately in union with the Father: in a natural outworking of the Chalcedonian formula, human agency here is not in competition with divine agency. Instead, human agency is at work without being in competition with God's own sovereign will. But much like in the prayers of Abraham and Moses, God's will, revealed in Jesus at prayer, is a desire for human well-being. Perhaps most importantly, as we look to our own lives of prayer, we are invited to pray like Jesus. But Jesus, as our intercessor, invites us into prayer with and in him, as our will comes into union with that divine will. This union with the divine will, a will revealed in Abraham, Moses, and ultimately in Jesus, is not the only end of prayer. We are welcomed, in and with Christ, to both express God's hopes and desires for others, and in that intercession, to take part in God's mission of the salvation and well-being of others.

15

Forming the
Pilgrim Fellowship

Joseph Ratzinger on Catechesis

JONATHAN WARREN P. (PAGÁN)

In the introduction to his survey of early Christian thought, Robert Louis
Wilken argues that "the Christian religion is inescapably ritualistic ...
uncompromisingly moral ... and unapologetically intellectual."[1] The long
ministry of Joseph Ratzinger, Pope Emeritus Benedict XVI, exemplifies this
point as well as any theologian in the twentieth century. Both his greatest
admirers and his most ardent detractors have identified Ratzinger as preeminently a catechist, a teacher of the faith, attendant not only to its intellectual
content but also to the formative liturgical and ecclesial context in which the
faith lives. Vittorio Messori's judgment of Ratzinger's vocation seems most
apropos: "He is a scholar with a concrete pastoral experience."[2]

To describe Ratzinger as a catechist is to draw attention, then, to the
pastoral character of his teaching. His teaching is not academic in the sense
of being detached and independent from the common life of the church,
but rather it has been devoted to the development of the deposit given in
Scripture and tradition. As Ratzinger argues, the task of theology differs
from other disciplines insofar as "it turns to something we ourselves have
not devised," which is authoritative over us and "is able to be the foundation

1. Robert Louis Wilken, *The Spirit of Early Christian Thought* (New Haven: Yale University
Press, 2005), xiii.
2. Joseph Ratzinger with Vittorio Messori, *The Ratzinger Report: An Exclusive Interview on the
State of the Church*, trans. Salvator Attanasio and Graham Harrison (San Francisco: Ignatius,
1985), 20.

of our life."[3] This essay focuses on the aspect of Ratzinger's catechesis that is most relevant to me as an Anglican parish priest: the consistent concern for the dense interweaving of dogma, liturgy, preaching, and Christian living that motivates his teaching and pastoral ministry.

If catechesis describes all of the church's efforts at "revitalizing the Church and making its members more self-conscious of their identity as Christians," as Berard Marthaler says,[4] then Ratzinger underscores that this revitalization cannot happen unless catechetical instruction takes place within a liturgical and moral environment that embodies and reinforces this instruction: "Catechesis is instruction. … But the actual living out of this doctrine is an essential component of it, and man's intellect sees properly only when the heart is integrated into the mind. Consequently, catechetical instruction also includes a pilgrim fellowship, a gradual familiarization with the new life-style of Christianity."[5]

CATECHESIS AND THE CHURCH AS CREATIVE MINORITY IN WESTERN SOCIETY

A number of scholars, including Ratzinger, have pointed out that in late modernity the revival of catechesis cannot be separated from the new evangelization. Michael Warren argues that catechesis involves the "entire process of handing on the word of God in the life of the Church," and evangelization is the first stage in catechesis, aimed at the initial conversion of the person. However, the great number of nominal Christians in the late modern West has created a context in which "evangelization must be undertaken within 'Christian' societies among those 'Christians' who have never been converted."[6]

---

3. Joseph Ratzinger, "What in Fact Is Theology?," in *Pilgrim Fellowship of Faith: The Church as Communion*, ed. Stephan Otto Horn and Vinzenz Pfnür, trans. Henry Taylor (San Francisco: Ignatius, 2005), 31.

4. Berard Marthaler, introduction to *Sourcebook for Modern Catechetics*, ed. Michael Warren (Winona, MN: Saint Mary's Press, 1983), 1:15.

5. Joseph Ratzinger, "Evangelization, Catechesis, Catechism," in *Gospel, Catechesis, Catechism: Sidelights on the Catechism of the Catholic Church* (San Francisco: Ignatius, 1995), 56–57.

6. Michael Warren, "Evangelization: A Catechetical Concern," in Warren, *Sourcebook for Modern Catechetics*, 330–31. See Joseph Ratzinger, "The New Evangelization," *Communio* 44, no. 2 (2017): 390–91.

Ratzinger often takes this lived reality of the increasingly post-Christian West as the point of departure for his speaking and writing. Over the course of the twentieth century, particularly following the two world wars, Christianity lost credibility and plausibility in the West, and the various philosophical and political projects of the early to mid-twentieth century all competed for the spiritual space that Christianity had once occupied. Ratzinger and many of his contemporaries realized that "what the Church was contending with was not so much poor philosophy, but competing humanisms, competing visions of the meaning of human life, and the nature of human dignity."[7] As Tracey Rowland argues, "The arrival of Marxism in the 1920s, Fascism in the 1930s, and New Ageism in the 1960s came with their own eschatologies (the Communist Utopia, the Third Reich, the Age of Aquarius), their own ecclesiologies (the authority of the Communist Party, the Nazi Party, and the enlightened pot-smoking gurus), and their own anthropologies (the Communist Man, the Master Race, the Flower Children), and so on."[8]

Ratzinger's speaking and writing on the *ressourcement* and retrieval of the Christian tradition and its relation to the exegesis of Scripture, his renewal and revival of Catholic liturgy and spirituality, his vehement emphasis on the inherently persuasive capacity of beauty, and his explorations of the catholicity of the church all stem from his desire to present the Catholic faith as an integral and authentic humanism that can command the affections and desires of late modern people.

To respond to these alternative humanisms, Ratzinger urges that the church must not simply demonstrate its goodwill in society as one more helping agency among others. The church must not be focused preeminently on running institutions efficiently, but rather on the personal and corporate holiness that makes the faith plausible and persuasive to those on the outside and the inside of the church. For Ratzinger, "Real 'reform' is to strive to let what is ours disappear as much as possible so that what belongs to Christ may become more visible. Saints ...

7. Tracey Rowland, *Ratzinger's Faith: The Theology of Pope Benedict XVI* (Oxford: Oxford University Press, 2008), 6.

8. Rowland, *Ratzinger's Faith*, 6. See also Tracey Rowland, *Benedict XVI: A Guide for the Perplexed* (London: T&T Clark, 2010), 99.

reformed the Church in depth ... by reforming themselves. What the Church needs in order to respond to the needs of man in every age is holiness, not management."[9] This holiness is not "visualized as untouchability by sin and evil," but rather it always expresses itself "precisely as mingling with the sinners whom Jesus drew into his vicinity." It is "the continuation of God's deliberate plunge into human wretchedness."[10]

The church for Ratzinger is a mystery in the Christian sense, an intelligible but never fully comprehensible reality, which always overspills its empirical boundaries and which always rewards deeper study and participation with a greater sense of the plenitude of the mystery. *Lumen Gentium*, which echoes Henri de Lubac's rediscovery of the church as primordial sacrament in the fathers of the church, proclaims that the "Church is in Christ like a sacrament or as a sign and instrument both of a very closely knit union with God and of the unity of the whole human race."[11]

But the sacramental or cosmic dimension of the church as Christ's body is not a bloodless abstraction. It must find local expression in contemporary proclamation and discipleship. To evangelize, Ratzinger argues, "means to show this path, to teach the art of living."[12] The gospel

9. Ratzinger with Messori, *Ratzinger Report*, 53. See also Ratzinger, "The Church on the Threshold of the Third Millennium," in *Pilgrim Fellowship of Faith*, 295: "If anyone knows the Church only from committee sessions and papers, they do not know her."

10. Joseph Ratzinger, *Introduction to Christianity*, trans. J. R. Foster (New York: Herder & Herder, 1969), 264–65.

11. *Lumen Gentium*, Dogmatic Constitution on the Church, Vatican II, November 21, 1964, §1, http://www.vatican.va/archive/hist_councils/ii_vatican_council/documents/vat-ii_const_19641121_lumen-gentium_en.html. Henri de Lubac, *The Splendor of the Church*, trans. Michael Mason (San Francisco: Ignatius, 1999), 202: "The Church is a mystery; that is to say that she is also a sacrament. She is 'the total *locus* of the Christian sacraments,' and she herself is the great sacrament that contains and vitalizes all the others. In this world she is the sacrament of Christ, as Christ himself, in his humanity, is for us the sacrament of God." Like de Lubac, Ratzinger argues that the church makes the Eucharist, and the Eucharist makes the church, because Christ unites worshipers to himself through the Eucharist: "We ask that the Logos, Christ, who is the true sacrifice, may himself draw us into his act of sacrifice, may 'logify' us, make us 'more consistent with the word,' 'more truly rational,' so that his sacrifice may become ours and maybe accepted by God as ours, may be able to be accounted as ours. We pray that his presence might pick us up, so that we become 'one body and one spirit' with him. We ask that his sacrifice might become present not just in an exterior sense, standing over against us and appearing, so to speak, like a material sacrifice. ... We are asking rather that we ourselves might become a Eucharist with Christ and, thus, become acceptable and pleasing to God." See Joseph Ratzinger, "Eucharist and Mission," in *Pilgrim Fellowship of Faith*, 116.

12. Ratzinger, "New Evangelization," 389.

requires conversion, which is a deeply personal but never individual-
istic action. "Certainly, conversion is above all a supremely personal
act," Ratzinger writes, "but true personalization is always also a new
and more profound socialization."[13] It is induction into a community
that lives by different standards and for a different telos than the culture that surrounds it.

The community that lives according to this alternative logic comes
to feel its distanciation from the prevailing culture that it is called to
evangelize. It comes to feel an aching gap between the object of its faith,
hope, and love, and the objects of desire most characteristic of its host
culture. The gap that opens in this way makes the church into a "sign
of contradiction" (Luke 2:34 in the Vulgate) opposed by the world,[14]
and the church under these conditions comes to play less an establish-
mentarian or chaplaincy role and more a missionary role in society. In
the extended interview with Peter Seewald *Salt of the Earth*, Ratzinger
speculates that the "de-secularization" of the church of the future will
require becoming a minority church again:

---

13. Ratzinger, "New Evangelization," 395.
14. "Ecce positus est hic in ruinam et resurrectionem multorum in Israhel et in signum cui
contradicetur." Ratzinger writes, on the basis of this passage, "We are not talking about
the past here. We all know to what extent Christ remains a sign of contradiction today,
a contradiction that in the final analysis is directed at God. God himself is constantly
regarded as a limitation placed on our freedom, that must be set aside if man is ever to
be completely himself. God, with his truth, stands in opposition to man's manifold lies,
his self-seeking and his pride. God is love. But love can also be hated when it challenges
us to transcend ourselves. But love can also be hated when it challenges us to transcend
ourselves. It is not a romantic 'good feeling.' Redemption is not 'wellness,' it is not
about basking in self-indulgence; on the contrary it is a liberation from imprisonment in
self-absorption. This liberation comes at a price: the anguish of the Cross. The prophecy
of light and that of the Cross belong together." Benedict XVI, *Jesus of Nazareth*, vol. 3, *The
Infancy Narratives*, trans. Philip J. Whitmore (New York: Image, 2012), 86. As John Paul
II recognized in *Redemptoris Mater*, as the church united with Christ becomes a sign of
contradiction, it faces increasing opposition from the world in imitation of Christ. "As
we see from the words of the Protogospel, the victory of the woman's Son will not take
place without a hard struggle, a struggle that is to extend through the whole of human
history. The 'enmity,' foretold at the beginning, is confirmed in the Apocalypse (the
book of the final events of the Church and the world), in which there recurs the sign of
the 'woman,' this time 'clothed with the sun' (Rev. 12:1). ... Mary, Mother of the Incar

She will be less identified with the great societies, more a minority Church; she will live in small, vital circles of really convinced believers who live their faith. But precisely in this way she will, biblically speaking, become the *salt of the earth* again. In this upheaval, constancy—keeping what is essential to man from being destroyed—is once again more important, and the powers of preservation that can sustain him in his humanity are even more necessary.[15]

Elsewhere Ratzinger describes this purified and purifying church as a "creative minority," a term he adapts from the historian Arnold Toynbee. Being a creative minority, as Rabbi Jonathan Sacks helpfully describes it, "involves maintaining strong links with the outside world while staying true to your faith, seeking not merely to keep the sacred flame burning but also to transform the larger society of which you are a part."[16] For Ratzinger, the church understood as a creative minority sees itself as participating in what John Meyendorff calls a "living tradition." A creative minority church sees itself as "carrying the fire," to adapt a phrase from Cormac McCarthy.[17] The church is enkindled with new life as it single-mindedly devotes itself to Christ, and it becomes capable, being so filled, of sharing that life with others:

> Something living cannot be born except from another living thing. Here is where I see the importance of creative minorities. ... This is why it is so important to have convinced minorities in the church, for the church, and above all beyond the Church and for society: human beings who in their encounters with Christ have discovered the precious pearl that gives value to

nate Word, is placed at the very center of that enmity, that struggle which accompanies the history of humanity on earth and the history of salvation itself." John Paul II, *Redemptoris Mater*, Encyclical Letter, March 25, 1987, §11, http://w2.vatican.va/content/john-paul-ii/en/encyclicals/documents/hf_jp-ii_enc_25031987_redemptoris-mater.html.

15. Joseph Ratzinger, *Salt of the Earth: The Church at the End of the Millennium; An Interview with Peter Seewald*, trans. Adrian Walker (San Francisco: Ignatius, 1997), 222.

16. Jonathan Sacks, "On Creative Minorities," *First Things*, January 2014, https://www.firstthings.com/article/2014/01/on-creative-minorities.

17. Cormac McCarthy, *The Road* (New York: Knopf Doubleday, 2007), 70, 109, 238.

all life ... assuring that the Christian imperatives are no longer ballast that immobilizes humanity, but rather wings that carry it upward. Such minorities are formed when a convincing model of life also becomes an opening toward a knowledge that cannot emerge amid the dreariness of everyday life. Such a life choice, over time, affirms its rationale to a growing extent, opening and healing a reason that has become lazy and tired. There is nothing sectarian about such creative minorities. Through their persuasive capacity and their joy, they reach other people and offer them a different way of seeing things.[18]

The creative-minority paradigm, as Ratzinger intimates above, does not mean that the church becomes a "sect" or withdraws from its fundamental engagement with the various sectors of public life. Christianity proposes an integral or authentic humanism, and therefore it cannot help but speak to all spheres of human life.[19] Christ is "the most human of men, the fulfilment of the whole concept of humanity."[20] Becoming a creative minority, however, must mean that the church shifts its expectations for how Western societies in particular will respond to it, expecting that its efforts will be met with both goodwill and with resistance, resentment, and hostility.

Second, in response to this mixed reception, it comes to see itself not as a secular, helping institution but as the site at which earth is opened to heaven and which seeks its own salvation and the salvation of the world. Paradoxically, it is only by being more "heavenly minded"

---

18. Joseph Ratzinger and Marcello Pera, *Without Roots: The West, Relativism, Christianity, Islam*, trans. Michael Moore (New York: Basic Books, 2006), 120.
19. In *Caritas in Veritate*, Benedict writes, "Only if we are aware of our calling, as individuals and as a community, to be part of God's family as his sons and daughters, will we be able to generate a new vision and muster new energy in the service of a truly integral humanism." Benedict XVI, *Caritas in Veritate*, Encyclical Letter, June 29, 2009, §78, http://w2.vatican.va/content/benedict-xvi/en/encyclicals/documents/hf_ben-xvi_enc_20090629_caritas-in-veritate.html.
20. Ratzinger, *Introduction to Christianity*, 156.

that the church becomes more capable of earthly good.[21] A recovery of catechesis—instruction in the content and practice of the faith—is a critical precondition to the renewed confidence of the church in its missionary posture for Ratzinger.

Ratzinger's work in this regard echoes *Lumen Gentium*, which declared that the "messianic people, although it does not actually include all men, and at times may appear as a small flock, is, however, a most sure seed of unity, hope and salvation for the whole human race."[22] The purification of the church through primary devotion to the salvation offered in Jesus Christ creates an inevitable distancing from the prevailing patterns of thought and practice in the culture of which the church is a part, a sense of its own strangeness and difference as a body set within a particular context. This differentiation must be practiced in order to be sustained. James K. A. Smith gives us the helpful language of liturgical "counter-formation" against the secular liturgies that entice and seduce us as a way to think about what this practice entails.[23] The space that this process of distanciation creates is actually necessary for the evangelization of any culture. The catechetical process is designed to inculcate this sense of being set apart while remaining in the tension of being an integral part of that culture.

But as the church becomes aware of its holiness—its set-apartness— it simultaneously becomes aware of its own catholicity, in what we might

---

21. Ratzinger writes, "This ontological precedence of the Church as a whole, of the one Church and the one body, of the one bride, over the empirical and concrete realizations in the various individual parts of the Church seems to me so obvious that I find it difficult to understand the objections raised against it. They seem to me to be possible at all only if one refuses to see God's great idea, the Church—perhaps through despair at her inadequacy here on earth—if one will no longer and can no longer see it at all. ... If you can no longer see the church except as existing in human organizations, then hopelessness is in fact all there is left." Joseph Ratzinger, "The Ecclesiology of the Constitution *Lumen Gentium*," in *Pilgrim Fellowship of Faith*, 135. As R. R. Reno puts it, the political implications of seeing the church as the site at which earth opens to heaven means that "we cannot serve the common good unless we seek higher things. We must seek to order public life in accord with metaphysical truths higher than the ersatz ends of maximizing utility, encouraging dialogue, and promoting diversity." Reno, *Resurrecting the Idea of a Christian Society* (Washington, DC: Regnery Faith, 2016), 141.

22. *Lumen Gentium*, §9.

23. James K. A. Smith, *Desiring the Kingdom: Worship, Worldview, and Cultural Formation* (Grand Rapids: Baker Academic, 2009), 88.

call its extensive, qualitative, and cosmic aspects.[24] It becomes aware of its participation in a worldwide, multiethnic, multilingual family, which has become breathtakingly more vibrant and confident in its proclamation in the Global South than in its historic homeland of the West. The church of the West is humbled as it realizes that this growth has taken place almost entirely after the dismantling of colonial structures.[25]

The church also recognizes, in its awareness of this extensiveness, the qualitative dimension of its catholicity, that this communion or fellowship creates unity across race, gender, nationality, and class. Finally, it sees that these two horizontal dimensions of catholicity are grounded by the vertical, cosmic dimension of catholicity, that the church lives on and is renewed exclusively by the life of the risen and ascended Christ, and that the visible church today participates in the life of the church in all ages by being united to Christ. Christianity is pluralistic, and the unified truth that its multiple instantiations across generations and geography is symphonic.[26]

The deeper catechists immerse themselves in history with the eyes of faith, the more this cosmic aspect of the church reveals itself. Catechists who see with the eyes of faith deepen in the conviction that the truth of the faith is not boring, but delightful and seductive. The truth "is never monotonous, nor is it ever exhausted in a single form, because our mind

---

24. In discussing the works of N. T. Wright, Jeremy Begbie distinguishes between "qualitative" and "extensive" catholicity: "qualitative catholicity speaking of the church's transcending all social and cultural divisions, as well as natural divisions such as age and gender; extensive catholicity speaking of the church's spatial extension, its comprising all professing Christians in all places." Begbie, "The Shape of Things to Come? Wright amidst Emerging Ecclesiologies," in *Jesus, Paul, and the People of God: A Theological Dialogue with N. T. Wright*, ed. Nicholas Perrin and Richard B. Hays (Downers Grove, IL: IVP Academic, 2011), 200. Ratzinger would agree that these aspects or dimensions pertain to catholicity, but would add to this a cosmic dimension, which accentuates the fellowship and sense of belonging that the visible body on earth has with the whole communion of saints.

25. See Scott Sunquist, *The Unexpected Christian Century: The Reversal and Transformation of Global Christianity, 1900–2000* (Grand Rapids: Baker Academic, 2015).

26. Hans Urs von Balthasar, *Truth Is Symphonic: Aspects of Christian Pluralism*, trans. Graham Harrison (San Francisco: Ignatius, 1987).

beholds it only in fragments, yet at the same time it is the power which unifies it. And only pluralism in relation to unity is great."[27]

TOOLS FOR THE RENEWAL OF CATECHESIS

For Ratzinger the tools for catechetical instruction include, first of all, the study of the history of the church in its most vital moments, the task of ressourcement and retrieval. As Henri de Lubac asked, "How should we rediscover Christianity if not by going back to its sources, trying to recapture it in its periods of explosive vitality?"[28] The exemplary saints that the church has produced in every age, along with the beauty that the church has produced on the basis of its worship and encounter with the Triune God, are a critical piece of the church's present capacity to form the faithful through catechesis and evangelize those outside of the body.

Ratzinger follows the lead of *Dei Verbum* and *Divino Afflante Spiritu* in reprioritizing sacred Scripture as the norming witness to the revelation of the Word of God in Christ.[29] At the same time, "Scripture is not a meteorite fallen from the sky," but rather "it is transmitted by a human history. It carries within it the life and thought of a historical society that we call the 'People of God.'" Thus there is a "reciprocal relationship" between the word of Scripture and the church: "This society is the essential condition for the origin and growth of the biblical Word; and conversely, this Word gives the society its identity and its continuity."[30] The project of *ressourcement* and retrieval is animated by the recovery not only of the drama of Scripture but also of the drama of

---

27. Joseph Ratzinger, *The Nature and Mission of Theology: Approaches to Understanding Its Role in the Light of Present Controversy*, trans. Adrian Walker (San Francisco: Ignatius, 1995), 97–98.

28. Henri de Lubac, *Paradoxes of Faith*, trans. Paule Simon and Sadie Kreilkamp (San Francisco: Ignatius, 1987), 57.

29. Rowland, *Ratzinger's Faith*, 55.

30. Ratzinger, "What in Fact Is Theology?," 33.

the incarnation of those Scriptures within the historical communities that have received Christ.[31]

The conviction that the church is the visible community extended through time devoted to Christ as revealed in the Scriptures shapes Ratzinger's repeated insistence that "the only really effective apologia for Christianity comes down to two arguments, namely, the *saints* the church has produced and the *art* which has grown in her womb."[32]

The church's history is a vital resource for the catechist not in its verbal aspects alone, but in its artistic expressions as well, because beauty is the radiance or splendor of truth, and hence to be indifferent to beauty is actually to be indifferent to the way in which the truth most persuasively presents itself to us. "A theologian who does not love art, poetry, music, and nature can be dangerous," Ratzinger reflects. "Blindness and deafness toward the beautiful are not incidental: they necessarily are reflected in his theology."[33] The images and iconography of the church are a critical catechetical resource here. The Western tradition, Ratzinger points out, has always emphasized, almost exclusively, the pedagogical value of images, but their value is equally their ability to draw us into the mystery of God, and to retrain our interior sense of sight. For that reason, "the complete absence of images is incompatible with faith in the Incarnation of God."[34]

---

31. Ratzinger's commitment to the ressourcement of word and church becomes clear in his reflections on what can be learned from St. Jerome: "What can we learn from St. Jerome? It seems to me, this above all: to love the Word of God in Sacred Scripture. St. Jerome said: 'Ignorance of the Scriptures is ignorance of Christ.' It is therefore important that every Christian live in contact and in personal dialogue with the Word of God given to us in Sacred Scripture. This dialogue must always have two dimensions: on the one hand, it must be a truly personal dialogue because God speaks with each one of us through Sacred Scripture and it has a message for each one. We must not read Sacred Scripture as a word of the past but as the Word of God that is also addressed to us, and we must try to understand what it is that the Lord wants to tell us. However, to avoid falling into individualism, we must bear in mind that the Word of God has been given to us precisely in order to build communion and to join forces in the truth on our journey towards God. Thus, although it is always a personal Word, it is also a Word that builds community, that builds the church. We must therefore read it in communion with the living Church." Benedict XVI, *The Fathers of the Church: From St. Clement of Rome to St. Augustine of Hippo*, ed. Joseph Lienhard (Grand Rapids: Eerdmans, 2009), 111.

32. Ratzinger with Messori, *Ratzinger Report*, 129.

33. Ratzinger with Messori, *Ratzinger Report*, 130.

34. Joseph Ratzinger, The Spirit of the Liturgy, trans. John Saward (San Francisco: Ignatius, 2000), 125, 131.

Beauty, as Balthasar realized, is perhaps most necessary in late modernity, in which the truthfulness of the truth has lost its capacity to persuade. Czesław Miłosz captures the evidential power of beauty in his poem "One More Day":

> And though the good is weak, beauty is very strong.Nonbeing
> sprawls, everywhere it turns into ash whole expanses of being,
> It masquerades in shapes and colors that imitate existence And
> no one would know it, if they did not know that it was ugly.[35]

Rich acquaintance with the moral beauty of the lives of the saints and with the beauty of its visual art and rhetorical eloquence can enflame the catechist with a sense that this richness of the past belongs also to us in the present, that we participate in its reality now, and that therefore these victories are not merely memories, but have the possibility of becoming reality now as well. It is not only in our personal encounter with these monuments of faith, but in sharing them with others, as St. Augustine argues, that we can have our delight in catechesis renewed. The delight that comes from sharing in these beautiful things is enhanced the closer and more vibrant the fellowship of this body is.[36]

The church does not simply glory in the past for its own sake, however. Rather, the project of *ressourcement* is in service of *aggiornamento*. The turn to the past is a turn that seeks inspiration for proclamation, catechesis, and evangelization in the contemporary context. Moreover, part of the purpose of *ressourcement* and retrieval of the past is to demonstrate to late moderns that they do not actually know Christianity at

35. Czesław Miłosz, "One More Day," in *The Collected Poems, 1931–1987* (New York: Ecco, 1988), 407.
36. Augustine writes, "Isn't it quite common that when we show certain beautiful, spacious locales, whether in town or out in the countryside, to those who have never seen them before, we who have been in the habit of passing them by without any enjoyment find our own delight renewed by their delight at the novelty of it all? And how much more enjoyable the closer our friendship, because as we come together more and more through this bond of love, what had gotten old becomes new to us all over again. ... How much more then ought we to rejoice when people now approach to learn of God Himself ... and how much more ought we to be renewed in their newness, so that if our preaching, now a routine, has cooled off, it may again catch fire because of our hearers." Augustine, quoted in William Harmless, *Augustine and the Catechumenate* (Collegeville, MN: Liturgical Press, 2014), 162.

all. Part of the church's challenge in late modernity is to overcome the sense among many, both among the baptized who are "over church," as a post-Christian acquaintance put it to me recently, and among secular observers, that they know what the gospel is and have rejected it. As Ratzinger argues, "An awareness needs to develop that in fact to a large extent we no longer know Christianity at all. ... There needs to be a renewal of what you could call a curiosity about Christianity, the desire really to discover what it's all about. It would be very important for preachers ... to create curiosity about the richness hidden in Christianity, so that this richness is regarded ... as a living treasure that is worth knowing." [37]

Second, it is crucial for Ratzinger that the church understand its place in the concrete, material conditions in which catechesis and evangelization must take place so that it can demonstrate how the Christian faith answers to both its longings and its aporias. In this he evidences a central concern for the churches of the West, the historic homeland of Christianity. The intellectual culture of the West is increasingly characterized by the dogma of relativism, Ratzinger argues, and has produced regimes whose most prominent institutions are committed to the popularization of normative relativism. Ratzinger famously referred to this reality as the "dictatorship of relativism that does not recognize anything as definitive and whose ultimate goal consists solely of one's own ego and desires." [38]

Relativistic societies above all reject the idea of any teleological framework for understanding human nature and maturity and celebrate authenticity and "expressive individualism." As Christian Smith

---

37. Ratzinger with Seewald, *Salt of the Earth*, 18.
38. Joseph Ratzinger, homily delivered at the Vatican Basilica, April 18, 2005, http://www.vatican.va/gpII/documents/homily-pro-eligendo-pontifice_20050418_en.html. Elsewhere Ratzinger argues that "in recent years I find myself noting how the more relativism becomes the generally accepted way of thinking, the more it tends toward intolerance, thereby becoming a new dogmatism. Political correctness ... seeks to establish the domain of a single way of thinking and speaking. Its relativism creates the illusion that it has reached greater heights than the loftiest philosophical achievements of the past. It prescribes itself as the only way to think and speak—if, that is, one wishes to stay in fashion. Being faithful to traditional values and to the knowledge that upholds them is labeled intolerance, and relativism becomes the required norm." Ratzinger, "Letter to Marcello Pera from Joseph Ratzinger," in Ratzinger and Pera, *Without Roots*, 128.

argues, the normative sacred vision of the person in late modernity is of an "autonomous, self-directing, therapeutically oriented individual."[39] Yuval Levin has argued in this connection that the strong institutions in American society promote "moral anarchy."[40] The National Survey of Youth and Religion, the most comprehensive study of its kind, indicates that this atmosphere has created a situation in which the vast majority of emerging adults in the United States are "moral individualists," that is, incapable of giving a nonsubjective justification for their moral beliefs, and a solid minority are moral relativists. Christian Smith and his team conclude that these emerging adults

> are morally at sea in boats that leak water badly. ... But if these emerging adults are lost, it is because the larger culture and society into which they are being inducted is also lost. ... The families, schools, religious communities, sports teams, and other voluntary organizations of civil society are failing to provide many young people with the kind of moral education and training needed for them even to realize, for example, that moral individualism and relativism make no sense, that they cannot be reasonably defended or sustained, that some alternative views must be necessary if we are to be at all reasonable when it comes to moral concerns.[41]

The embrace of relativism produces an inertia in the soul associated with the traditional monastic vice of acedia on a grand scale. The daughters of acedia, according to the tradition, include "apathy (*torpor*) with regard to everything man needs for salvation, faintheartedness (*pusillanimitas*); nursing grudges (*rancor*); and spitefulness (*malitia*)." All of these manifestations of acedia are on powerful display in modern society, as anyone who spends time on social media can attest. Ratzinger goes so

---

39. Christian Smith, *The Sacred Project of American Sociology* (New York: Oxford University Press, 2014), 130.
40. Yuval Levin, *The Fractured Republic: Renewing America's Social Contract in the Age of Individualism* (New York: Basic Books, 2017), 173.
41. Christian Smith, with Kari Christofferson, Hilary Davidson, and Patricia Snell Herzog, *Lost in Transition: The Dark Side of Emerging Adulthood* (New York: Oxford University Press, 2014), 60–61.

far as to say that "rancor, the nursing of grudges, is today included by many as a component of the modern catalogue of virtue."[42]

For Ratzinger, then, catechesis must be more than the mere communication of information about the faith, it must be an immersive formation in the spiritual exercises that can rouse Christians to pursue greatness of soul (*magnanimitas*). Acedia is actually a kind of sorrow that comes "from an incapability of believing in the greatness of the human vocation that has been destined for us by God."[43] Catechesis, for Ratzinger, therefore means to connect dogma, spirituality, and morality seamlessly so that the church may regain its awareness of the triune mystery in which it participates for the life of the world. It is incumbent on the church not to "presuppose" the faith in such a context, but to "propose" it as the only true basis for an authentically human existence, to offer this hope to the world as a foundation on which to build their lives, and then to show them how to do it, to embody the "greatness of soul" that is the evidence of holiness among both clergy and laity in particular congregations.[44]

Because moderns have lost a sense of teleology, we have also lost a sense of how history and ontology are related. Time for us is simply "secular" or "profane" time, that is, linear time. We have no sense of "higher time," a time which is capable of gathering up the moments of history into the presence of eternity and making them contemporary with one another. Thus time for us is meaningless except insofar as we impose our own meaning on it. The liturgy and sacraments hinge on the possibility of higher time, on the possibility of God supervening on ordinary time to fill it with meaning given by sacred history.

Our baptism is our present immersion in Christ's death and resurrection (Rom 6:3–4), which we also experience together with the Israelites who were baptized into Moses in the Red Sea (1 Cor 10:1–2). In the Eucharist, "we are caught up and made contemporary with the

42. Joseph Ratzinger, *To Look on Christ: Exercises in Faith, Hope, and Love,* trans. Robert Nowell (New York: Crossroad, 1991), 74.
43. Ratzinger, *To Look on Christ,* 70–71.
44. Ratzinger, "What Is the Meaning of Faith?," in *Gospel, Catechesis, Catechism,* 24.

Paschal Mystery of Christ."[45] "The Eucharist is an entry into the liturgy of heaven; by it we become contemporaries with Jesus Christ's own act of worship, into which, through his Body, he takes up worldly time and straightway leads it beyond itself, snatching it out of its own sphere and enfolding it into the communion of eternal love."[46] The Eucharist is a sacrifice, not because Christ is "resacrificed" on the altar, but because the memorial unites us substantially with Christ's once-for-all sacrifice: "What is perpetual takes place in what happens only once."[47] As Charles Taylor argues, higher time creates "warps" between events in history, which link events distant in time from one another together and cause them to participate in one another.[48]

Ratzinger's ecclesiological and liturgical writing is dedicated to a presentation of these historic ways of understanding time and its profound difference from the "disenchanted" time of modernity. The church's liturgy, architecture, and ceremonial ought all to reflect the fact that in Christ time and eternity have converged, so that our "today" is contemporary with the today of the paschal mystery.[49]

Late modernity in the West represents a point of crisis, in which the historic underpinnings related to theological anthropology and the ability history to transmit the truth about being have been eroded. The latter point, the relationship between ontology and history, is identified

---

45. Ratzinger, *Spirit of the Liturgy*, 57.
46. Ratzinger, *Spirit of the Liturgy*, 70.
47. Ratzinger, *Spirit of the Liturgy*, 56.
48. Taylor argues that "'Secular' time is what to us is ordinary time, indeed, to us it's just time, period. One thing happens after another, and when something is past, it's past. Time placings are consistently transitive. A is before B and B before C, then A is before C. The same goes if we want to quantify these relations: if A is long before B, and B long before C, then A is very long before C. ... Now higher times gather and re-order time. They introduce 'warps' and seeming inconsistencies in profane time-ordering. Events which were far apart in profane time could nevertheless be closely linked." Charles Taylor, *A Secular Age* (Cambridge: Belknap Press of Harvard University Press, 2007), 55.
49. Rowland write that for Ratzinger, "the Catholic liturgy is a cosmic drama. When celebrated as Ratzinger envisions there is a dramatic tension in the Mass which builds to the consecration. The festive joy that is subsequently experienced is also related to the release of tension. Protestant liturgy, by contrast, lacks the dramatic tension because there is no sacrifice, there is only the reading of scripture and fellowship. When the Catholic liturgy begins to take on the form of Protestant liturgy, and the sacrificial dimension is played down, it becomes banal and, at best, pedagogy, not liturgy. There is nothing cosmic about it. In contrast ... Ratzinger's experience of good liturgy is deeply sensual, communal, incarnational, and cosmic." Rowland, *Ratzinger's Faith*, 134.

by Ratzinger as "fundamental crisis of our age." Ratzinger, like many of his generation, found himself increasingly frustrated with neo-scholastic retrenchment, "a Thomism which prides itself on being 'above history'" and rebuttals to modernism which responded that "history is irrelevant and only heretics think about it."[50]

In the West, the church's catechesis therefore must be aware of both the twin dangers of neo-scholastic retrenchment against the relativizing effects of history, and the modernistic embrace of historicism to the disintegration of the faith, so that proclamation of the gospel must be "somewhere between mummification and evaporation." The church "must find the way to serve the Word and to establish, based on the Word, unity among past, present, and future time."[51]

DEVELOPMENT OF THE CATECHISM OF THE CATHOLIC CHURCH

The Catechism of the Catholic Church (released in 1992) is one of Ratzinger's chief contributions to the catechesis of the Roman Catholic Church. Twenty years after the close of the Second Vatican Council, a memorial synod was convoked at which Ratzinger was present. In the conversations at that synod, "there arose the idea of a catechism of the universal Church, analogous to the Roman Catechism of 1566, which in its day had made an essential contribution to the renewal of catechesis in the spirit of the Council of Trent."[52]

In place of the various catechisms that had been used during the twentieth century—successful ones such as the Baltimore Catechism, as well as less satisfactory catechisms such as the Dutch Catechism of 1968, of which Ratzinger is profoundly critical[53]—there would be one catechism demonstrating how the insights of Vatican II fit into the overall

50. Rowland, *Ratzinger's Faith*, 6.
51. Joseph Ratzinger, *Dogma and Preaching: Applying Christian Doctrine to Daily Life*, trans. Michael J. Miller and Matthew O'Connell, ed. Michael J. Miller (San Francisco: Ignatius, 2005), 24.
52. Joseph Ratzinger, "Introduction to the Catechism of the Catholic Church," in Joseph Ratzinger and Christoph Schönborn, *Introduction to the Catechism of the Catholic Church* (San Francisco: Ignatius, 1994), 11.
53. Ratzinger, *Dogma and Preaching*, 59–76.

magisterial teaching of the Catholic Church rather than accenting the originality of the "spirit of Vatican II."

That the catechism should express the unity and coherence of the church's teaching was fundamental to Ratzinger. One of his deepest worries, expressed in various writings, was the increasing fragmentation of the West, not only in political life, but also in the church itself. The purpose of an updated catechism was the unity of the church, which could then produce the resources for overcoming social divisions. Ratzinger argues that "the decomposition of ecclesiastical unity goes hand in hand with the disintegration of civil unity,"[54] and he believes that the reverse is true as well.

Thus the catechism was not to state the theological predilections of one group, but rather to state in plain language "the faith of the Church, which is no one's personal invention."[55] The catechism would express this faith in content, adopting the traditional loci of catechesis, the Apostles' Creed, the sacraments, the Ten Commandments, and the Lord's Prayer, a structure that was shared equally by the Catechism of the Council of Trent and Luther's *Large Catechism*.[56]

It would also express this commitment to universality in structure and approach to the presentation of the faith. Ratzinger notes that initial discussions about the catechism focused on whether it should proceed "inductively," guiding the person in modern society from "today's questions" to the "solutions" of God, Christ, and the church, or whether the faith should be set out according to its own logic, thus shifting the purpose of the catechism from arguing to "bearing witness." Eventually it was concluded that since there is "no one global state of affairs" and thus no single narrative of modernization that can be addressed, an inductive approach to the catechism would address only one type of society, becoming less useful or even irrelevant in other contexts.[57]

---

54. Ratzinger, "Introduction to the Catechism," 20.
55. Ratzinger, "Introduction to the Catechism," 20.
56. Ratzinger, "Introduction to the Catechism," 28–30; Christoph Schönborn, "A Short Introduction to the Four Parts of the Catechism," in Ratzinger and Schönborn, *Introduction to the Catechism of the Catholic Church*, 63–64.
57. Ratzinger, "Introduction to the Catechism," 20–21.

Thus it takes as its starting point the life of the church both synchronically and diachronically, which has as its source and its goal communion with the Triune God. As Cardinal Schönborn has pointed out, the *Catechism* is structured as a whole by the Trinity, and at several places this foundation is evident and visible, in the missionary connection between the missions of Son and Spirit that ground the mission of the church; in the Trinitarian works of creation, redemption, and sanctification; and in the work of the liturgy.[58] Especially noteworthy in this regard is the Trinitarian logic of the resurrection highlighted in the *Catechism*:

Christ's Resurrection is an object of faith in that it is a transcendent intervention of God himself in creation and history. In it the three divine persons act together as one, and manifest their own proper characteristics. The Father's power "raised up" Christ his Son and by doing so perfectly introduced his Son's humanity, including his body, into the Trinity. Jesus is conclusively revealed as "Son of God in power according to the Spirit of holiness by his Resurrection from the dead." St. Paul insists on the manifestation of God's power through the working of the Spirit who gave life to Jesus' dead humanity and called it to the glorious state of Lordship.[59]

A second crucial focus of the *Catechism* is the christological basis of the faith. "Christ crucified" is the center of all authentically Christian preaching, and maturity in Christ is the goal of all catechesis. As John Paul II wrote, "At the heart of catechesis we find, in essence, a Person, the Person of Jesus of Nazareth, the only Son from the Father ... who suffered and died for us and who now, after rising, is living with us forever." Thus the *Catechism* says that to catechize is " 'to seek to understand the meaning of Christ's actions and words and of the signs worked by him.' Catechesis aims at putting 'people ... in communion ... with Jesus

58. Christoph Schönborn, "Major Themes and Underlying Principles of the Catechism of the Catholic Church," in Ratzinger and Schönborn, *Introduction to the Catechism of the Catholic Church*, 43–44.
59. *Catechism of the Catholic Church*, §648.

Christ: only he can lead us to the love of the Father in the Spirit and make use share in the life of the Holy Trinity.'"[60]

Together these Trinitarian and christological foundations make clear the primacy of God's grace to any authentically Christian life. As Cardinal Schönborn has said, the "primacy in catechesis is to be given to God and to his works. Whatever man has to do will always be a response to God and his works. ... *God is first; grace is first.*"[61] Striking and compelling preaching of the sacrifice of Christ and its basis in the Trinitarian life must ground Christian catechesis if it is not to result in an arid moralism.

Crucial to Ratzinger's vision for the catechism as well was that it would not simply be exclusively accessible to specialists and experts, but that it would be a resource that could be read and embraced with profit by the faithful: "It was a matter of principle that the work also be accessible to interested laymen as a tool of their Christian maturity and of their responsibility for the faith. They are not merely instructed from above but can also say themselves: This is our faith."[62]

Here we see expressed in the form and simplicity of Ratzinger's vision for the *Catechism* a commitment to see catechesis extended in parishes being revived into creative minorities in the increasingly secular nations of the West. As the *Catechism* itself says, "Periods of renewal in the Church are also intense moments of catechesis."[63] The plain style of the *Catechism* was directed not only to the faithful but to the evangelization of secular and non-Christian audiences as well. Ratzinger says that "among its intended readership are agnostics, seekers and inquirers, to whom it is offered as a help to become acquainted with what the Church teaches and tries to live."[64]

In light of these priorities, the decision that the *Catechism* be written "not by scholars, but by pastors drawing on their experience of

60. John Paul II, *Catechesi Tradendae,* quoted in *The Catechism of the Catholic Church,* §426, http://www.vatican.va/archive/ENG0015/_INDEX.HTM.
61. Schönborn, "A Short Introduction," 48–49.
62. Ratzinger, "Introduction to the Catechism," 18.
63. *Catechism,* prologue, II.8.
64. Ratzinger, "Introduction to the Catechism," 19.

the Church and the world" was indispensable.[65] The editorial team selected for the three parts of the *Catechism* consisted of three pairs of bishops: Bishops Estepa (Spain) and Maggiolini (Italy) on the creed; Bishops Medina (Chile) and Karlic (Argentina) on the sacraments; and Honoré (France) and Konstant (England) on morality, with Christoph Schönborn serving as secretary to synthesize different modes of thought and stylistic differences into a unity.[66]

When a fourth part needed to be added, on prayer, the editorial team wished to have an Eastern representative but could not secure a bishop for the author, choosing instead Jean Corbon, a French priest serving in war-torn Beirut, "who wrote the beautiful concluding text on prayer while in beleaguered Beirut, frequently in the midst of dramatic situations, taking shelter in his basement in order to continue working during the bombardments."[67] Embedded within the *Catechism* itself, in other words, was the work of a priest embodying the posture of the creative minority, praying and writing on prayer in a basement while bombs fell around him. The harmony between word and deed in the *Catechism* reflects Benedict's own priorities for catechesis: "Whoever, in fact, wishes to become a Christian must learn to believe. He must, in addition, make his own the Christian way of life, the Christian 'lifestyle,' as it were. He has also to be able to pray as a Christian and, lastly, he must enter into the mysteries, into the Church's liturgical cult."[68]

Christian catechesis is no mere transmission of a theory, but rather it means "to learn to pray, which in its turn means learning to live, inasmuch as prayer includes the dimension of moral conduct."[69] The goal of catechesis, as the *Catechism* puts it, is that "by looking to him in faith ... Christ's faithful can hope that he himself fulfills his promises in them, and that, by loving him with the same love with which he has loved them, they may perform works in keeping with their dignity."[70]

---

65. Ratzinger, "Introduction to the Catechism," 23.
66. Ratzinger, "Introduction to the Catechism," 23.
67. Ratzinger, "Introduction to the Catechism," 23.
68. Ratzinger, "Introduction to the Catechism," 29.
69. Ratzinger, "Introduction to the Catechism," 29.
70. *Catechism of the Catholic Church,* §1698.

The initial goal when the *Catechism* was first drafted in 1987 was to translate the different sections from the contemporary languages in which they were written into Latin, but the drafters discovered that misunderstandings occurred in the translation process. The drafters therefore switched to writing in an agreed on contemporary language. It turned out all drafters had at least some basic competency in French.[71] The final text was, however, translated and published in Latin and then retranslated into contemporary languages, reflecting Ratzinger's own commitment to the Latin language as preserving diachronic continuity within the church and unity within an international body that speaks almost all the languages of the earth.[72]

CONCLUSION

I have focused in this essay on Ratzinger's concern that catechesis be not only instruction but also training in Christianity. The church's decline in the West requires that the church again become a creative minority that can feel its difference from the prevailing culture without becoming sectarian. Among the tools for this difficult task are a deep immersion in the lives of the saints and the beauty the church has created, as well as a depth of understanding of the critical presuppositions of our time. If the church accepts this task, becoming a "sign of contradiction," it is guaranteed opposition: "Anything that does not meet with opposition has obviously not dealt at all with the urgent needs of its time."[73] But it is also guaranteed to encounter the risen and ascended Christ, and to help others do the same.

---

71. Ratzinger, "Introduction to the Catechism," 24.
72. As the church's culture grew on Latin-speaking soil, Ratzinger regards the preservation of the Latin language as crucial to the preservation of the church's patrimony: "Precisely in the multiplicity of languages and cultures, Latin, for so many centuries the vehicle and instrument of Christian culture, not only guarantees continuity with our roots but continues to be as relevant as ever for strengthening the bonds of unity of the faith in the communion of the Church." Benedict XVI, "Presentation of the Compendium of the *Catechism of the Catholic Church*," June 28, 2005, §8. https://w2.vatican.va/content/benedict-xvi/en/speeches/2005/june/documents/hf_ben-xvi_spe_20050628_compendium.html.
73. Ratzinger, "Evangelization, Catechesis, and Catechism," 36–37.

Afterword

After a lecture given by a distinguished evangelical theologian, a liberal Catholic colleague of mine asked: "Why do evangelicals dialogue with conservative Catholics? Why not dialogue with liberal Catholics whose views of Roman Catholicism cohere much more closely with Protestant ecclesiology?" Already, many Catholic parishes in the various regions of the United States do not differ much from liberal Episcopalian parishes in the same region. In a number of European countries, too, the theological and practical differences between Catholic parishes and many mainline Protestant ones are hardly noticeable.

My colleague's question was understandable. After all, as a private theologian and in his official church capacities, Joseph Ratzinger worked hard to accentuate the distinctively Catholic elements of the Roman Catholic Church. He did so without slighting ecumenical outreach; nonetheless, he often emphasized and defended aspects of the liturgy and the church that remain in dispute between Catholics and Protestants. He frequently stood in sharp and explicit contrast with his erstwhile friend and colleague, the well-known liberal Catholic theologian Karl Rahner.

After Vatican II, Rahner promoted an ecumenical outreach that he hoped would prove attractive to both Catholics and Protestants. Rahner looked forward to a worldwide Roman Catholic Church in which the question of whether a priest is needed in order to celebrate the Eucharist can be left open. Likewise, intercommunion—an open Eucharistic table, at least for anyone who believes in God and Christ—should now be thinkable. As for the question of who should exercise the priestly ministry, Rahner holds that it should be the person who, due to his or her spiritual and pastoral gifts, has received the community's recognition as its leader. When the congregation identifies its leader, the church should establish this person as the congregation's "priest," and he or she should preside at the Eucharistic table.

Gifted laypeople should be welcome to preach regurlarly in the liturgy. The Catholic Church should be rooted not in episcopally defined parishes but in communities of faith that arise "as a result of free initiative and association."[1] Priests and laypeople should expect to elect bishops, at least in societies where democratic elections are the norm, and to "co-operate ... in a deliberative and not merely consultative way in the Church's decisions."[2]

While affirming that in some sense the church should be able to make binding decisions and that there should be a Petrine office of headship of some kind, Rahner emphasizes that the church should have "open doors" and be an "open Church," "open even in regard to orthodoxy."[3] The papacy may continue to exist in the Catholic Church but only in service to unity in the most essential matters (God and Christ). It should not be allowed to proclaim any new dogmas, and it should not be able to enforce doctrinal unity throughout the broader church. Other than the fundamental affirmations about God and Jesus Christ, all Catholic dogma and traditional teachings should be reevaluated, since much of what was held to be dogmatically definitive can now be seen to have met a need in the past but perhaps not in the future. From this perspective, the need for believers to be united in dogmatic faith can suitably give way to a doctrinal and moral pluralism. Moral norms that were thought binding in the past should be reconsidered today given the scientific, political, and anthropological developments that have brought about new understandings of the human person.

If this was the ecumenical future of the Roman Catholic Church envisioned by Rahner—a future in which the post-Tridentine Roman Catholicism of the councils and popes would essentially be reversed— why is it that evangelical theologians actively draw from and dialogue with Ratzinger rather than with his ecclesiastical opponent Rahner?

---

1. Karl Rahner, *The Shape of the Church to Come*, trans. Edward Quinn (New York: Seabury Press, 1974), 108.
2. Rahner, *The Shape of the Church to Come*, 121.
3. Rahner, *The Shape of the Church to Come*, 94. See also Rahner, *The Shape of the Church to Come*, 95, 112.

In part this is because Rahner did not become pope, but Rahner's theology also has proved much less interesting to evangelical theologians. Indeed, I recently asked a dear evangelical friend whether he would not be happier if the Roman Catholic Church moved in Rahner's direction. My friend knew that this would mean that Roman Catholics would essentially relinquish all the claims of the Council of Trent and many of the more ecumenically painful claims of Vatican I and II—even if in the name of a historicist hermeneutic rather than in the name of the Protestant *solas*. My friend certainly would be glad to see Catholics relinquish such claims. But far from wishing to see the triumph of Rahner's thought in the Roman Catholic Church, my evangelical friend deeply appreciated the work done by Pope John Paul II and, especially, by Pope Benedict XVI against the pressures tending toward theological liberalism. My friend was not expressing a Catholic-leaning admiration for the post-Tridentine period of Roman Catholic history and practice. By no means; his perspective is quite the opposite. Instead, he was speaking in accord with what we find in this amazing book that Tim Perry has given us.

Here we have evangelical Christians, critical of the theology of Joseph Ratzinger in numerous areas, nonetheless finding a tremendous amount to treasure in the thought of this Catholic theologian and churchman. Above all, the contributors to this volume appreciate that Ratzinger is a defender of divine revelation, of the revealing and revealed realities of faith. They appreciate that he believes in a cognitively communicated, hearable, followable word of God and that he believes that Scripture is trustworthy and true. As they know, Ratzinger holds that Scripture must be read by the same Spirit in which it was written, and Scripture cannot be separated from the matrix to which it testifies (the church founded upon the apostles). But Scripture is not a wax nose for Ratzinger. He affirms in faith that the living Word, Jesus Christ, has really made himself known and that our ancestors in faith truthfully proclaimed this living Word in the Spirit. He is a man of prayer and worship, a defender of the reasonableness of faith against those who consider faith to be irrational, a preacher and evangelizer to the whole world, a person who seeks the Spirit's gifts of transformation in hope and charity. He is an opponent of the historicizing and ideological trends that imagine Christianity to be simply the humanly invented product of ever-evolving cultural and political situations. He navigates carefully between the twin pitfalls of fundamentalism and liberalism.

Many of the essays in the present volume are brilliant, and all are good. This book stands in the very first rank—the top handful—of studies on Ratzinger's thought. This is first and foremost a testimony to the extraordinary intellectual caliber of evangelical theology today, but it is also a testimony to the immense richness of Ratzinger's thought. As a Catholic theologian, I rejoice in this exchange of gifts: a magnificent Catholic theologian and pastor producing fruit for all Christians, and evangelical theologians responding in kind, "rooted and grounded in love" (Eph 3:17 RSV). Surely, after centuries of mutual condemnations, this book and others like it are a sign of great hope. Though we are still divided, we can say together: "Now to him who by the power at work within us is able to do far more abundantly than all that we ask or think, to him be glory in the church and in Christ Jesus to all generations, for ever and ever" (Eph 3:20–21 RSV).

Matthew Levering
University of Saint Mary of the Lake

Ratzinger Sources

Benedict XVI. Angelus Address, St. Peter's Square. January 28, 2007. http://
w2.vatican.va/content/benedict-xvi/en/angelus/2007/documents/hf_ben-
xvi_ang_20070128.html.

———. Anglicanorum Coetibus. Apostolic Constitution. November 4, 2009. http://
w2.vatican.va/content/benedict-xvi/en/apost_constitutions/documents/
hf_ben-xvi_apc_20091104_anglicanorum-coetibus.html.

———. "Appendix I: The Subiaco Address." In Rowland, Ratzinger's Faith, 156–65.

———. "Appendix II: The Regensburg Address." In Rowland, Ratzinger's Faith,
166–74.

———. Caritas in Veritate. Encyclical Letter. June 29, 2009. http://w2.vatican.va/con-
tent/benedict-xvi/en/encyclicals/documents/hf_ben-xvi_enc_20090629_
caritas-in-veritate.html.

———. Charity in Truth: Caritas in Veritate. San Francisco: Ignatius, 2009.

———. Deus Caritas Est. Encyclical Letter. December 25, 2005. https://w2.vat-
ican.va/content/benedict-xvi/en/encyclicals/documents/hf_ben-xvi_
enc_20051225_deus-caritas-est.html.

———. Deus Caritas Est. Vatican City: Libreria Editrice Vaticana, 2006.

———. The Essential Pope Benedict XVI: His Central Writings and Speeches. Edited by
John F. Thornton and Susan B. Varenne. San Francisco: HarperOne, 2007.

———. "Faith, Reason and the University: Memories and Reflections." University
of Regensburg. September 12, 2006. http://w2.vatican.va/content/
benedict-xvi/en/speeches/2006/september/documents/hf_ben-xvi_
spe_20060912_university-regensburg.html.

———. The Fathers of the Church: From St. Clement of Rome to St. Augustine of Hippo.
Edited by Joseph Lienhard. Grand Rapids: Eerdmans, 2009.

———. General Audience. December 5, 2012. http://w2.vatican.va/content/bene-
dict-xvi/en/audiences/2012/documents/hf_ben-xvi_aud_20121205.html.

———. General Audience. November 14, 2012. http://w2.vatican.va/content/bene-
dict-xvi/en/audiences/2012/documents/hf_ben-xvi_aud_20121114.html.

———. General Audience. November 21, 2012. http://w2.vatican.va/content/bene-
dict-xvi/en/audiences/2012/documents/hf_ben-xvi_aud_20121121.html.

———. General Audience. October 17, 2012. http://w2.vatican.va/content/bene-
dict-xvi/en/audiences/2012/documents/hf_ben-xvi_aud_20121017.html.

———. General Audience. October 24, 2012. http://w2.vatican.va/content/ben-edict-xvi/en/audiences/2012/documents/hf_ben-xvi_aud_20121024. html.

———. General Audience. October 31, 2012. http://w2.vatican.va/content/ben-edict-xvi/en/audiences/2012/documents/hf_ben-xvi_aud_20121031. html.

———. *Gesammelte Schriften: Einführung in das Christentum: Bekenntnis—Taufe—Nachfolge*. Freiburg: Herder, 2014.

———. *Heart of the Christian Life: Thoughts on Holy Mass*. San Francisco: Ignatius, 2010.

———. Homily at First Vespers, Vatican Basilica, December 1, 2012. http://w2.vatican.va/content/benedict-xvi/en/homilies/2012/documents/hf_ben-xvi_hom_20121201_vespri-avvento.html.

———. Homily at the Cathedral of Santa Maria la real de la Almudena, Madrid, World Youth Day. August 20, 2011. https://w2.vatican.va/content/ben-edict-xvi/en/homilies/2011/documents/hf_ben-xvi_hom_20110820_seminaristi-madrid.html.

———. Homily delivered at San Patrizio Al Colle Prenestino, Rome. December 16, 2012. http://w2.vatican.va/content/benedict-xvi/en/homilies/2012/documents/hf_ben-xvi_hom_20121216_parrocchia.html.

———. Homily delivered at the Vatican Basilica. June 12, 2011. http://w2.vatican.va/content/benedict-xvi/en/homilies/2011/documents/hf_ben-xvi_hom_20110612_pentecoste.html.

———. Homily delivered at the Vatican Basilica. September 12, 2009. http://w2.vatican.va/content/benedict-xvi/en/homilies/2009/documents/hf_ben-xvi_hom_20090912_ord-episcopale.html.

———. Interview. May 11, 2010. http://w2.vatican.va/content/benedict-xvi/en/speeches/2010/may/documents/hf_ben-xvi_spe_20100511_portogal-lo-interview.html.

———. *Jesus of Nazareth*. Vol. 1, *From the Baptism in the Jordan to the Transfiguration*. Translated by Adrian J. Walker. New York: Doubleday, 2007.

———. *Jesus of Nazareth*. Vol. 2, *Holy Week: From the Entrance into Jerusalem to the Resurrection*. Translated by Philip J. Whitmore. San Francisco: Ignatius, 2011.

———. *Jesus of Nazareth*. Vol. 3, *The Infancy Narratives*. Translated by Philip J. Whitmore. New York: Image; London: Bloomsbury, 2012.

———. *Light of the World: The Pope, The Church and the Signs of the Times*; An Interview with Peter Seewald. Translated by Michael J. Miller and Adrian J. Walker. San Francisco: Ignatius, 2010.

———. Message on World Youth Day. March 28, 2010. http://w2.vatican.va/content/benedict-xvi/en/messages/youth/documents/hf_ben-xvi_mes_20100222_youth.html.

———. "The Praying Presence of Mary." In *Prayer*, 175–80. Huntington, IN: Our Sunday Visitor, 2013.

———. "Presentation of the Compendium of the Catechism of the Catholic Church." June 28, 2005. https://w2.vatican.va/content/benedict-xvi/en/speeches/2005/june/documents/hf_ben-xvi_spe_20050628_compendium.html.

———. Sacramentum Caritatis. Post-Synodal Apostolic Exhortation, February 22, 2007. http://w2.vatican.va/content/benedict-xvi/en/apost_exhortations/documents/hf_ben-xvi_exh_20070222_sacramentum-caritatis.html.

———. *A School of Prayer: The Saints Show Us How to Pray*. Translated by L'Osservatore Romano. San Francisco: Ignatius, 2016.

———. *Spe Salvi: Encyclical Letter*. November 30, 2007. http://w2.vatican.va/content/benedict-xvi/en/encyclicals/documents/hf_ben-xvi_enc_20071130_spe-salvi.html.

———. *Spe Salvi: Saved in Hope*. San Francisco: Ignatius, 2007.

———. "To the Catholics of Ireland." March 19, 2010. http://w2.vatican.va/content/benedict-xvi/en/letters/2010/documents/hf_ben-xvi_let_20100319_church-ireland.html.

———. *Verbum Domini: The Word of the Lord*. Boston: Pauline Books & Media, 2010.

Benedict XVI with Peter Seewald. *Last Testament: In His Own Words*. Translated by Jacob Phillips. London: Bloomsbury, 2016.

Ratzinger, Joseph. *Behold the Pierced One: An Approach to a Spiritual Christology*. Translated by Graham Harrison. San Francisco: Ignatius, 1986.

———. "Biblical Foundations of Priesthood." *Communio* 17, no. 4 (1990): 617–27.

———. "Biblical Interpretation in Crisis" (1988). *First Things*, April 26, 2008. https://www.firstthings.com/web-exclusives/2008/04/biblical-interpretation-in-crisis.

———. "Biblical Interpretation in Crisis: On the Question of the Foundations and Approaches of Exegesis Today." In Neuhaus, *Biblical Interpretation in Crisis*, 1–23.

———. *Christianity and the Crisis of Cultures*. Translated by Brian McNeil. San Francisco: Ignatius, 2006

———. *Church, Ecumenism, and Politics: New Endeavors in Ecclesiology*. Translated by Michael J. Miller et al. San Francisco: Ignatius, 2008.

———. *Collected Works*. Vol. 2, *Theology of the Liturgy: The Sacramental Foundation of Christian Existence*. Edited by Michael J. Miller. Translated by John Saward et al. San Francisco: Ignatius, 2014.

———. "Commentary on Dei Verbum." In *Commentary on the Documents of Vatican II*, edited by Herbert Vorgrimler, 3:184–98. New York: Crossroad, 1989.

———. *Daughter Zion: Meditations on the Church's Marian Belief*. Translated by John M. McDermott, SJ. San Francisco: Ignatius, 1983.

———. *Der Gott des Glaubens und der Gott der Philosophen* [The God of faith and the God of the philosophers]. Munich: Verlag Schnell und Steiner, 1960.

———. *Der Gott Jesu Christi: Betrachtungen uber den Dreieinigen Gott*. Munich: Kosel-Verlag, 1976.

———. *Dogma and Preaching: Applying Christian Doctrine to Daily Life*. Translated by Michael J. Miller and Matthew J. O'Connell. Edited by Michael J. Miller. San Francisco: Ignatius, 2011.

———. *Eschatology: Death and Eternal Life*. Translated by Michael Waldstein and Aidan Nichols. Washington, DC: Catholic University of America Press, 1988.

———. *Europe: Today and Tomorrow; Addressing the Fundamental Issues*. Translated by Michael J. Miller. San Francisco: Ignatius, 2007.

———. "Exegesis and the Magisterium of the Church." In *Opening Up the Scriptures: Joseph Ratzinger and the Foundations of Biblical Interpretation*, edited by José Granados, Carlos Granados, and Luis Sánchez-Navarro. Grand Rapids: Eerdmans, 2008.

———. *Faith and the Future*. Chicago: Franciscan Herald Press, 1971. Reprint, San Francisco: Ignatius, 2009.

———. *The Feast of Faith: Approaches to a Theology of the Liturgy*. Translated by Graham Harrison. San Francisco: Ignatius, 1986

———. *God and the World: A Conversation with Peter Seewald*. Translated by Henry Taylor. San Francisco: Ignatius, 2002.

———. *The God of Jesus Christ: Meditations on the Triune God*. Translated by Brian McNeil. San Francisco: Ignatius, 2008.

———. *Gospel, Catechesis, Catechism: Sidelights on the Catechism of the Catholic Church*. San Francisco: Ignatius, 1997.

———. Homily delivered at the Vatican Basilica. April 18, 2005. http://www.vatican.va/gpII/documents/homily-pro-eligendo-pontifice_20050418_en.html.

———. *"In the Beginning": A Catholic Understanding of the Story of Creation and the Fall*. Translated by Boniface Ramsey. Grand Rapids: Eerdmans, 1995.

———. *Introduction to Christianity*. Translated by J. R. Foster. London: Search Press, 1969.

——. *Introduction to Christianity*. Translated by J. R. Foster. New York: Herder & Herder, 1969.

——. *Introduction to Christianity*. Translated by J. R. Foster. Rev. ed. San Francisco: Ignatius, 2004

——. "Introduction to the Catechism of the Catholic Church." In Joseph Ratzinger and Christoph Schönborn, *Introduction to the Catechism of the Catholic Church*, 9–36. San Francisco: Ignatius, 1994.

——. *Joseph Ratzinger in Communio*. Vol. 2, *Anthropology and Culture*. Edited by David L. Schindler and Nicholas J. Healy. Grand Rapids: Eerdmans, 2013.

——. *Many Religions, One Covenant: Israel, the Church and the World*. Translated by Graham Harrison. San Francisco: Ignatius, 1999.

——. Introduction to _Mary: God's Yes to Man_ (Encyclical Letter: _Redemptoris Mater_), by John Paul II. Translated by Lothar Krauth. San Francisco: Ignatius, 1987.

——. *Milestones: Memoirs 1927–1977*. Translated by Erasmo Leiva-Merikakis. San Francisco: Ignatius, 1998.

——. *The Nature and Mission of Theology: Essays to Orient Theology in Today's Debates*. Translated by Adrian Walker. San Francisco: Ignatius, 1991.

——. *The Nature and Mission of Theology: Understanding Its Role in the Light of the Present Controversy*. Translated by Adrian Walker. San Francisco: Ignatius, 1995.

——. "The New Pagans and the Church: A 1958 Lecture by Joseph Ratzinger (Pope Benedict XVI)." Translated by Kenneth Baker, SJ. *Homiletic and Pastoral Review*, January 30, 2017. https://www.hprweb.com/2017/01/the-new-pagans-and-the-church/.

——. *A New Song for the Lord: Faith in Christ and Liturgy Today*. Translated by Martha M. Matesich. 2nd ed. New York: Crossroad, 2005.

——. *On Conscience*. San Francisco: Ignatius, 2007.

——. *On the Way to Jesus Christ*. Translated by Michael J. Miller. San Francisco: Ignatius, 2005.

——. *Pilgrim Fellowship of Faith: The Church as Communion*. Edited by Stephan Otto Horn and Vinzenz Pfnür. Translated by Henry Taylor. San Francisco: Ignatius, 2005.

——. *Politik und Erlösung: zum Verhältnis von Glaube, Rationalität und Irrationalem in der sogenannten Theologie der Befreiung* [Politics and redemption: the relation between faith, rationality, and the irrational in the so-called theology of liberation]. Düsseldorf: Westdeutscher, 1986.

——. Preface to *The Interpretation of the Bible in the Church*, edited by J. L. houlden. London: SCM, 1995.

290

———. *Principles of Catholic Theology: Building Stones for a Fundamental Theology*. Translated by Mary Frances McCarthy. San Francisco: Ignatius, 1987.

———. "Relationship between Magisterium and Exegetes." Address to the Pontifical Biblical Commission. May 10, 2003. http://www.vatican.va/roman_curia/congregations/cfaith/pcb_documents/rc_con_cfaith_doc_20030510_ratzinger-comm-bible_en.html.

———. "Revelation Itself." In *Commentary on the Documents of Vatican II*, edited by Herbert Vorgrimler, 3:170–80. Translated by W. Glen-Doepel, H. Graef, J. M. Jakubiak, S. Young, and E. Young. New York: Crossroad, 1989.

———. "The Theological Locus of Ecclesial Movements." *Communio* 25, no. 3 (1998): 480–504.

———. *A Turning Point for Europe? The Church in the Modern World*. Translated by Brian McNeil. San Francisco: Ignatius, 1994

———. *Salt of the Earth: The Church at the End of the Millennium; An Interview with Peter Seewald*. Translated by Adrian Walker. San Francisco: Ignatius, 1996.

———. *The Spirit of the Liturgy*. Translated by John Saward. San Francisco: Ignatius, 2000.

———. *Teaching and Learning the Love of God: Being a Priest Today*. Translated by Michael J. Miller. San Francisco: Ignatius, 2017.

———. *To Look on Christ: Exercises in Faith, Hope, and Love*. Translated by Robert Nowell. New York: Crossroad, 1991.

———. *Truth and Tolerance: Christian Belief and World Religions*. Translated by Henry Taylor. San Francisco: Ignatius, 2004.

———. *Volk und Haus Gottes in Augustins Lehre von der Kirche* [The people of God and the house of God in Augustine's doctrine of the church], Munich: Zink, 1954.

Ratzinger, Joseph, and Marcello Pera. *Without Roots: The West, Relativism, Christianity, Islam*. Translated by Michael Moore. New York: Basic Books, 2006.

Ratzinger, Joseph, with Vittorio Messori. *The Ratzinger Report: An Exclusive Interview on the State of the Church*. Translated by Salvator Attanasio and Graham Harrison. San Francisco: Ignatius, 1985.

Works Cited

Adam, A. K. M., Stephen E. Fowl, Kevin J. Vanhoozer, and Francis Watson. *Reading Scripture with the Church: Toward a Hermeneutic for Theological Interpretation.* Grand Rapids: Baker Academic, 2006.

Allen, Michael, and Scott R. Swain. *Reformed Catholicity: The Promise of Retrieval for Theology and Biblical Interpretation.* Grand Rapids: Baker Academic, 2015.

Allison, Gregg R. *Roman Catholic Theology and Practice: An Evangelical Assessment.* Wheaton: Crossway, 2014.

Allison, Gregg, and Chris Castaldo. *The Unfinished Reformation: What Unites and Divides Catholics and Protestants after 500 Years.* Grand Rapids: Zondervan, 2016.

Augustine. *The City of God against the Pagans.* Edited by R. W. Dyson. Cambridge: Cambridge University Press, 1998.

———. *City of God.* Translated by Henry Bettenson. New York: Penguin, 1972.

Bacon, Francis. *The New Organon.* Edited by Lisa Jardine. Cambridge: Cambridge University Press, 2000.

Balthasar, Hans Urs von. *Truth Is Symphonic: Aspects of Christian Pluralism.* Translated by Graham Harrison. San Francisco: Ignatius, 1987.

Balthasar, Hans Urs von, and Joseph Cardinal Ratzinger. *Mary: The Church at the Source.* Translated by Adrian Walker. San Francisco: Ignatius, 2005.

Barth, Karl. *Homiletics.* Translated by Geoffrey William Bromiley and Donald E. Daniels (Louisville: Westminster John Knox, 1991.

———. "The Need and Promise of Christian Preaching." In *The Word of God and the Word of Man,* 97–135. Translated by Douglas Horton. New York: Harper, 1957.

Begbie, Jeremy. "The Shape of Things to Come? Wright amidst Emerging Ecclesiologies." In *Jesus, Paul and the People of God: A Theological Dialogue with N. T. Wright,* edited by Nicholas Perrin and Richard B. Hays, 183–207. Downers Grove, IL: IVP Academic, 2011.

Billings, Todd J. *The Word of God for the People of God: An Entryway to the Theological Interpretation of Scripture.* Grand Rapids: Eerdmans, 2010.

Bonhoeffer, Dietrich. *Letters and Papers from Prison.* Edited by Eberhard Bethge. New York: Touchstone, 1997.

Boone, Kathleen C. *The Bible Tells Them So: The Discourse of Protestant Fundamentalism*. Albany: State University of New York Press, 1989.

Brownlee, Annette. *Preaching Jesus Christ Today: Six Questions for Moving from Scripture to Sermon*. Grand Rapids: Baker Academic, 2018.

Brunner, Emil, and Karl Barth. *Natural Theology: Comprising "Nature and Grace" by Professor Dr. Emil Brunner and the Reply "No!" by Dr. Karl Barth*. Translated by Peter Fraenkel. London: Bles; the Centenary Press, 1946.

Calvin, John. *Commentary on Galatians, Ephesians, Philippians, Colossians, I & II Timothy, Titus, and Philemon*. Calvin's Commentary Series 21. Grand Rapids: Baker, 1979.

————. *Institutes of the Christian Religion*. Edited by John T. McNeill. Translated by Ford Lewis Battles. Philadelphia: Westminster, 1960.

Campbell, Charles. *Preaching Jesus: New Directions for Homiletics in Hans Frei's Postliberal Theology*. Grand Rapids: Eerdmans, 1997.

Carbajosa, Ignacio. *Faith, the Fount of Exegesis: The Interpretation of Scripture in Light of the History of Research on the Old Testament*. Translated by Paul Stevenson. San Francisco: Ignatius, 2013.

Carl, Scott, ed. *Verbum Domini and the Complementarity of Exegesis and Theology*. Grand Rapids: Eerdmans, 2015.

Catechism of the Catholic Church. Toronto: Random House Canada, 1995.

Catechism of the Catholic Church. http://www.vatican.va/archive/ENG0015/_INDEX.HTM.

Congregation for the Doctrine of the Faith *Dominus Iesus*. August 6, 2000. http://www.vatican.va/roman_curia/congregations/cfaith/documents/rc_con_cfaith_doc_20000806_dominus-iesus_en.html.

Cortez, Marc. *Christological Anthropology in Historical Perspective: Ancient and Contemporary Approaches to Theological Anthropology*. Grand Rapids: Zondervan, 2016.

Cross, F. L., and E. A. Livingstone, eds. *The Oxford Dictionary of the Christian Church*. 3rd ed. Oxford: Oxford University Press, 2005.

de Chirico, Leonardo. "The Blurring of Time Distinctions in Roman Catholicism." *Themelios* 29, no. 2 (2004): 40–46.

de Gaál, Emery. *The Theology of Pope Benedict XVI: The Christocentric Shift*. New York: Palgrave Macmillan, 2010.

de Lubac, Henri. *Paradoxes of Faith*. Translated by Paule Simon and Sadie Kreilkamp. San Francisco: Ignatius, 1987.

————. *The Splendor of the Church*. Translated by Michael Mason. San Francisco: Ignatius, 1999.

Duffy, Eamon. "Benedict XVI and the Eucharist." *New Blackfriars* 88, no. 1014 (2007): 195–212.

Feiner, Johannes, and Magnus Löhrer, "Einleitung." In *Mysterium Salutis: Grundriss Heilsgeschichtlicher Dogmatik*. Vol. 1, *Die Grundlagen Heilsgeschichtlicher Dogmatik*, edited by Johannes Feiner and Magnus Löhrer, xxiii–xliv. Zurich: Benziger, 1965.

Flannery, Austin, ed. *Vatican Council II: The Conciliar and Post Conciliar Documents*. Collegeville, MN: Liturgical Press, 1975.

———, ed. *Vatican Council II*. Vol. 1, *The Conciliar and Post Conciliar Documents*. Rev. ed. Northport, NY: Costello, 1996.

First Anglican/Roman Catholic International Commission. Eucharistic Doctrine. 1971. http://www.vatican.va/roman_curia/pontifical_councils/chrstuni/angl-comm-docs/rc_pc_chrstuni_doc_1971_eucharistic-doctrine_en.html.

Gadenz, Pablo. "Overcoming the Hiatus between Exegesis and Theology: Guidance and Examples from Pope Benedict XVI." In Carl, *Verbum Domini*, 41–62.

Gay, Peter. *Weimar Culture: The Outsider as Insider*. New York: W. W. Norton, 2001.

General Assembly of the Synod of Bishops. The Word of God in the Life and Mission of the Church: Instrumentum Laboris. Synod of Bishops, Twelfth Ordinary General Assembly. 2008. http://www.vatican.va/roman_curia/synod/documents/rc_synod_doc_20080511_instrlabor-xii-assembly_en.html.

Gese, Hartmut. "Die Herkunft des Herrenmahls." In *Zur biblische Theologie*, 107–27. Munich: Kaiser, 1977.

———. "The Origin of the Lord's Supper." In *Essays on Biblical Theology*, 117–40. Translated by Keith Crim. Minneapolis: Augsburg, 1981.

Ginther, James R. *The Westminster Handbook to Medieval Theology*. Louisville: Westminster John Knox, 2009.

Gray, Tim. *From Jewish Passover to Christian Eucharist: The Todah Sacrifice as Background for the Last Supper*. Steubenville, OH: Emmaeus Road, 2006.

Guardini, Romano. *The Art of Praying: The Principles and Methods of Christian Prayer*. Manchester, NH: Sophia Institute, 1985.

Hahn, Scott W. *Covenant and Communion: The Biblical Theology of Pope Benedict XVI*. Grand Rapids: Brazos, 2009.

Häring, Hermann. *Theologie und Ideologie bei Joseph Ratzinger*. Dusseldorf: Patmos, 2001.

Harmless, William. *Augustine and the Catechumenate*. Collegeville, MN: Liturgical Press, 2014.

Hart, John W. *Karl Barth vs. Emil Bruner: The Formation and Dissolution of a Theological Alliance, 1916–1936*. New York: Peter Lang, 2001.

Hooper, John, and Stephen Bates. "Dismay and Anger as Pope Declares Protestants Cannot Have Churches." *The Guardian*. July 11, 2007. https://www.theguardian.com/world/2007/jul/11/catholicism.religion.

Horton, Michael. *Covenant and Salvation: Union with Christ*. Louisville: Westminster John Knox, 2007.

Ignatius Catholic Study Bible. San Francisco: Ignatius, 2010.

International Theological Commission. *Theology Today: Perspectives, Principles, and Criteria*. Washington, DC: Catholic University of America Press, 2012.

———. *Sensus Fidei* in the Life of the Church. 2004. http://www.vatican.va/roman_curia/congregations/cfaith/cti_documents/rc_cti_20140610_sensus-fidei_en.html.

Janz, Denis R. *The Westminster Handbook to Martin Luther*. Louisville: Westminster John Knox, 2010.

Jenson, Robert W. "Scripture's Authority in the Church." In *The Art of Reading Scripture*, edited by Ellen F. Davis and Richard B. Hays, 27–37. Grand Rapids: Eerdmans, 2003.

John Paul II. Redemptoris Mater. Encyclical Letter. March 25, 1987. http://w2.vatican.va/content/john-paul-ii/en/encyclicals/documents/hf_jp-ii_enc_25031987_redemptoris-mater.html.

Johnson, P. W. T. *The Mission of Preaching: Equipping the Community for Faithful Witness*. Downers Grove, IL: IVP Academic, 2015.

Jones, C. P. M., and C. J. A. Hickling. "The New Testament." In *The Study of Liturgy*, edited by Cheslyn Jones, Geoffrey Wainwright, Edward Yarnold, SJ, and Paul Bradshaw, 184–209. Oxford: Oxford University Press, 1992.

Jones, L. Gregory. "Embodying Scripture in the Community of Faith." In Davis and Hays, *Art of Reading Scripture*, 145.

Kasper, Walter. *The God of Jesus Christ*. Translated by Matthew J. O'Connell. New York: Crossroad, 1984.

Kendall, Daniel. *The Blessed Virgin Mary*. Grand Rapids: Eerdmans, 2013.

Küng, Hans. *On Being a Christian*. Translated by Edward Quinn. New York: Doubleday, 1976). German original: *Christ Sein*. Munich: Piper, 1974.

LaCugna, Catherine Mowry. *God for Us: The Trinity and Christian Life*. San Francisco: HarperSanFrancisco, 1991.

Legaspi, Michael C. *The Death of Scripture and the Rise of Biblical Studies*. Oxford: Oxford University Press, 2011.

Levering, Matthew. *Engaging the Doctrine of the Holy Spirit: Love and Gift in the Trinity and the Church*. Grand Rapids: Baker Academic, 2016.

———. *An Introduction to Vatican II as an Ongoing Theological Event*. Washington, DC: Catholic University of America Press, 2017.

Levin, Yuval. *The Fractured Republic: Renewing America's Social Contract in the Age of Individualism*. New York: Basic Books, 2017.

Lindbeck, George. *The Nature of Doctrine: Religion and Theology in a Postliberal Age*. Louisville: Westminster, 1984.

Lose, David. *Confessing Jesus Christ: Preaching Jesus Christ in a Postmodern World*. Grand Rapids: Eerdmans, 2003.

Lumen Gentium. Dogmatic Constitution on the Church. November 21, 1964. http://www.vatican.va/archive/hist_councils/ii_vatican_council/documents/vat-ii_const_19641121_lumen-gentium_en.html.

Luther, Martin. *Luther's Works*. Vol. 2, *Lectures on Genesis, Chapters 6–14*. Edited by Jaroslav Pelikan and Daniel E. Poellot. Translated by George V. Schick. St. Louis: Concordia, 1960.

———. *Luther's Works*, vol. 41, *Church and Ministry III*. Edited by Helmut T. Lehmann and Eric W. Gritsch. Translated by Charles M. Jacobs, W. P. Stephens, and Eric W. Gritsch. Philadelphia: Fortress, 1966.

Marthaler, Berard. *Introduction to Sourcebook for Modern Catechetics*, edited by Michael Warren, oo–oo. Winona: Saint Mary's Press, 1983.

McCabe, Herbert. *God Matters*. Springfield, IL: Templegate, 1991.

McCarthy, Cormac. *The Road*. New York: Knopf Doubleday, 2007.

McGrath, Alister. "Natural Theology? The Barth-Brunner Debate of 1934." In *Emil Brunner: A Reappraisal*, 90–132. Chichester, UK: Wiley Blackwell, 2014.

McGregor, Peter John. *Heart to Heart: The Spiritual Christology of Joseph Ratzinger*. Eugene, OR: Pickwick, 2016.

Miłosz, Czesław. "One More Day." In *The Collected Poems, 1931–1987*, 407. New York: Ecco, 1988.

Moreland, J. P., and John Mark Reynolds, eds. *Three Views on Creation and Evolution*. Grand Rapids: Zondervan, 1999.

Murray, Paul D. "Roman Catholic Theology after Vatican II." In *The Modern Theologians*, edited by David F. Ford with Rachel Muers, 265–86. 3rd ed. Malden, MA: Blackwell, 2005.

Nagel, Thomas. *The View from Nowhere*. Oxford: Oxford University Press, 1986.

Neuhaus, Richard John, ed. *Biblical Interpretation in Crisis: The Ratzinger Conference on Bible and Church*. Grand Rapids: Eerdmans, 1989.

Nichols, Aidan. *Catholic Thought Since the Enlightenment*. London: Gracewing, 1998.

———. *The Thought of Pope Benedict XVI: An Introduction to the Theology of Joseph Ratzinger*. London: Burns & Oates, 2007.

Nygren, Anders. *Agape and Eros.* Translated by Philip Watson. Philadelphia: Westminster, 1953.

O'Malley, John W. *What Happened at Vatican II.* Cambridge: Harvard University Press, 2008.

O'Regan, Cyril. "Benedict the Augustinian." In *Explorations in the Theology of Benedict XVI,* edited by John C. Cavadini, 21–62. Notre Dame, IN: University of Notre Dame Press, 2012.

Oberman, Heiko A. *Forerunners of the Reformation: The Shape of Late Medieval Thought.* New York: Holt, Rinehart & Winston, 1966.

Ott, Heinrich. *Fundamentals of Catholic Dogma.* Edited by James Canon Bastible. Charlotte: TAN, 1974.

Paul VI. *Marialis Cultus.* Apostolic Exhortation. February 2, 1974. http://w2.vatican.va/content/paul-vi/en/apost_exhortations/documents/hf_p-vi_exh_19740202_marialis-cultus.html.

Perry, Tim. *Mary for Evangelicals.* Downers Grove, IL: IVP Academic, 2006.

Pitre, Brant. "Verbum Domini and Historical-Critical Exegesis." In Carl, *Verbum Domini,* 26–40.

"Pope Asserts Order to Reinstate Old Latin Mass." *National Post,* May 15, 2011. https://nationalpost.com/holy-post/pope-asserts-order-to-reinstate-old-latin-mass.

Rahner, Karl. "Der Dreifaltige Gott als Transzendenter Urgrund der Heilsgeschichte." In *Mysterium Salutis: Grundriss Heilsgeschichtlicher Dogmatik.* Vol. 2, *Die Heilsgeschichte vor Christus,* edited by Johannes Feiner and Magnus Löhrer, 317–97. Einsiedeln: Benziger, 1967.

———. *The Trinity.* Translated by Joseph Donceel. New York: Crossroad, 1997.

Ramm, Bernard. *The Pattern of Religious Authority.* Grand Rapids: Eerdmans, 1957.

Rausch, Thomas P. *Pope Benedict XVI: An Introduction to His Theological Vision.* New York, Paulist, 2009.

Reid, Alcuin. *The Organic Development of the Liturgy.* 2nd ed. San Francisco: Ignatius, 2005.

Reno, R. R. *Resurrecting the Idea of a Christian Society.* Washington, DC: Regnery Faith, 2016.

Rowland, Tracey. *Benedict XVI: A Guide for the Perplexed.* London: T&T Clark, 2010.

———. *Ratzinger's Faith: The Theology of Pope Benedict XVI.* Oxford: Oxford University Press, 2008.

Sacks, Jonathan. "On Creative Minorities." *First Things,* January 2014. https://www.firstthings.com/article/2014/01/on-creative-minorities.

Sanders, Fred. *The Image of the Immanent Trinity: Rahner's Rule and the Theological Interpretation of Scripture*. New York: Peter Lang, 2004.

Schmitt, Ron. "Attempt to Resurrect pre–Vatican II Mass Leaves Church at Crossroads." *National Catholic Reporter*, December 8, 2012. https://www.ncronline.org/news/spirituality/attempt-resurrect-pre-vatican-ii-mass-leaves-church-crossroads.

Schnackenburg, Rudolf. *Jesus in the Gospels: A Biblical Christology*. Louisville: Westminster John Knox, 2005.

Schönborn, Christoph. "A Short Introduction to the Four Parts of the Catechism." In Ratzinger and Schönborn, *Introduction to the Catechism of the Catholic Church*, 63–64.

Smith, Christian. *The Sacred Project of American Sociology*. New York: Oxford University Press, 2014.

Smith, Christian, with Kari Christofferson, Hilary Davidson, and Patricia Snell Herzog. *Lost in Transition: The Dark Side of Emerging Adulthood*. New York: Oxford University Press, 2014.

Smith, James K. A. *Desiring the Kingdom: Worship, Worldview, and Cultural Formation*. Grand Rapids: Baker Academic, 2009.

Stallsworth, Paul T. "The Story of an Encounter." In Neuhaus, *Biblical Interpretation in Crisis*, 102–90. Grand Rapids: Eerdmans, 1989.

Stott, John. *Evangelical Truth: A Personal Plea for Unity, Integrity, and Faithfulness*. Rev. ed. Downers Grove, IL: InterVarsity Press, 2003.

Sunquist, Scott. *The Unexpected Christian Century: The Reversal and Transformation of Global Christianity, 1900–2000*. Grand Rapids: Baker Academic, 2015.

Tanner, Kathryn. *God and Creation in Christian Theology*. Minneapolis: Fortress, 2005.

Taylor, Charles. *A Secular Age*. Cambridge: Belknap Press of Harvard University Press, 2007.

Turner, Frederick. "The Significance of the Frontier in American History." *Annual Report of the American Historical Association* (1893): 197–227.

Vanhoozer, Kevin J. *Biblical Authority after Babel: Retrieving the Solas in the Spirit of Mere Protestant Christianity*. Grand Rapids: Brazos, 2016.

———. "A Mere Protestant Response." In Matthew Levering and Kevin Vanhoozer, *Was the Reformation a Mistake? Why Catholic Doctrine Is Not Unbiblical*, 191–231. Grand Rapids: Zondervan, 2017.

Warner, Greg. "Conservative Evangelicals Hope for New Ally in Pope Benedict XVI." *Baptist Standard*, April 22, 2005. https://www.baptiststandard.com/archives/2005-archives/conservative-evangelicals-hope-for-ally-in-new-pope-benedict-xvi50205/.

Warren, Michael. "Evangelization: A Catechetical Concern." In *Sourcebook for Modern Catechetics*, edited by Michael Warren, 330–31. Winona, MN: Saint Mary's Press, 1983.

Wilken, Robert Louis. *The Spirit of Early Christian Thought*. New Haven: Yale University Press, 2003.

Williams, A. N. *The Architecture of Theology: Structure, System, and Ratio*. Oxford: Oxford University Press, 2011.

Williams, Rowan. *Christ: The Heart of Creation*. London: Bloomsbury, 2018.

Wilson, Paul Scott. *Preaching and Homiletical Theory*. St. Louis: Chalice, 2004.

Subject Index

Scripture Index

Old Testament

New Testament

314

THE THEOLOGY OF BENEDICT XVI

Deuterocanonical Books